THE BRAND PHOTOGRAPHY PLAYBOOK

The Insider's Guide to Planning Your Photo Shoot and Building a Stand-Out Brand

BY MALLIKA MALHOTRA

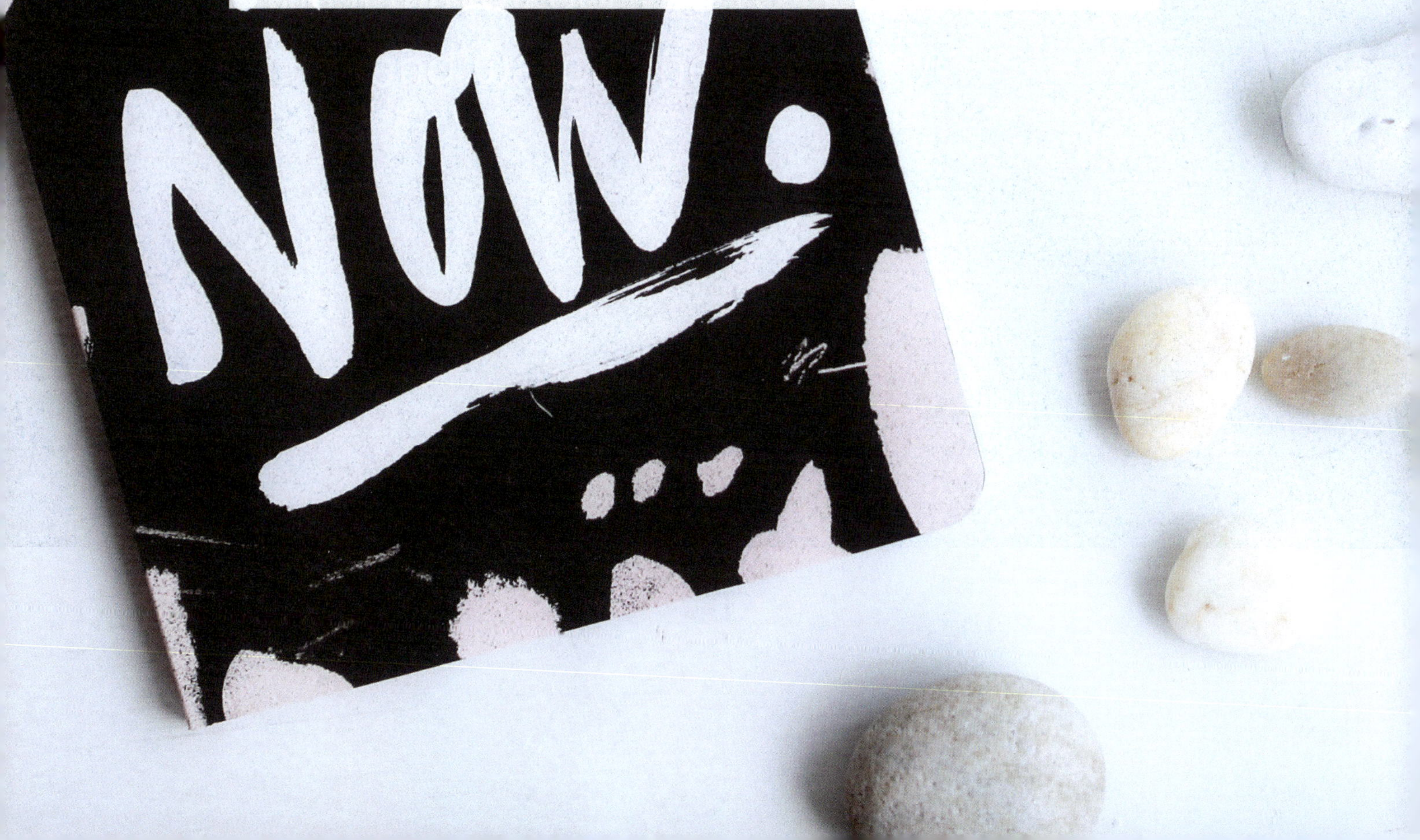

ISBN 978-0-692-88793-6

Editor : Jodi Brandon
Designer : Samantha Grose
Cover Photograph : Laura Neff

More information about MikiFoto + Co and Mallika Malhotra can be found at www.mikifoto.com.

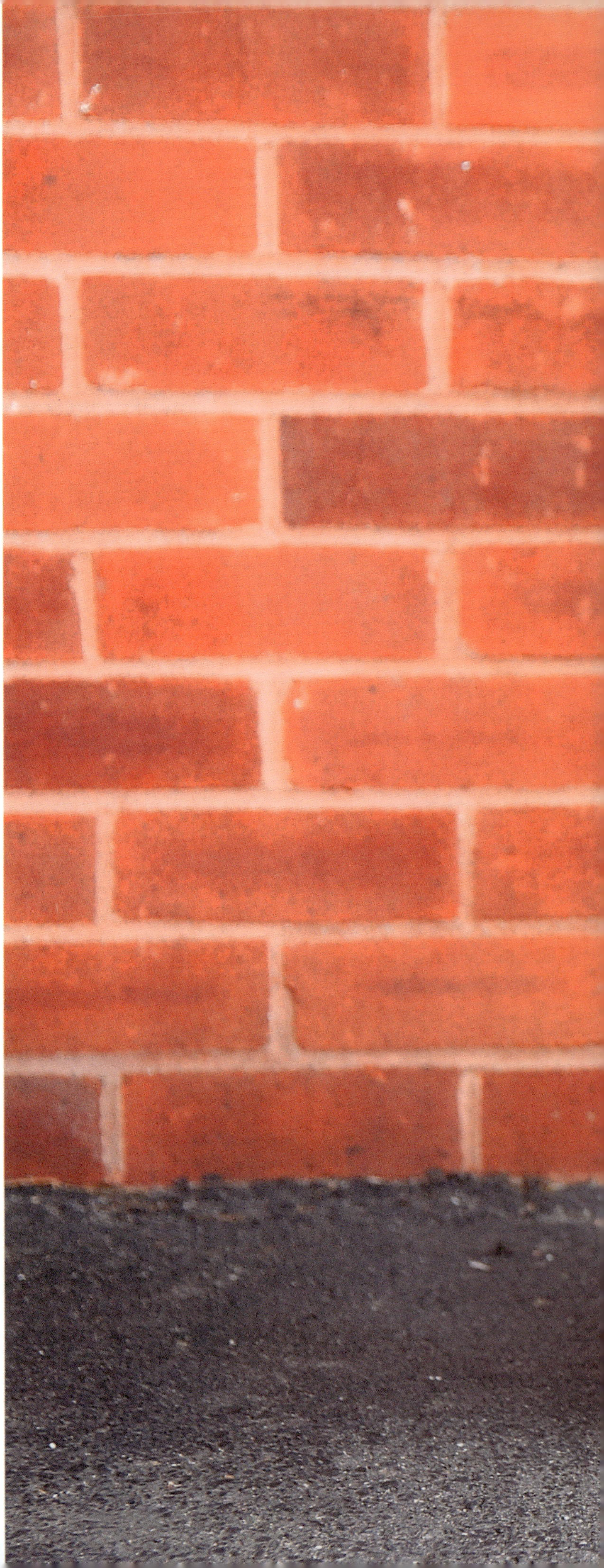

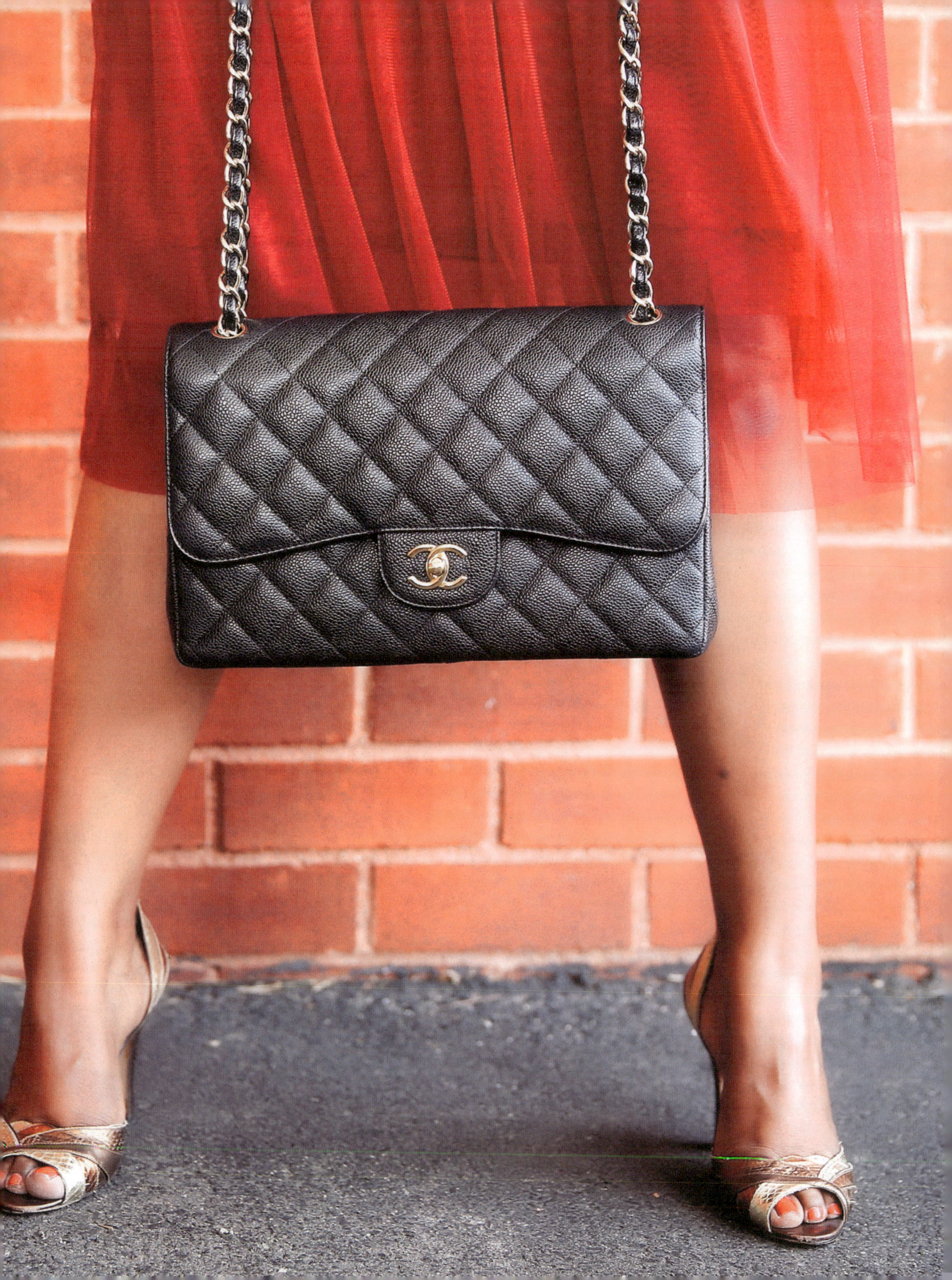

TABLE OF CONTENTS

NICE TO MEET YOU

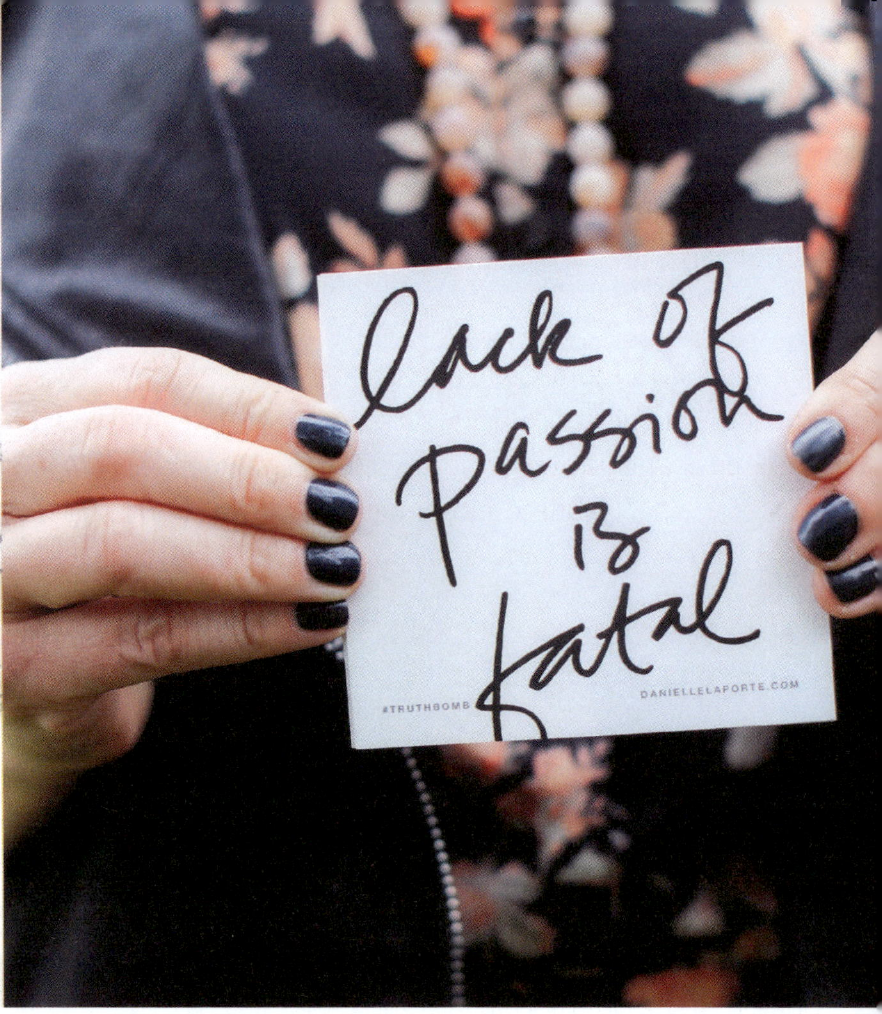

I'm thrilled that you're here. My name is Mallika, and I can't wait to share with you all the insider information to planning a brand photography shoot. Over the past several years as a professional photographer, I've worked with hundreds of entrepreneurs to help them tell their brand stories through a visual strategy. Yes, it's all about the strategy and planning, because this kind of photo shoot is a big deal — a big investment for your business. It should be treated with more than a "show up and shoot" plan. There's so much to think about, from shot lists to logistics to styling. There are so many emotions that arise when we know the camera lens will be on us. It can feel quite overwhelming!

But don't you worry. I've got your back.

This guide was created to encourage you. To show you that you CAN get it all done — beautifully. You can be informed and empowered about the process. You can arrive to your shoot feeling confident and calm. You can finally create those show-stopping images that you've always dreamed about. Use this playbook as a tool to gain clarity on your brand story. Find inspiration and ideas in the featured photographs. Share this guide with your photographer to ensure you both are on the same page for your photo goals.

So whether you have already booked your photo session, you are simply curious about

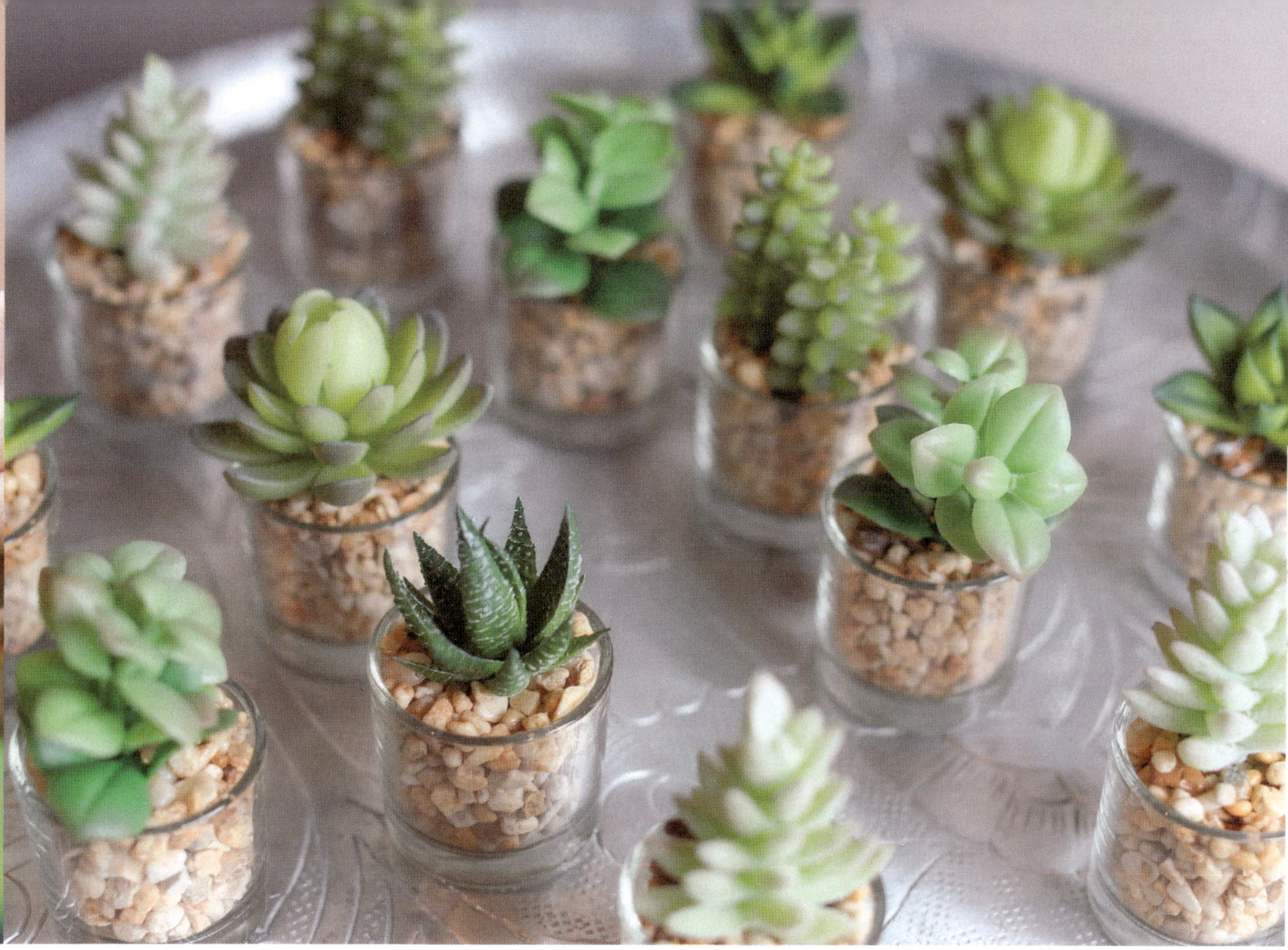

WELCOME

what a brand photo shoot actually looks like, or maybe you are a fellow photographer considering offering brand photography in your business in the future, this playbook will cover all the things and is meant to be a valuable resource that you can return to again and again.

I am excited that you are here! You're on your way to creating images that connect, energize and bring personality to your business. This guide was created to help you feel prepared, empowered, and confident for your upcoming brand photo shoot.

You are so much more than just a pretty headshot. The world is waiting to see and learn your full brand story. Let's dig deep together and get you ready for the center stage of success. I will walk you every step of the way.

Cheers,
Mallika

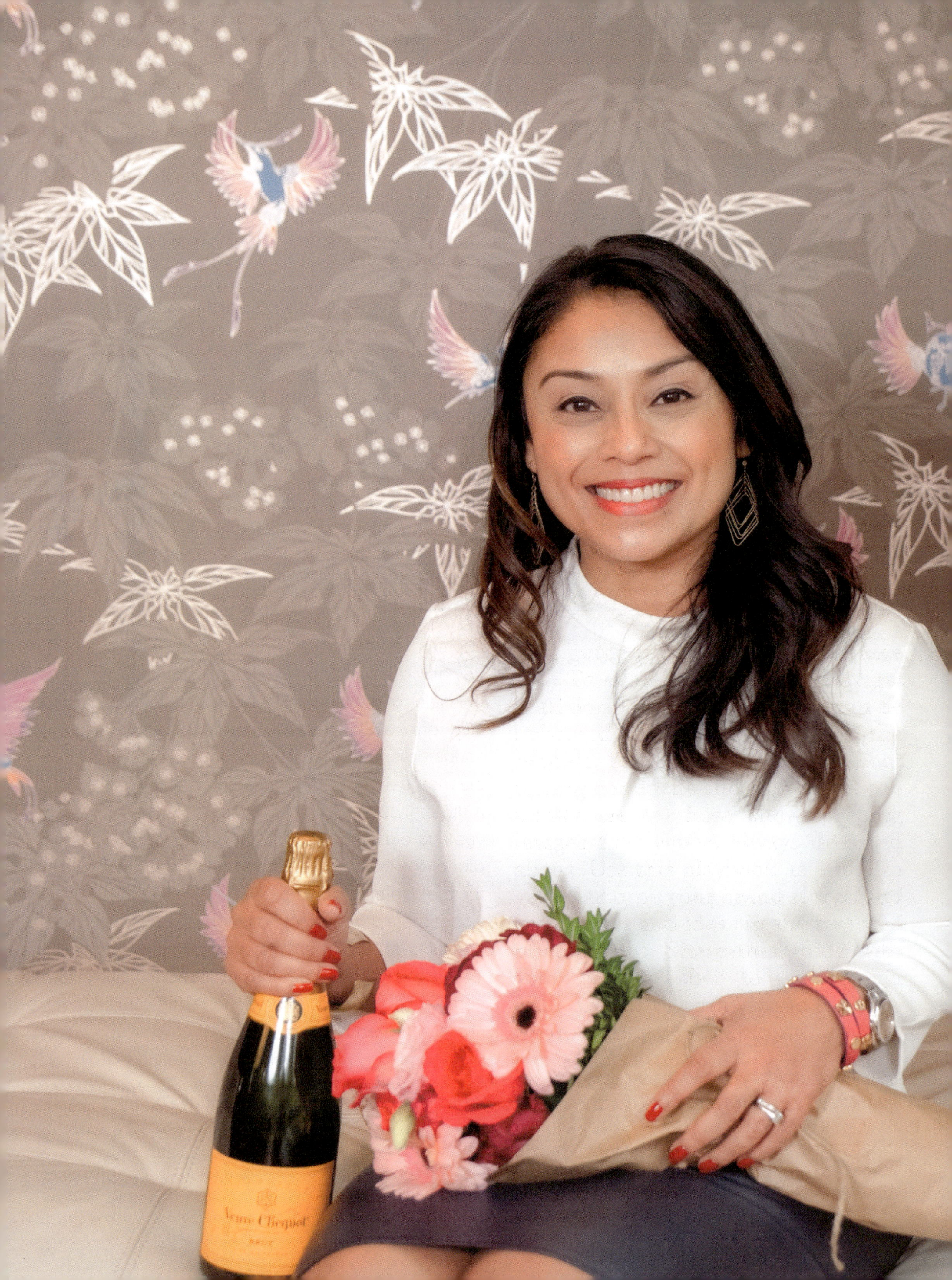

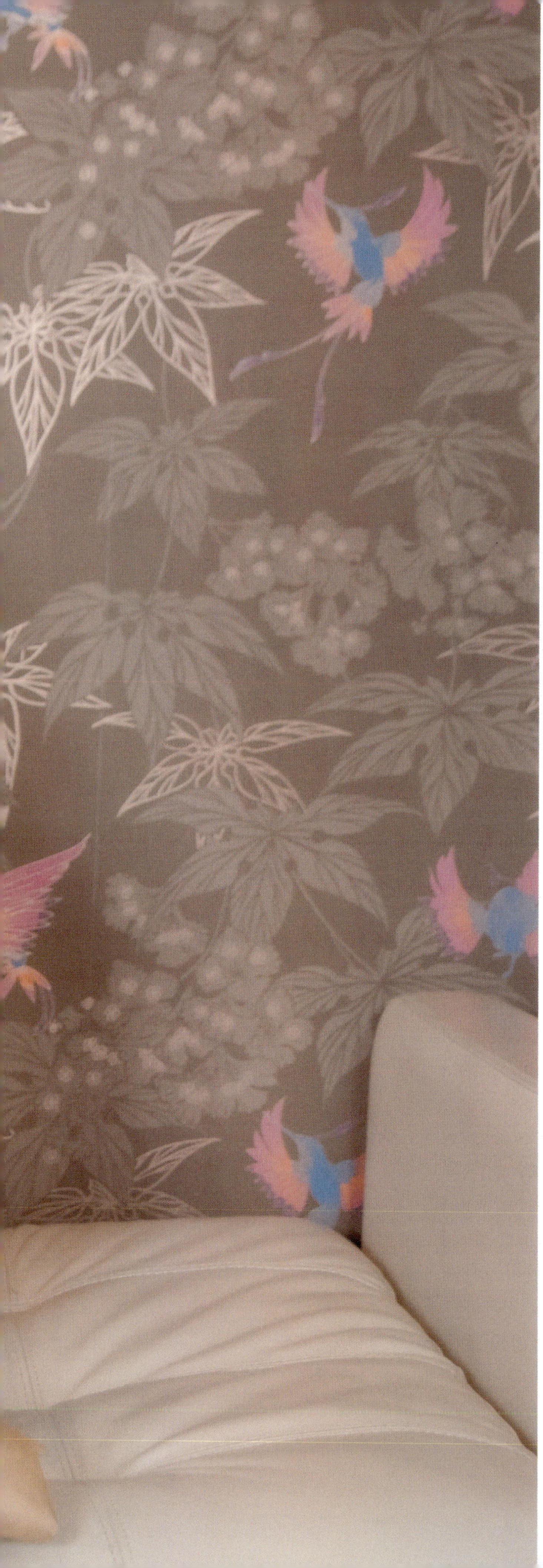

WHO AM I?

My name is Mallika Malhotra, and I'm on a mission to inspire thousands of women to boldly own their brand and share their message with confidence. I am not only a photographer but a strategist, a storyteller, and a confidence-stirring coach. I work with passionate, go-getter entrepreneurs like you to create images that not only will have you turning heads but also have you turning hearts. I take you from feeling lost and invisible to getting noticed as a leader in your industry.

Based in northern New Jersey, I also teach live workshops on branding, social media, vision boarding, photo styling, and iPhoneography. When I am not taking photos or building brands, I am home with my three sons and husband, drinking coffee or red wine and dreaming about our next global adventure.

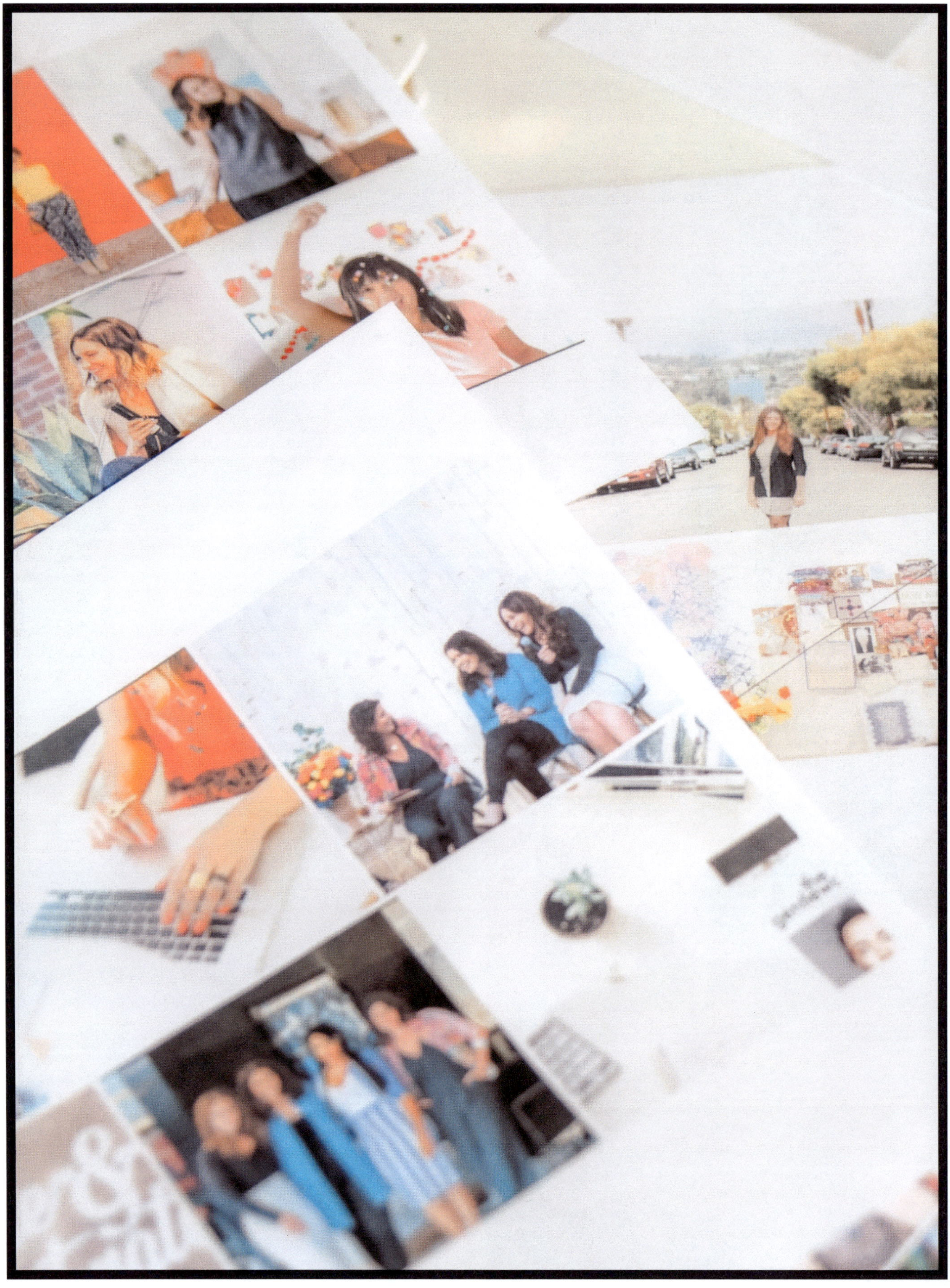

BRAND

PHOTOGRAPHY BASICS

01

WHAT IS BRAND PHOTOGRAPHY?

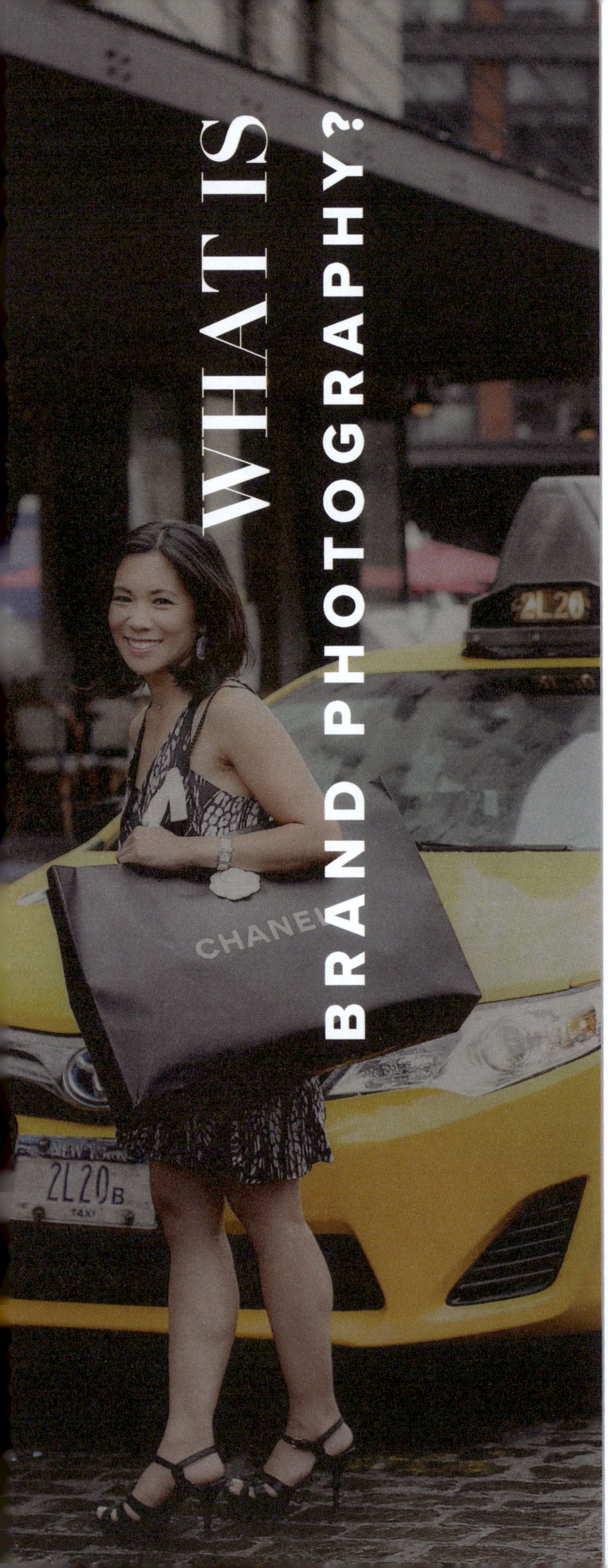

If you search Google or Wikipedia for "brand photography," you will not find a clear definition. Although definitions exist for portrait photography, branding, personal branding, and even headshots, brand photography is a newer niche in the photography industry. It is not widely known yet and can often be mistaken for other things.

Brand photography is a collection of professional and customized images that represent the essence of your brand. This type of photography communicates who you are, what you do, how it feels to work with you, and what differentiates you.

Brand photography visuals share your personality, your process, and your core message. Consider these images a visual journey that educates your audience about the many layers of your business. Brand photography should be both aspirational and authentic.

Brand Photography Is NOT:

- Your logo.
- Your tagline.
- Your colors.
- Your fonts.
- Your selfies.
- A headshot.
- Generic stock photos.
- Fashion photography.
- Your Instagram feed.
- Advertising.

WHY YOU NEED BRAND PHOTOGRAPHY?

So what's the big deal? Isn't a headshot enough? Don't DIY photos and selfies work?

These other kinds of images can help your brand, but they often struggle to communicate your complete message. When you are finally ready to up-level and position yourself as a leader, your images have to follow suit. Your business can't rely only on a single headshot or styled stock photography. Although DIY photos may be "on brand," they are not professional and don't necessarily communicate that you are the go-to expert. Imagine having a library of professional brand images that tell a strong visual story without you ever having to say a word. The end result is that you will not only have images that radiate who you are, but you will also:

Connect with your audience.

We live in a visual world where visual content is king! Storytelling images allow us to breathe life and personality into our brands. As we share our story, our audience starts to know, like, and trust us.

Stand out.

We live in a noisy world where we are being bombarded with messages and distractions. Professional photos help us get noticed, grab our audience's attention, and make our brands memorable.

Elevate your expert status.

We live in a competitive world where our industries are saturated. Professional photos differentiate the leaders from the amateurs. Great photos can position you as the authority or go-to expert in your market. Take that step to view yourself as an expert, and others will too.

Share your depth.

Your brand is more than a pretty headshot. Share the foundation of your brand, your process, your personality and your experience through visuals. This meaningful reveal will start to attract your dreamy clients and inspire them into action.

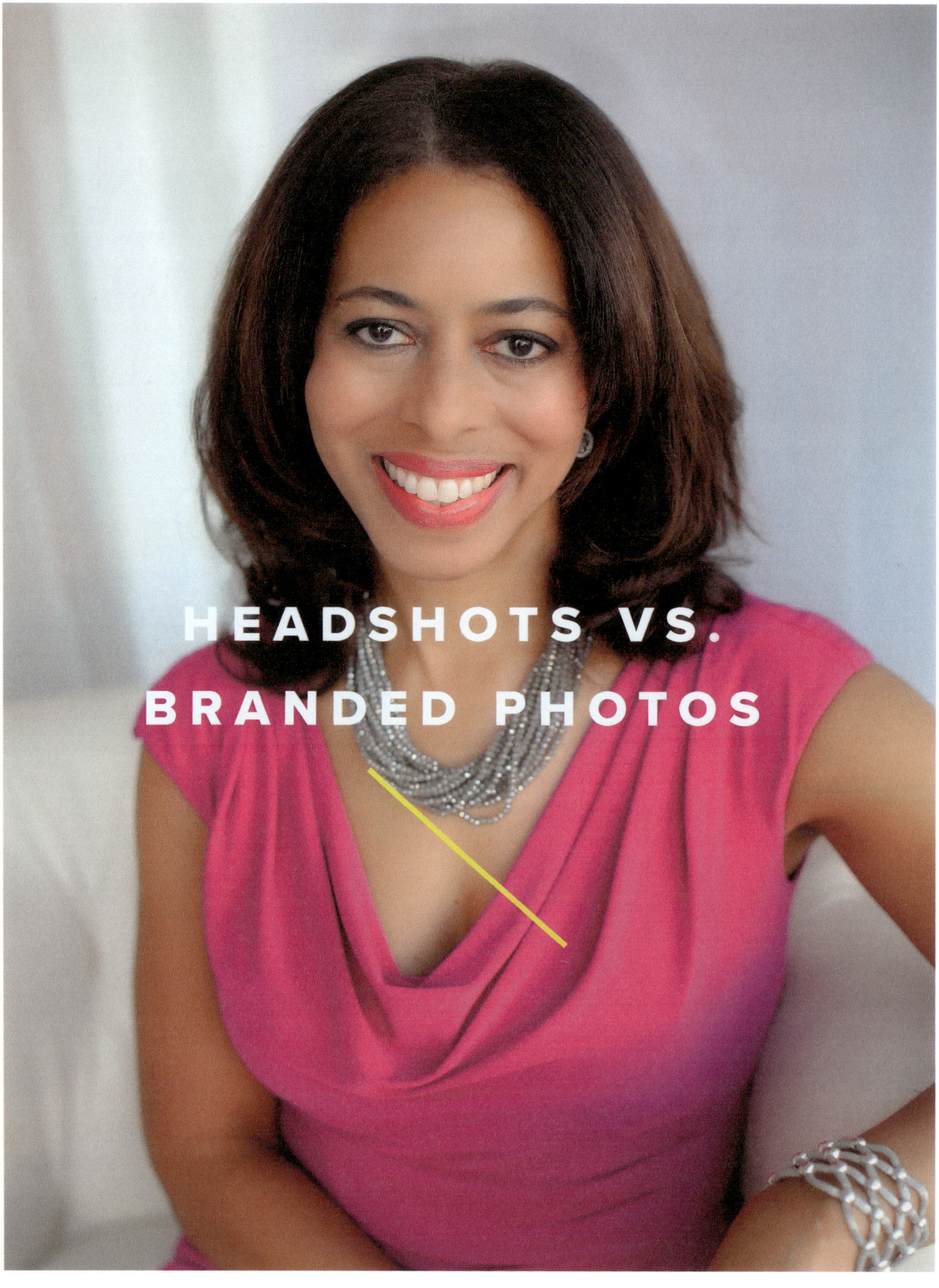

HEADSHOTS VS. BRANDED PHOTOS

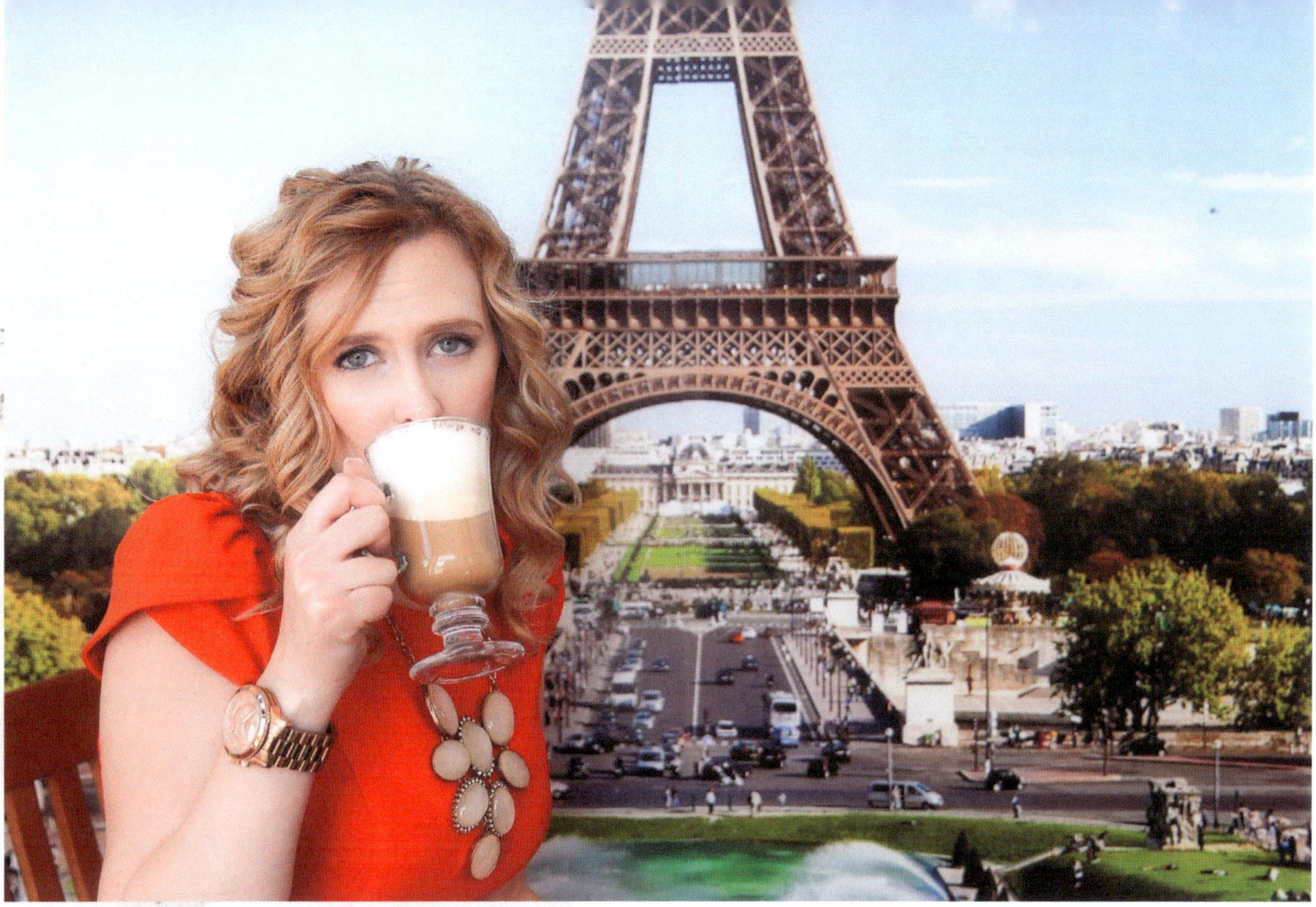

*h*eadshots can be the first point of contact with your audience. They're normally used as your profile pic on social media platforms like Facebook and Instagram, as well as on your website's "About Me" page. It's a portrait primarily focused on a person's face and taken from the shoulders up. I call headshots your virtual handshake. They should communicate that you are a professional and a legitimate business owner. While we all need a good headshot, headshots can often be one-dimensional and not great at communicating the layers of your business.

Brand photography takes the audience on a deeper look into your business. Think images that share your process, your workspace, your personality, and your community, and include environments, styling, and props. These types of photos connect and engage with your audience.

PEOPLE DO BUSINESS WITH PEOPLE, SO IT'S TIME TO SHOW UP AND BE THE FACE OF YOUR BRAND.

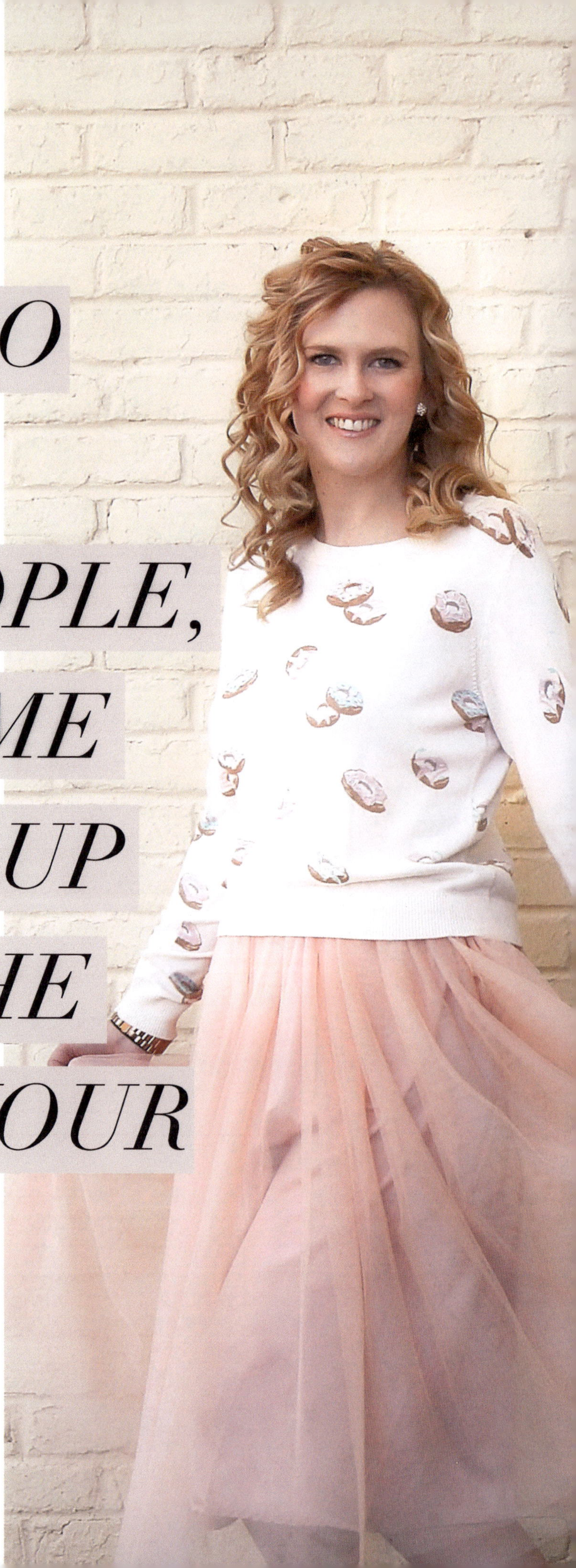

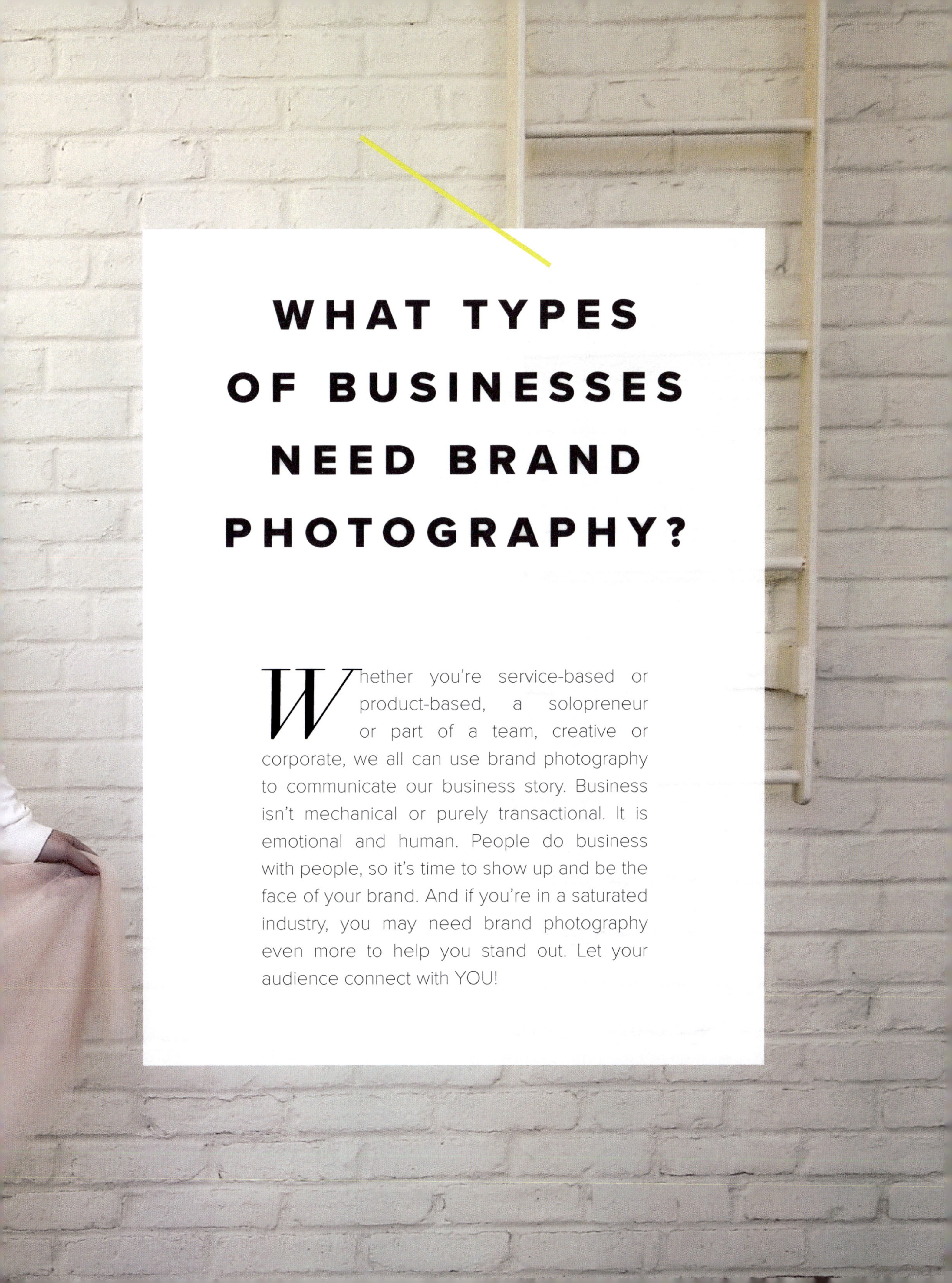

WHAT TYPES OF BUSINESSES NEED BRAND PHOTOGRAPHY?

Whether you're service-based or product-based, a solopreneur or part of a team, creative or corporate, we all can use brand photography to communicate our business story. Business isn't mechanical or purely transactional. It is emotional and human. People do business with people, so it's time to show up and be the face of your brand. And if you're in a saturated industry, you may need brand photography even more to help you stand out. Let your audience connect with YOU!

WHEN IS IT TIME TO
CONSIDER BRAND PHOTOGRAPHY?

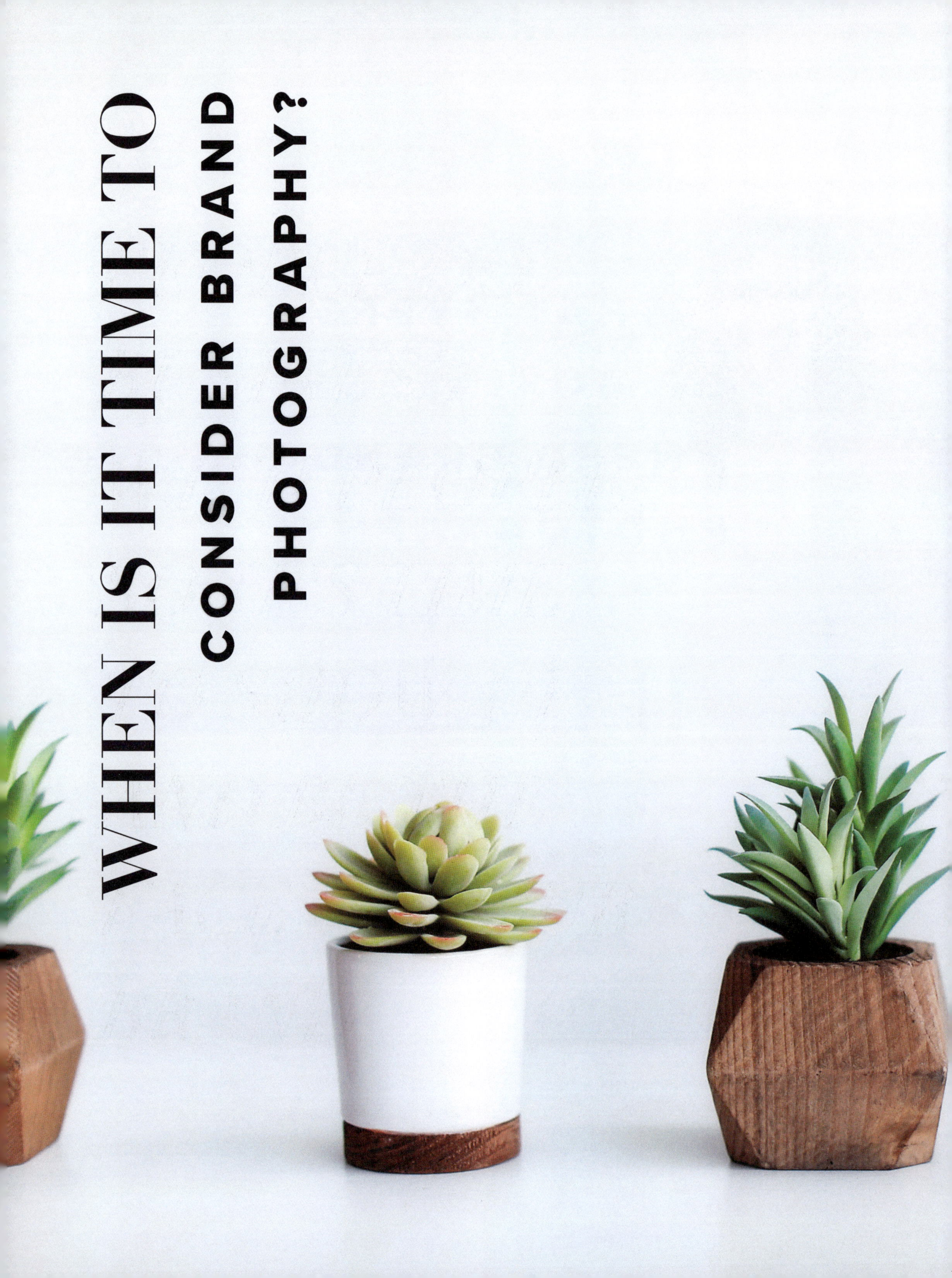

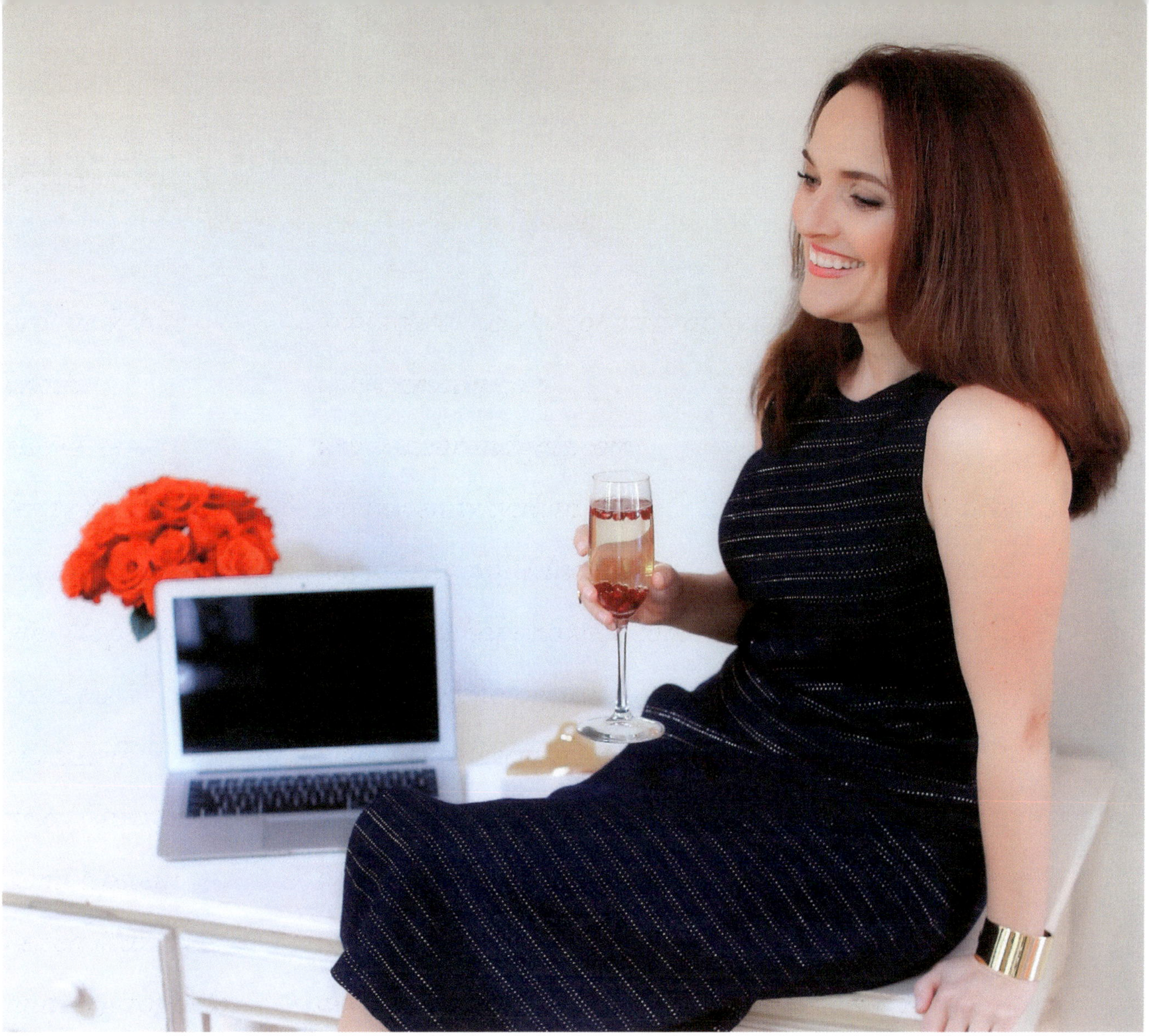

The entrepreneurial journey can vary for all of us. I've had clients who are fresh to business and others who have 10 years of experience under their belt. In my opinion, it's best to make the investment when you are clear on your brand story and messaging. When you have a concrete business plan and marketing strategy, brand photo visuals can pull everything together. If you already have that in place and you're ready to up-level your business, then brand photography may be the right next step for you. If you're still defining your brand, you may want to work with a business mentor or a specialized brand photographer to help you get ready.

Consider my client Sarah Walton. She is an author and speaker who was about to launch her first online "Money Mindset" course when I met her. Sarah wanted new visuals to communicate her financial expertise, her passion for women empowerment, and her fun-loving personality. She wanted to build connection with her audience as a mentor they could trust. New brand photos were her way to communicate a deeper story to her brand and build excitement for her launch. Examples of her new brand photos included Sarah at her laptop with the course title on the screen, her holding cash in her hands, a "behind the scenes" of Sarah speaking in front of a video camera, and Sarah drinking a celebratory champagne.

HERE ARE THE TOP 10 REASONS WHY MY CLIENTS APPROACH ME FOR BRAND PHOTOS

1

LAUNCHING A NEW BUSINESS.

5

TIME TO REVITALIZE! AMP UP MARKETING. KEEP THINGS FRESH.

6

BRAND IS STUCK; NEED TO GAIN MOMENTUM AND GROWTH.

9

NEW PRESS OPPORTUNITIES (CONFERENCES, PODCASTS, TV).

RE-BRANDING. NEW MESSAGING OR NEW POSITIONING.

LAUNCHING A WEBSITE.

LAUNCHING A COURSE OR OFFERING.

PROMOTE EXPERT STATUS (SPEAKER, INFLUENCER, AUTHOR).

PHYSICAL TRANSFORMATION. NEW YOU!

GET PERSONAL! NEED TO HUMANIZE AND CONNECT WITH AUDIENCE.

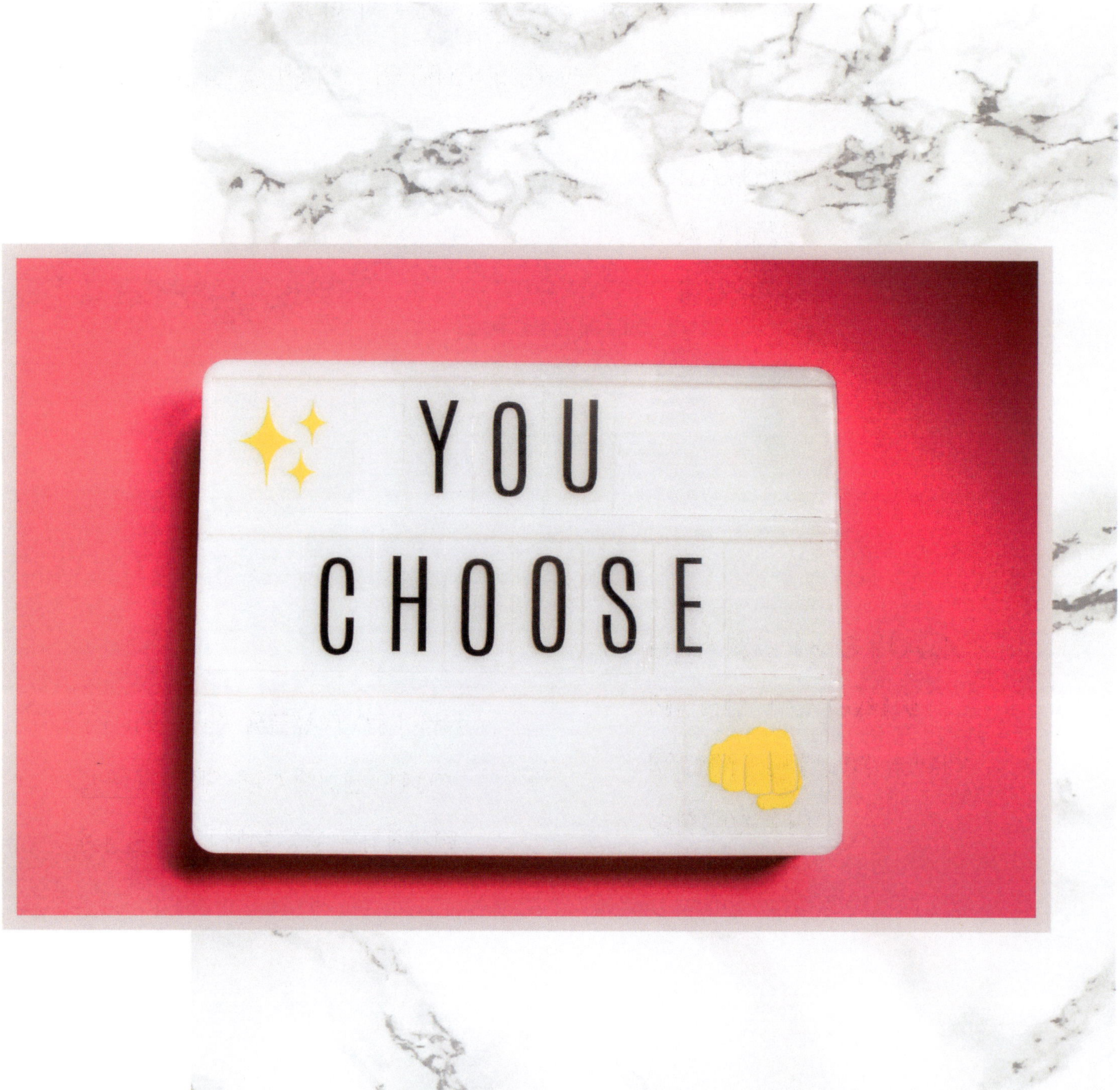
YOU
CHOOSE

QUESTIONS TO ASK BEFORE HIRING A BRAND PHOTOGRAPHER

02

If you're ready to take the leap and be the face of your brand, then it's time to find a brand photographer. Keep in mind that not all photographers are created equal, so it's necessary to do some due diligence before hiring someone. Brand photography is a new concept, so you may not have a specialist in your area. You may notice that there are only wedding, portrait, and event photographers in your town. Take time and do the research, ask questions, and set up discovery calls.

Following are some questions you should consider and ask as you find your best match.

STYLE & PORTFOLIO

Do I like the look and feel of their work?

Does the photographer's style fit with my brand?

Is their style consistent in the photos on their website?

Do the subjects in their photos look natural and relaxed?

Do the images look natural or over edited/processed?

Is the work creative and eye-catching?

EXPERIENCE

How long have they been in business?

Are they professional, or is this a hobby?

Do they have a degree in photography, or are they self-taught?

SKILL SET

What is the photographer's area of expertise (portraits, events, documentary)?

Have they done brand or business photography before?

Do they shoot in natural light, a studio, or both?

What other expertise or talents does the photographer offer (e.g., branding, styling, social media)?

Are they savvy in business and branding?

Do they have an understanding of strategy and storytelling?

Do they have a strong social media presence?

Is the photographer creative and visionary?

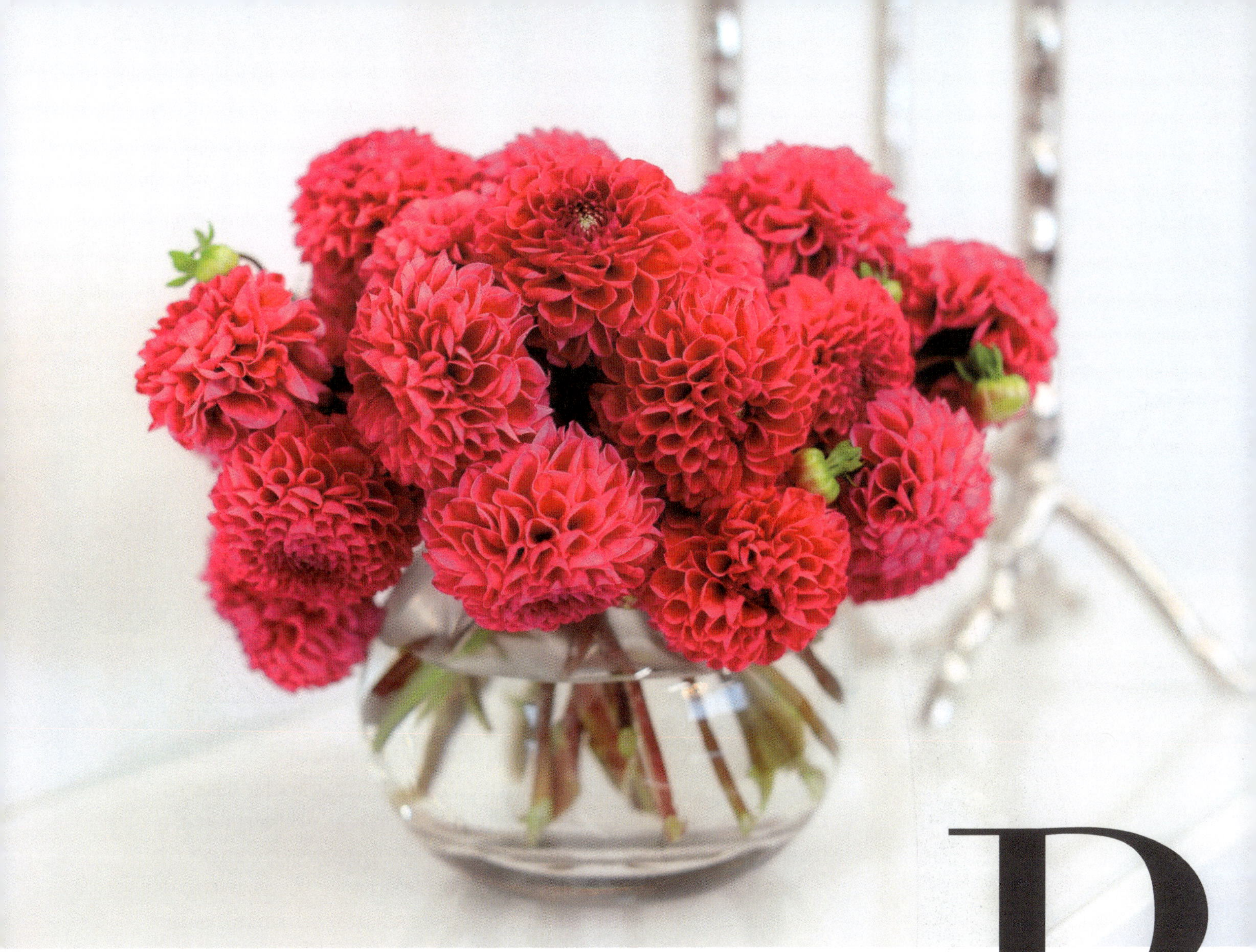

P

PERSONALITY

Do I like this person?

Are they easy to talk with?

Do I feel comfortable with them?

Can I be myself and relax around them?

Do they pick up the phone to talk live or correspond by email?

Are they a good listener; do they ask questions?

RECOMMENDATIONS

What do their reviews say?

How do previous clients describe the experience and relationship?

Are there any negative comments?

PRICE

How much do they charge?

Is there a fee for the session and a separate fee for the digitals?

Do they offer all-inclusive packages?

Are hair and makeup included in the fee?

How many digitals are included in the fee?

What if I want to purchase more images? How much would it cost?

Is there an archiving fee (i.e., fee to re-upload gallery after time has passed)?

How much is the deposit to secure my date?

Can I pay in installments?

What is the fee for a re-shoot?

PROCESS

How do we work together?

What process will they take me through to understand my business and story?

Is there a questionnaire?

How do I share my vision with them (e.g., Pinterest board, sketch, phone call)?

Do we create a mood board?

Do they have a team? An assistant?

Who does hair/makeup and where?

Any special instructions on how I should prep and arrive for the shoot (e.g., bare faced, clean hair)?

How will I select and style my outfits?

What should I wear?

Do they work with a stylist? Is this an additional fee?

How many outfits should I bring?

What colors should I wear?

How long is the shoot day?

What is the best time of day to shoot?

How many locations?

How do we get around from place to place?

Do I need props at the photo shoot to help tell my story?

What kind of props and how many (e.g, books, mugs, journal, candles)?

Who gets the props?

How will I transport and organize all of my stuff?

Where will I change between shots?

How do I pose?

Will they direct me on how to move my body?

What else should I bring to the shoot?

Do they take a range of photos at different angles?

How will I view the image gallery?

Do I view my gallery online, or can I have a proof sheet?

Do I see all the photos that they take?

How do they select the images that I see in my gallery?

How long does it take for them to edit?

What kind of editing do they do?

Can they help me choose the images?

What happens if it rains or the weather interferes?

What happens if I am sick or need to cancel?

What do I need to do before the photo shoot?

PRODUCT

What are the deliverables?*

Do they shoot film or digital?

How many images do I get?

How are the images delivered?

What format do I get the images? (High-resolution? Web-sized?)

Are the images proofs or edited?

Do they watermark the images?

Do they use Photoshop?

How much retouching do they do?

Can I retouch/edit/add filters to the photos later?

What happens if I don't like the final product/photos?

What if I want to purchase more?

Do I have usage and printing rights?

Do they have any rights to my photo?

Will they be using it in any way?

Are there any restrictions around how I can use the photos?

Do I have to credit them when using the images?

**This is a very important question to ask because each photographer operates differently. Some may offer a specific number of edited high-res images; others may give you all the proofs, which are un-finished. Some photographers may even do a combination of both. I suggest you pick a package with finished, edited images. You may think that you want ALL the proofs from your photo shoot, but if you don't know how to edit yourself, will you really share an unfinished photo to represent your brand?*

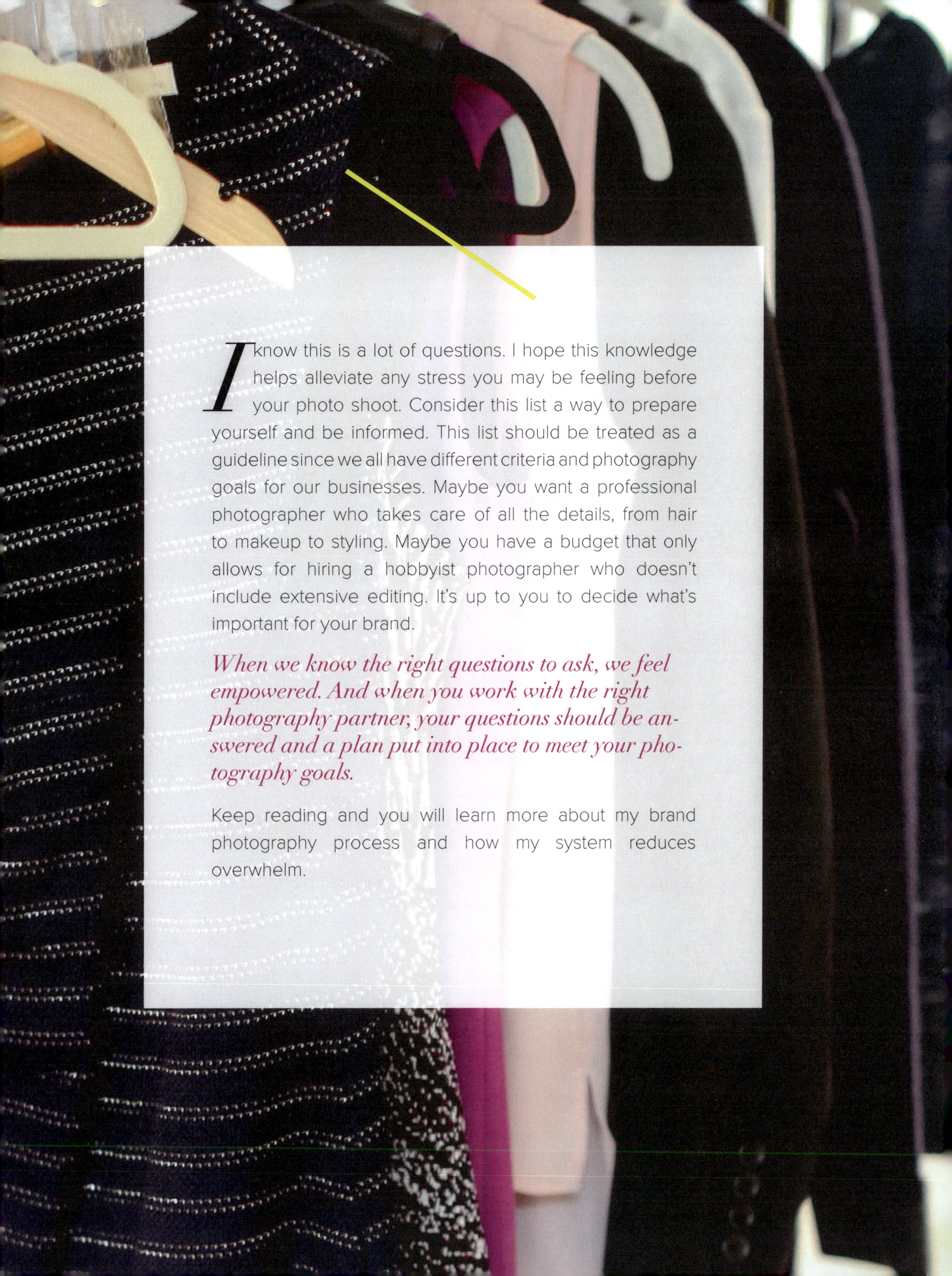

I know this is a lot of questions. I hope this knowledge helps alleviate any stress you may be feeling before your photo shoot. Consider this list a way to prepare yourself and be informed. This list should be treated as a guideline since we all have different criteria and photography goals for our businesses. Maybe you want a professional photographer who takes care of all the details, from hair to makeup to styling. Maybe you have a budget that only allows for hiring a hobbyist photographer who doesn't include extensive editing. It's up to you to decide what's important for your brand.

When we know the right questions to ask, we feel empowered. And when you work with the right photography partner, your questions should be answered and a plan put into place to meet your photography goals.

Keep reading and you will learn more about my brand photography process and how my system reduces overwhelm.

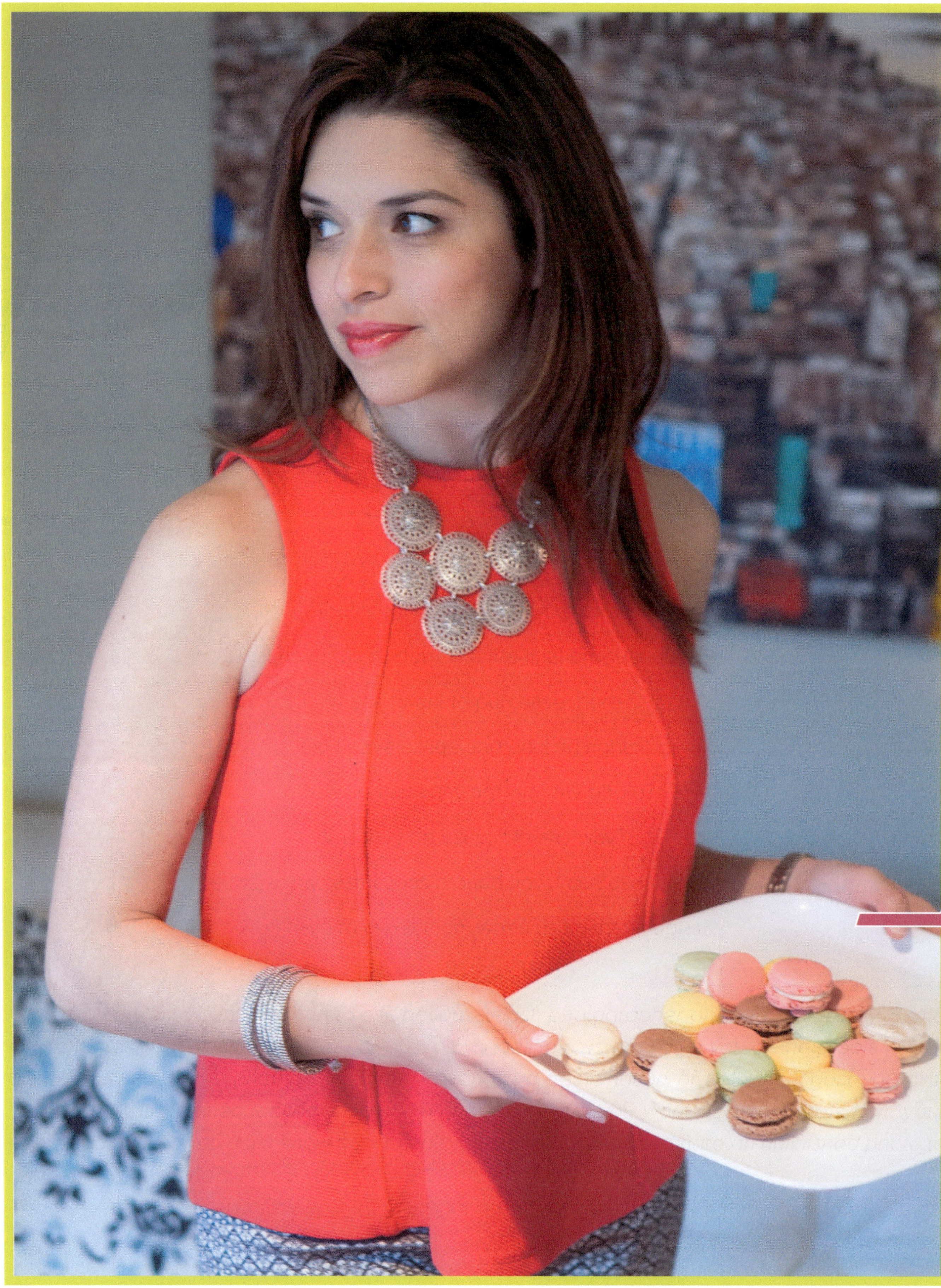

03

A TYPICAL BRAND PHOTOGRAPHY SHOOT

Curious to know what a brand photography shoot looks like from start to finish? Let me take you through my signature process. Remember: Not every photographer has the same system, but this is how I partner with my clients to create their brand photography libraries.

MIKIFOTO PROCESS

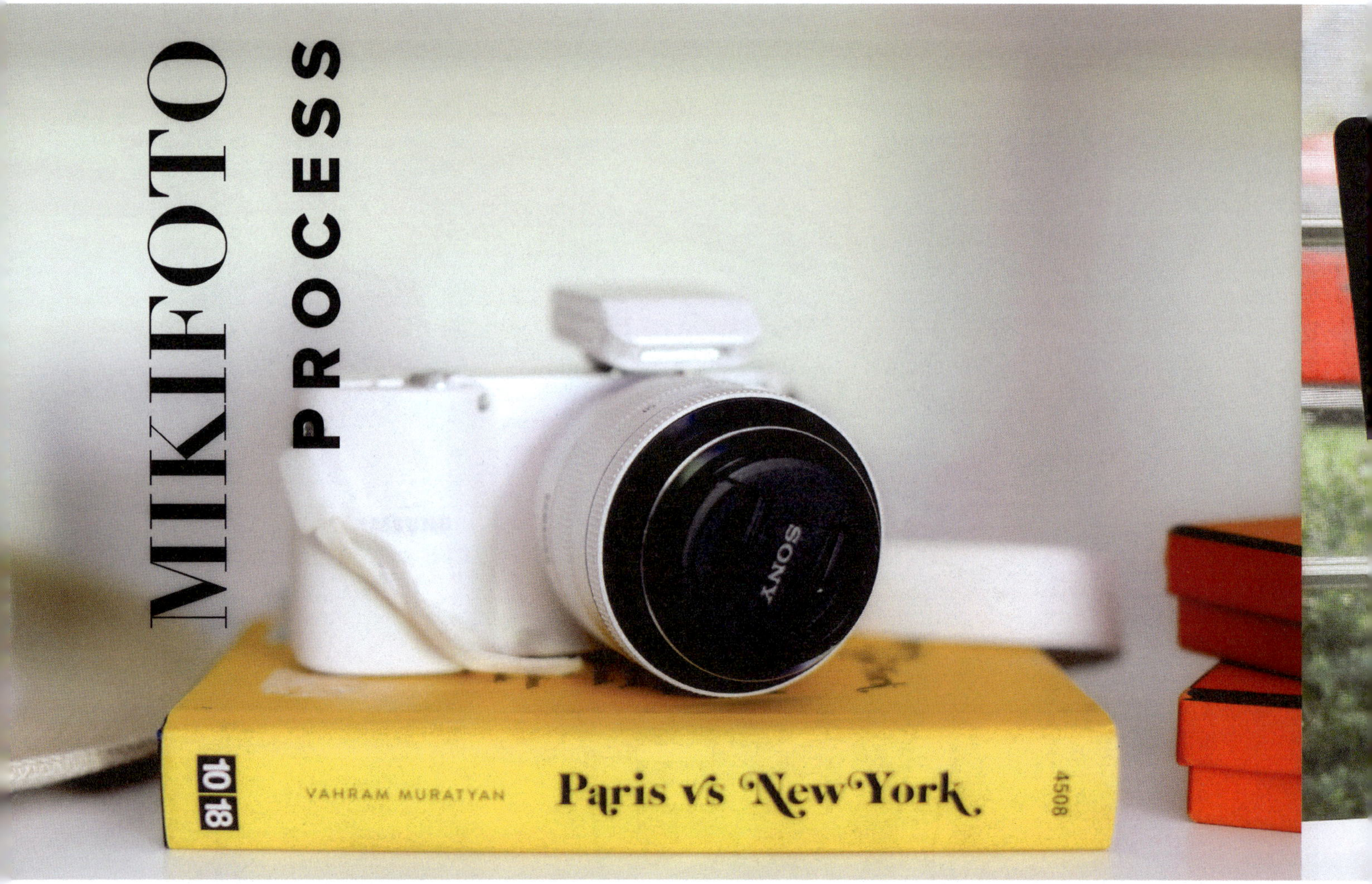

01 Introductory Chat

We start with a 15-minute phone conversation/consultation to see if we are a good fit. We make sure your photography goals and budget meet what I offer and can deliver. Let's say you only need a headshot, for example. In that case, a larger package wouldn't be the right fit and we would discuss alternate options.

02 Tell Me Your Story

Once the contract and estimate are approved, I send a detailed questionnaire for you to fill out on your own. This survey explores your brand foundation like your purpose, values, and core message, along with your photography goals.

03 Creative Brainstorming

After the questionnaire is complete, I ask you to create a Pinterest board, to which you pin visuals and ideas that inspire you and represent the look and feel of your brand. We use this tool as a starting point for the creative discussion and then I create a brand inspiration/mood board for our photo shoot.

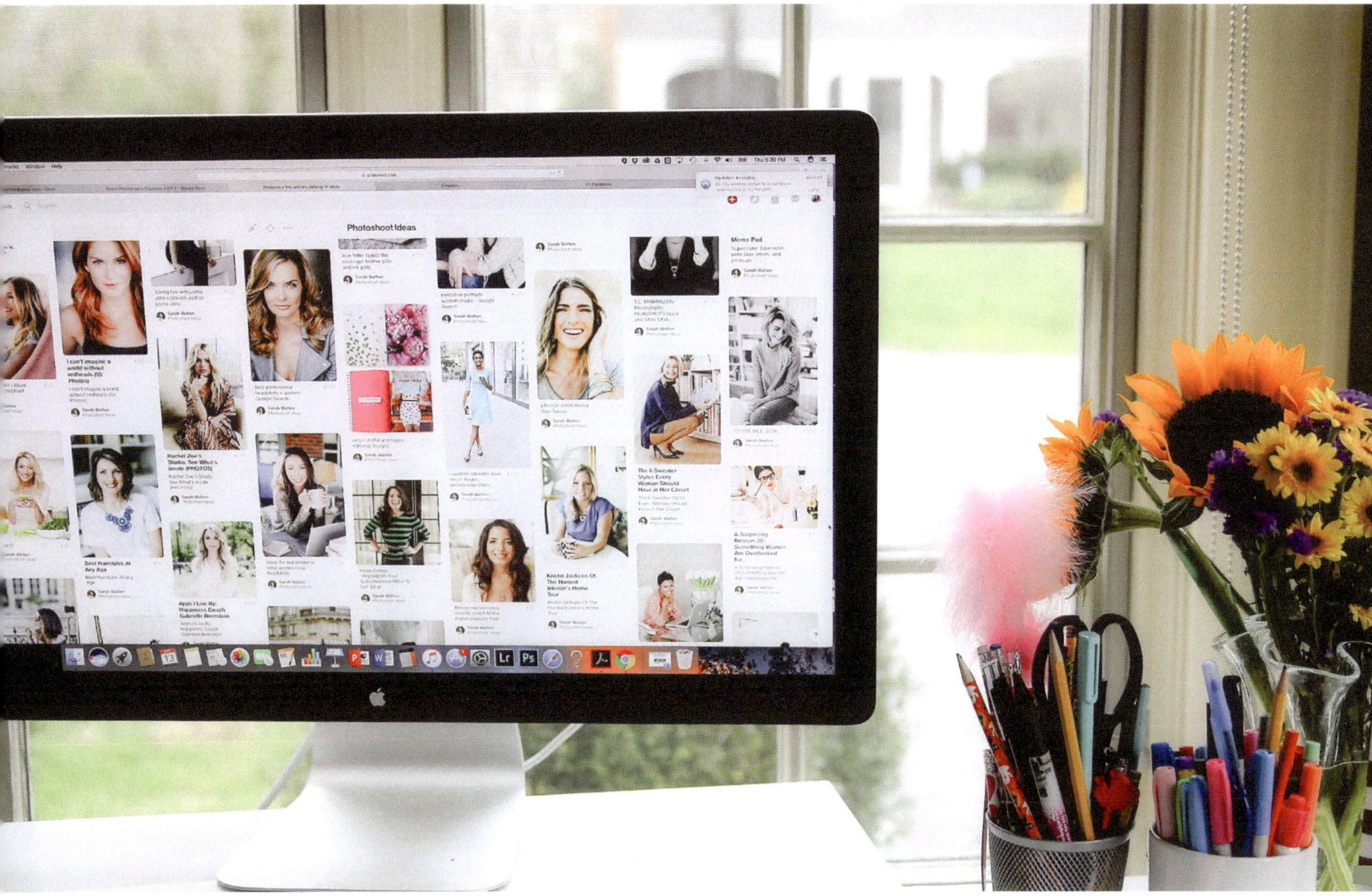

04

Strategy Session

After your questionnaire and mood board are complete, we set up a meeting in person or by Skype to review your answers and the visual inspiration. We brainstorm ideas and outline story concepts. We chat about locations and props. We discuss outfits and accessories. This is when the creative storytelling unfolds and when we define our creative photography strategy.

05

Creative Team on Board

Once the strategy is in place, we share the mood board and strategic direction with the entire team of creatives: hair, makeup, and stylist (if hiring). We make sure everyone is on board and understands the branding photo goals.

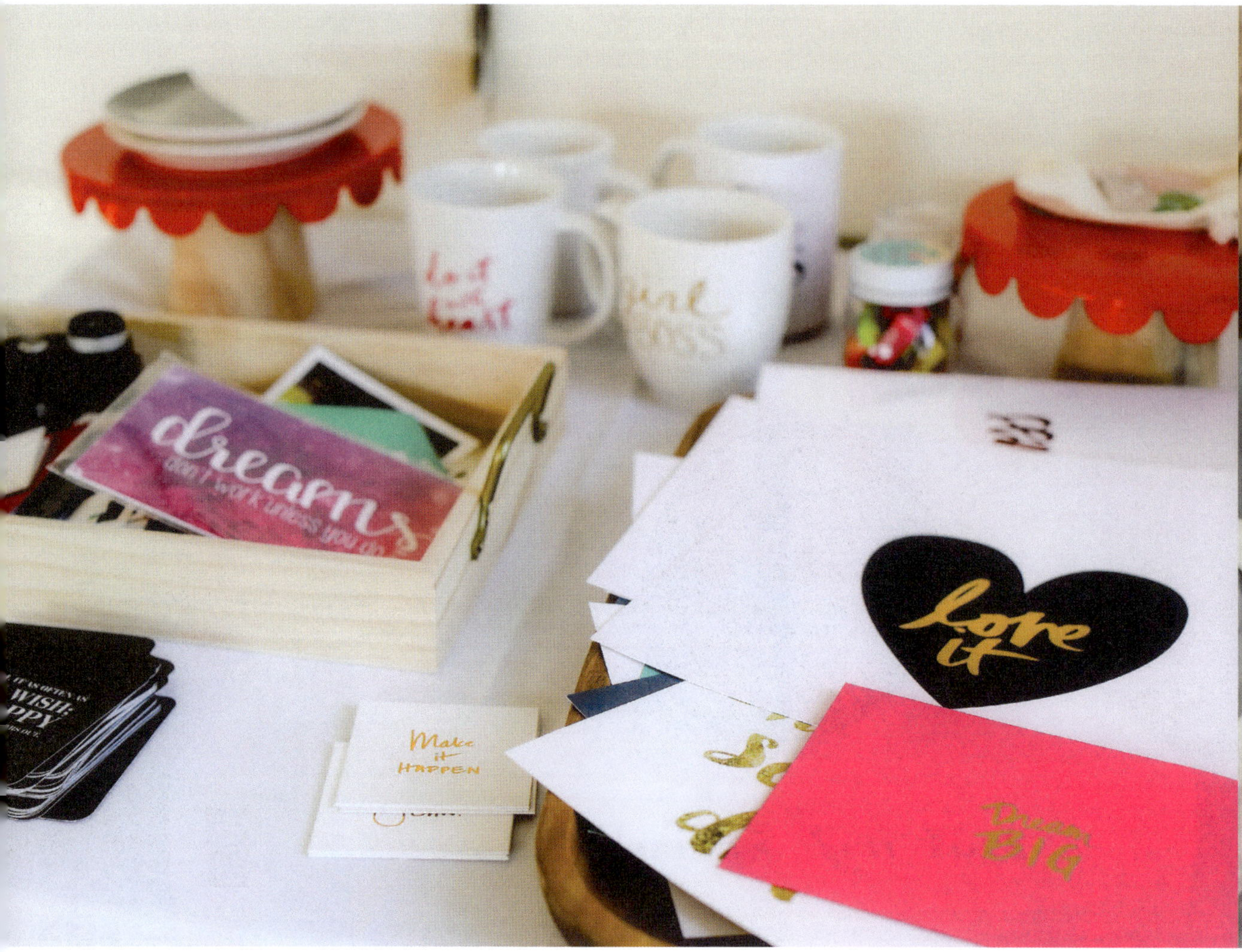

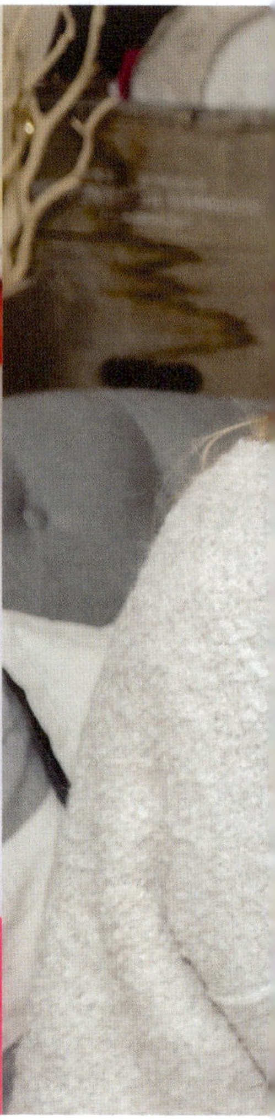

06

Shoot Schedule

We pick a shoot date (and rain date) based on everyone's availability: yours, mine, the hair/makeup artists, and the wardrobe stylist (if you choose to hire one). I create a detailed outline of the day and plan out every hour of our time together. I provide a shot list that we review together to ensure that every picture we want to capture is covered in our schedule. Expect to be shooting from about 9 a.m. until 2 p.m., with lots of traveling and wardrobe changes. We select three to four locations for the shoot. You should have three to five outfits prepared from head to toe (tops, bottoms, accessories, shoes).

07

Showtime (Session Day)

Prepare for an early wakeup call for hair and makeup. The team of stylists (hair, makeup, and wardrobe) usually arrives by 8 a.m. to get started. They work with you in the morning for one to two hours to get you ready for the day's shoot. I arrive at 8:30 a.m. to start photographing some of your props and favorite things

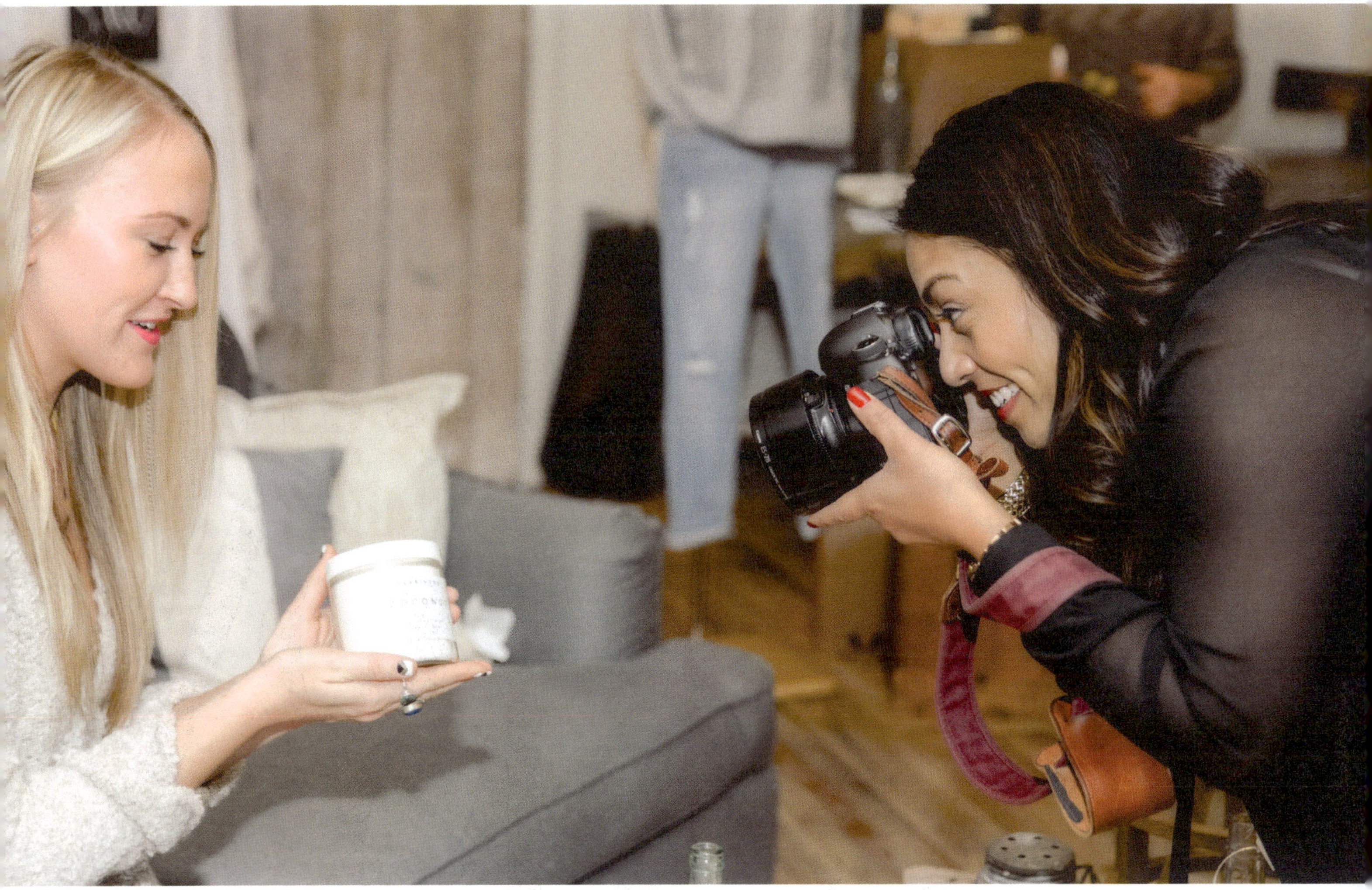

to create your customized, styled stock photos. Once you are ready, we get started and usually drive in my car together to the different locations. For the next five hours, I take a combination of photos: headshots, lifestyle (you in action), environmental (you with the setting/location), closeups, action shots, product shots, and various moods, expressions, and emotions. It's a busy, fun-filled day celebrating you and your brand story.

08 Gallery Review

Within 10 business days of your photo session, I have your private online gallery of proofs ready for your review. The images in your gallery are all soft edits and not fully finished. You pick your favorite 40 images (with my help if necessary) and once your selections are made, I will start editing.

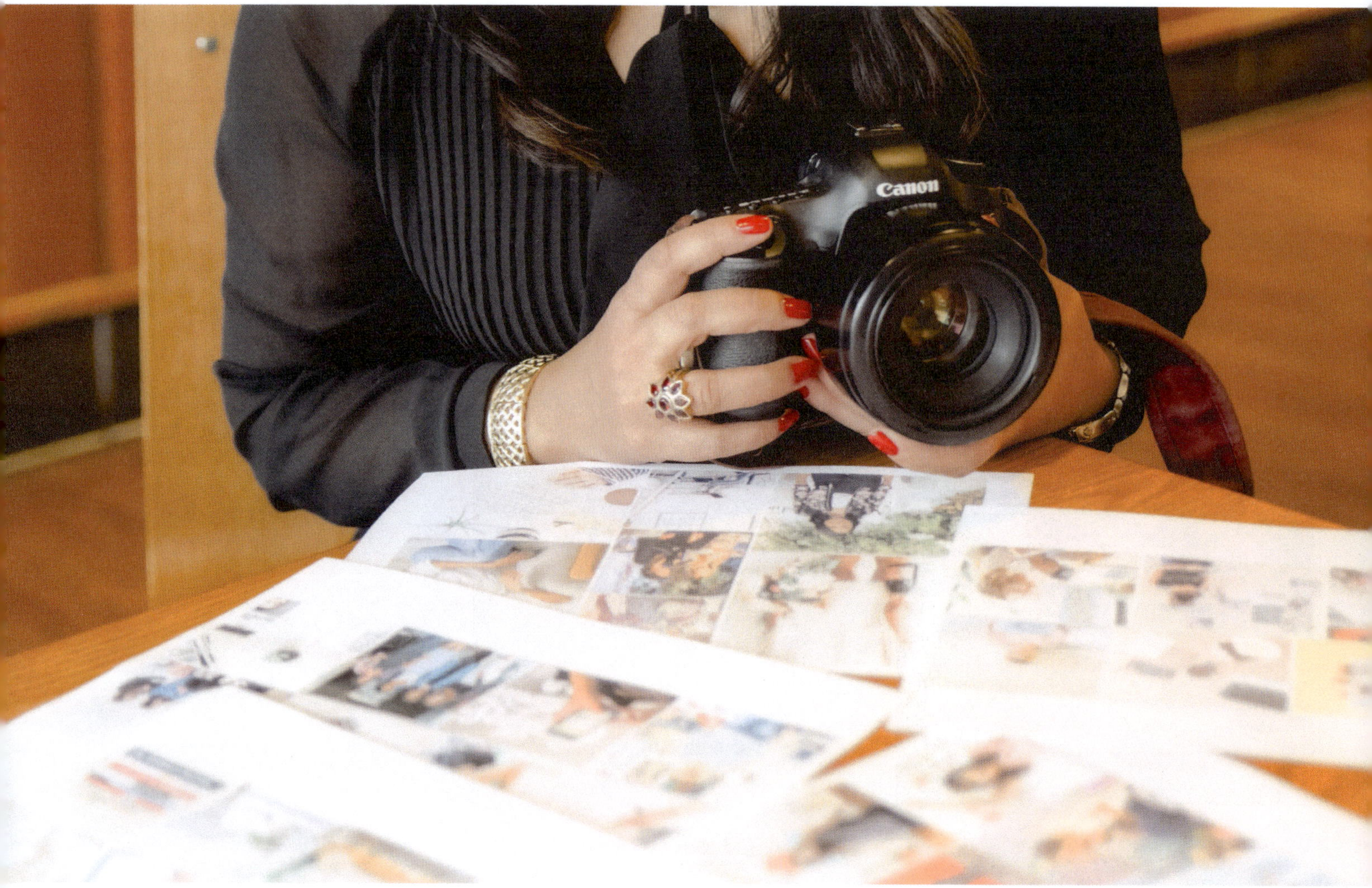

09

Library Download

Once your images are fully edited and finished, you are able to download by Dropbox. You now have a complete library of storytelling visuals that you can use across all marketing platforms. I send you a high-resolution (for printing) and Web-sized (for online) version of each of the selected images.

10

Continued Support

After the shoot and images are delivered, I continue to highlight your photos on my website, newsletters, social media, and so forth as they fit in my branding. I always tag you in order to share your brand with my audience. I am passionate about building community and supporting my fellow entrepreneurs!

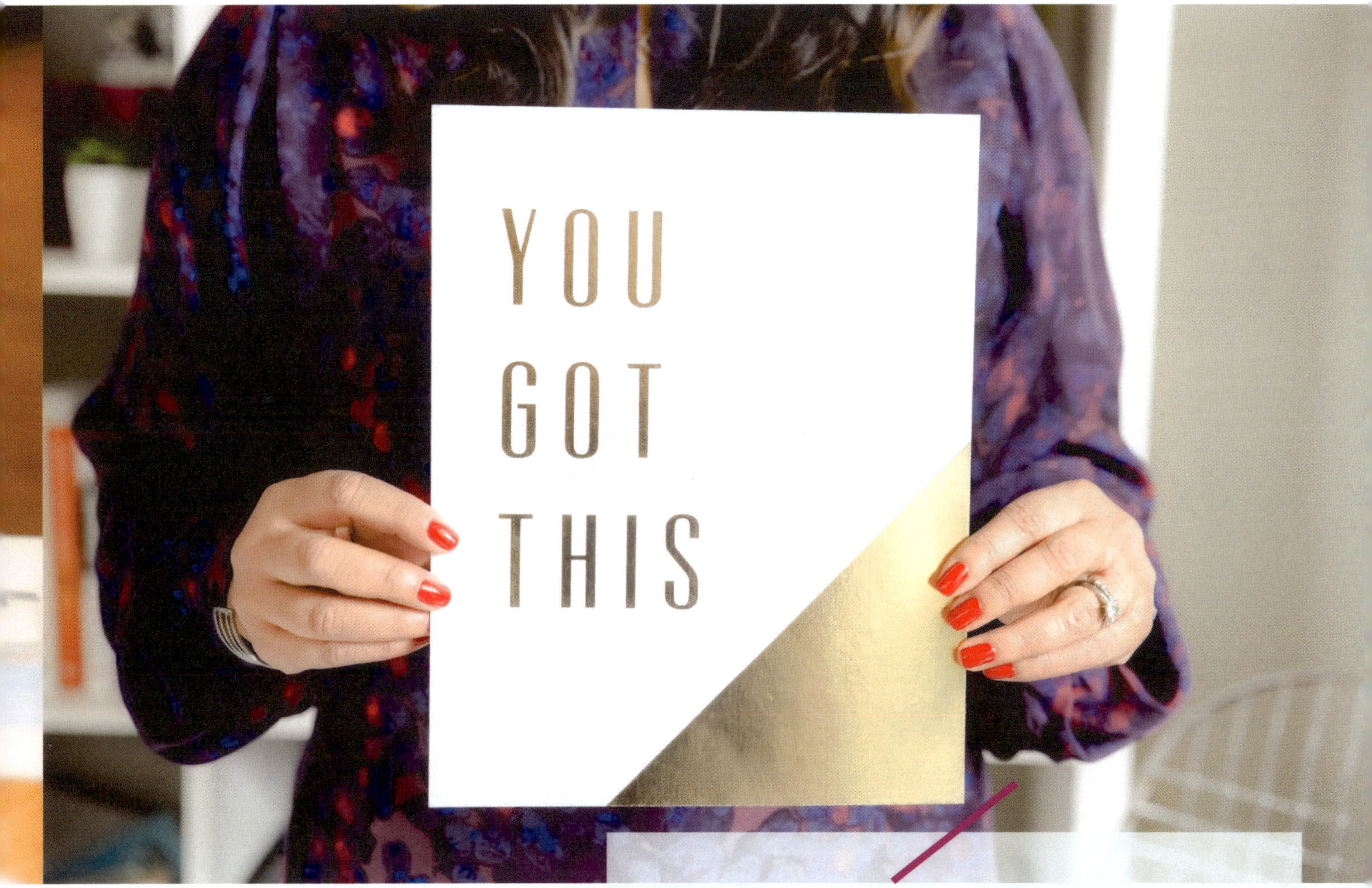

As you can see, there are many moving parts to a brand photography shoot. Every photographer has their own process, so the experience may be slightly different than mine. It can seem overwhelming, but with the right photographer and proper preparation, the shoot details can all come together to run smoothly and be loads of fun. Just remember that this is not a "show up and shoot" type of photo session. It's an investment that requires work. But it will all be worth it to help grow your business.

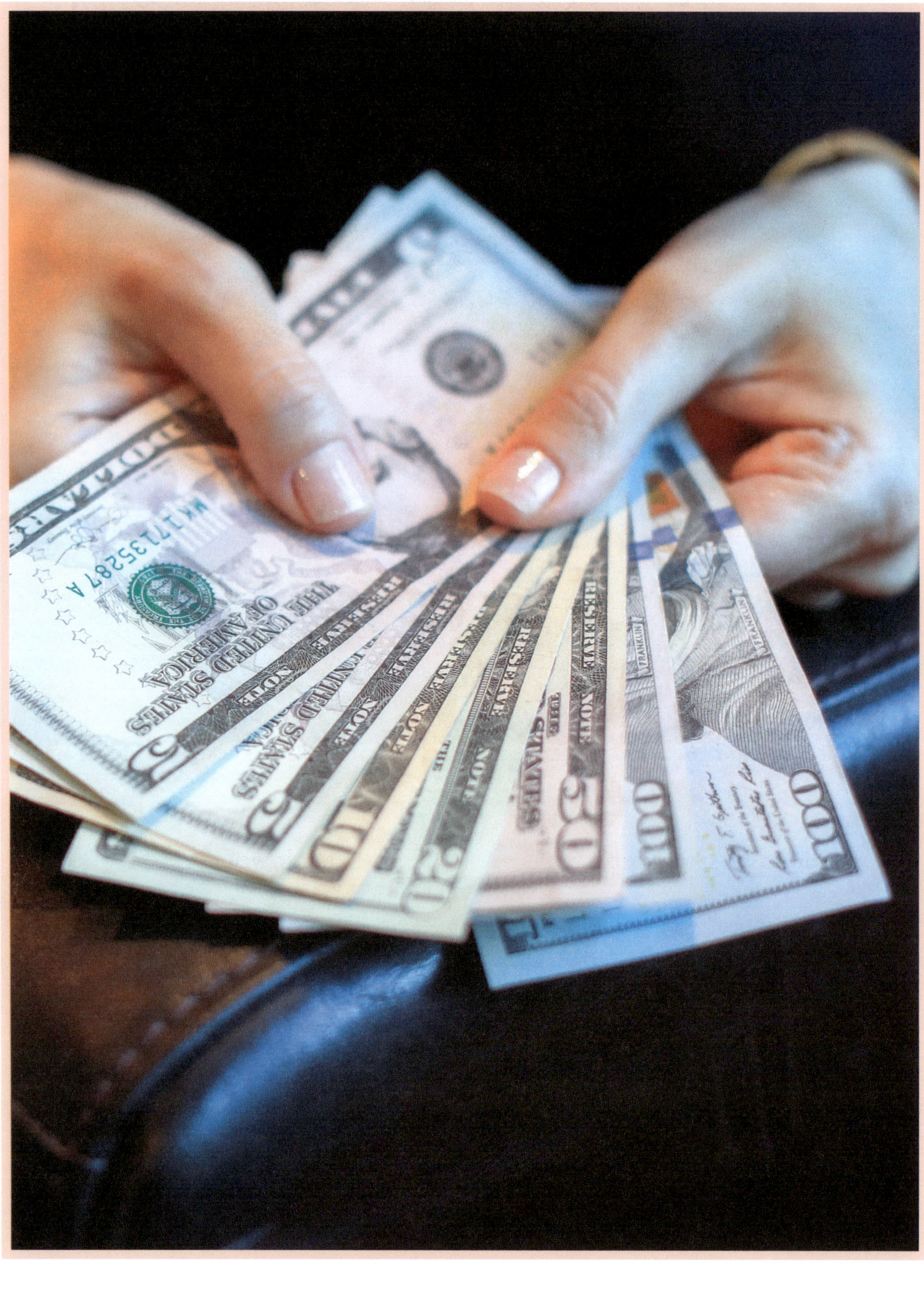
THE UNITED STATES OF AMERICA
MK17135287A
RESERVE NOTE

04

WHAT'S THE INVESTMENT?

Pricing is never definitive and can fluctuate depending on where you live, how many years of experience the photographer has, and what is included in the package. Unlike a headshot, brand photography is an investment in both time and money. The package fee is usually higher because this kind of session is robust and time-intensive. It can include strategy, pre-production, creative counsel, hair, makeup, location scouting, the actual photo shoot, curating, editing, retouching, and digital files. Not to mention, you may work with a team of creatives.

To give you a guideline and benchmark, I'm sharing my brand photography packages and pricing (as of spring 2017). Keep in mind that I live in New Jersey close to New York City, so my fees may be different than a photographer's fee based in a smaller community. Plus, I have nine years of experience and have photographed hundreds of women in business.

SMALLER BRAND PHOTOGRAPHY SHOOT

$999

Pre-shoot brand story consultation
Pre-shoot creative strategy discussion
One-hour photo session at one location
Photography of two looks
Headshots and lifestyle shots
Wardrobe and styling assistance
Hair blowout and makeup application
Access to private online gallery of proofs
Your choice of 15 edited images
Additional images at $50 each

SIGNATURE BRAND PHOTOGRAPHY SHOOT

$2,499

Pre-shoot brand story questionnaire and consultation
Pre-shoot creative strategy discussion
Four-hour photo session time at three locations
Photography of up to four outfits/looks
Headshots, lifestyle shots, and stock photography
Wardrobe and styling assistance
Hair blowout and makeup application
Brand library of 40 edited, high-resolution images
Spotlight on MikiFoto social media
Storytelling collages for social media
Additional images at $50 each

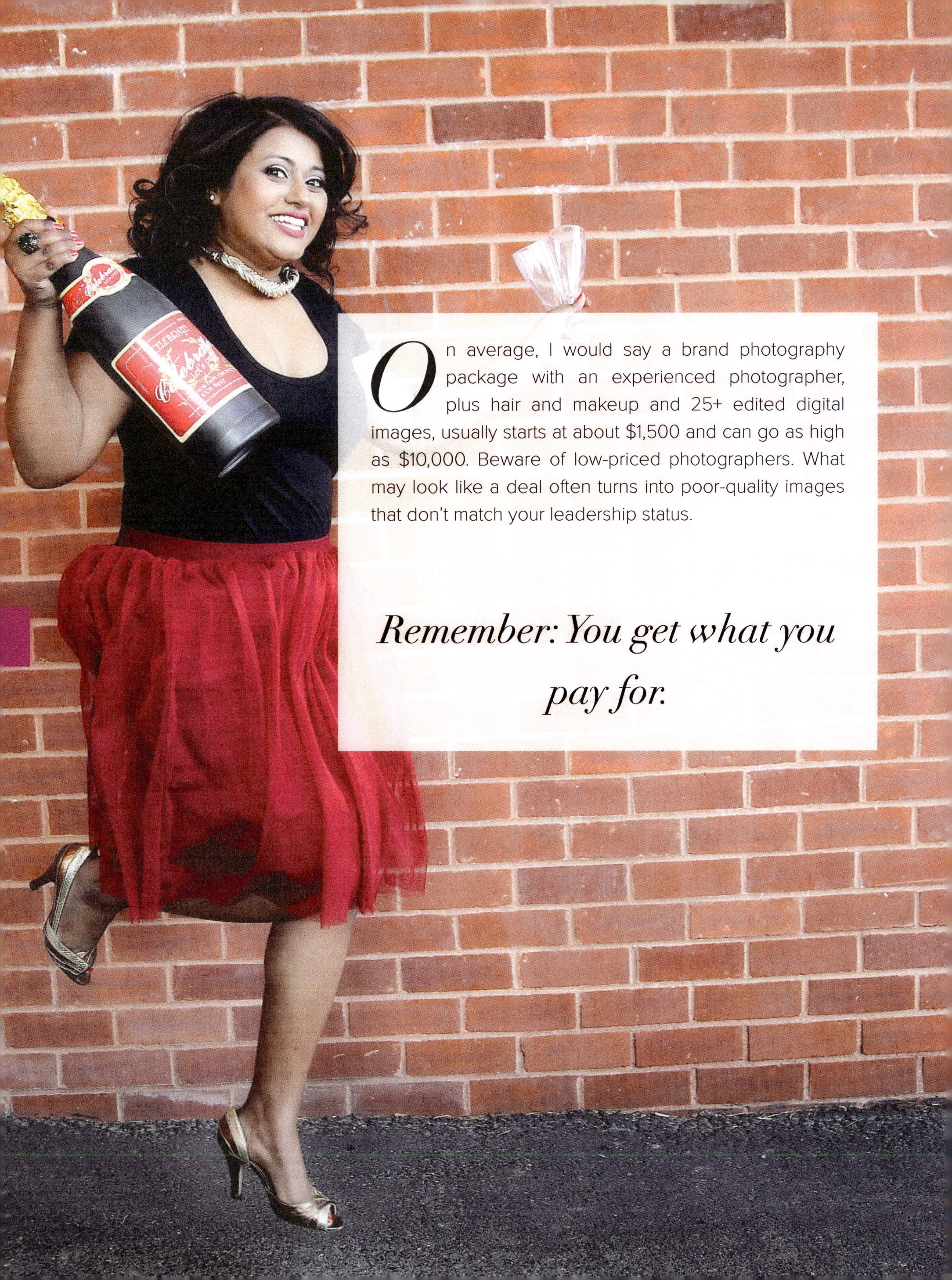

On average, I would say a brand photography package with an experienced photographer, plus hair and makeup and 25+ edited digital images, usually starts at about $1,500 and can go as high as $10,000. Beware of low-priced photographers. What may look like a deal often turns into poor-quality images that don't match your leadership status.

Remember: You get what you pay for.

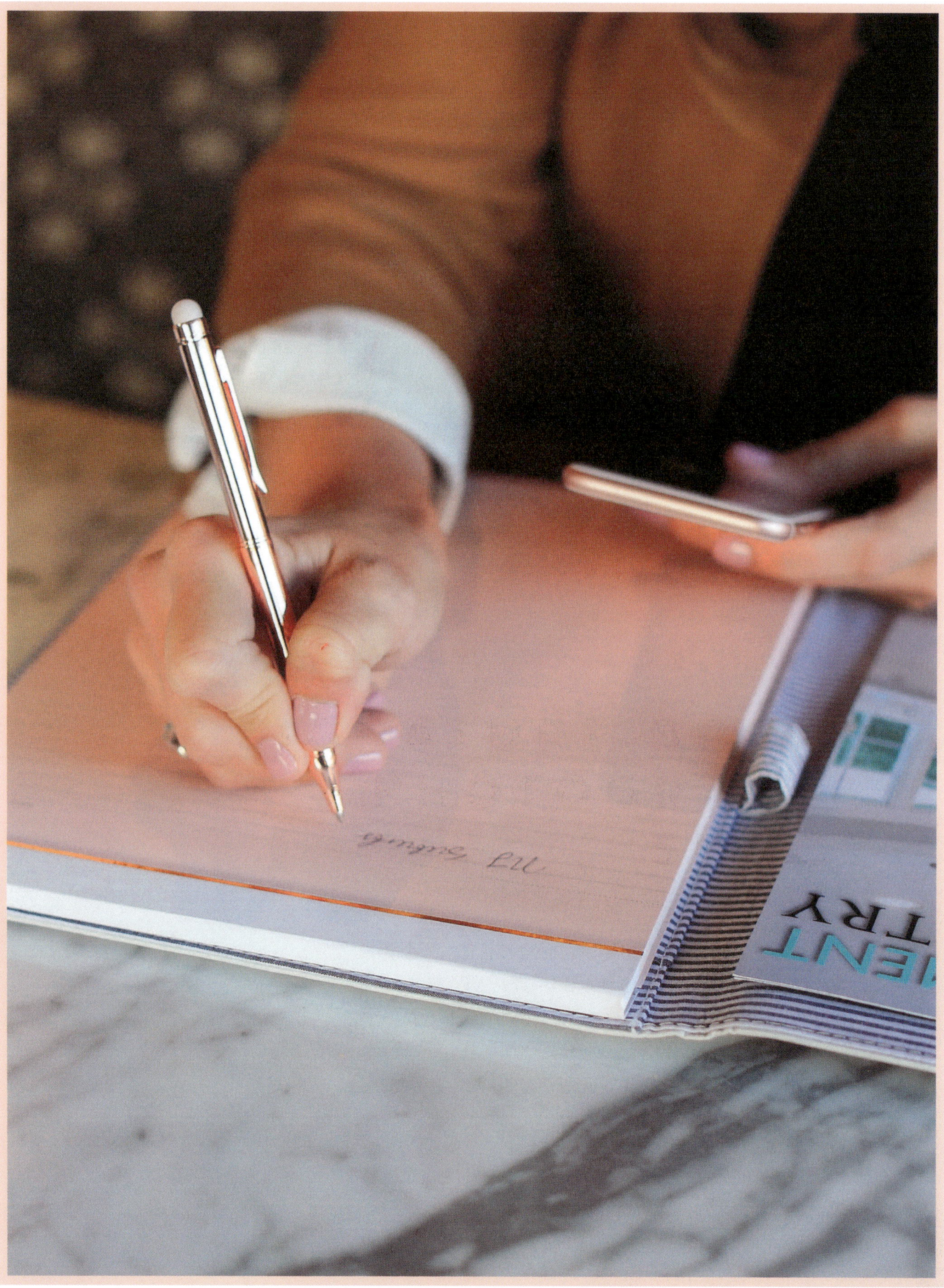

05

HOW SHOULD I PREPARE FOR A BRAND PHOTOSHOOT?

Congrats! Your photographer is booked. The date is on your calendar. Now is the time to do the pre-shoot work. Here is an outline of steps you should consider with your photographer before your shoot day. This preparation stage can take six to 10 weeks. Give yourself time! Each step is so important for to creating images that are impactful and authentic.

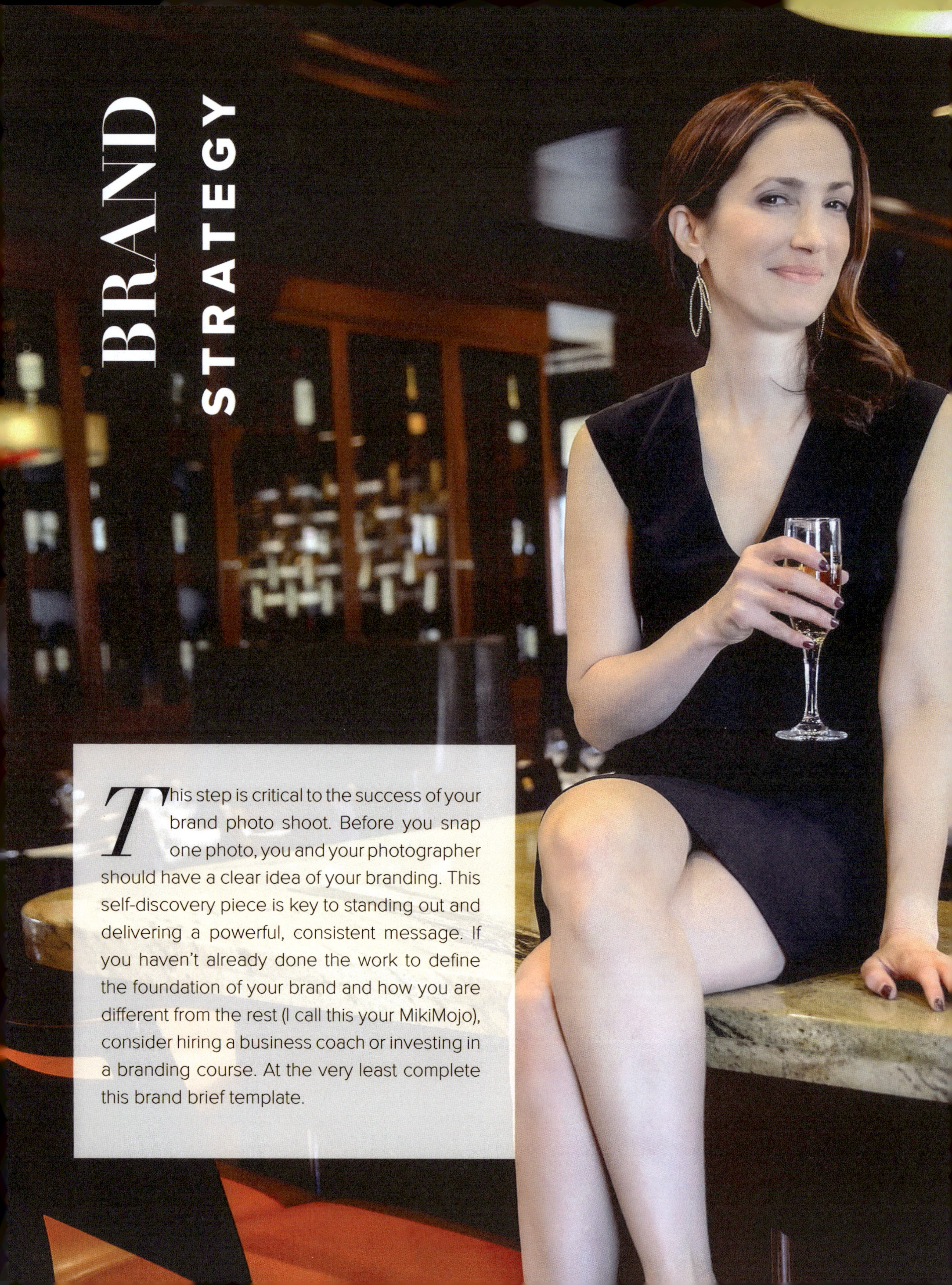

BRAND STRATEGY

This step is critical to the success of your brand photo shoot. Before you snap one photo, you and your photographer should have a clear idea of your branding. This self-discovery piece is key to standing out and delivering a powerful, consistent message. If you haven't already done the work to define the foundation of your brand and how you are different from the rest (I call this your MikiMojo), consider hiring a business coach or investing in a branding course. At the very least complete this brand brief template.

BRAND NAME

WEBSITE

SOCIAL MEDIA HANDLES

PRODUCT / SERVICE : What are you selling?

INTENTION: What do you want the brand photos to do for you?

PURPOSE: Why do you do this work?

VALUES: List 3–5 values that you believe in.

CLIENT: Who is your ideal customer?

PROBLEM: What are they struggling with?

END RESULT: What problem are you solving?

PERSONALITY: What are you and your brand like?

MOOD: How do you want your client to feel?

STYLE: What is the look/feel of your brand?

MESSAGE: What is your one key story that you want your client to know/learn?

EXPERTISE: What do you specialize in and want your brand to be known for?

PROCESS: How do you work with your clients?

DIFFERENTIATOR: What is your point of difference and how do you stand out?

VISION: What is your future goal for your business?

KEY WORDS: What are 3–5 words that describe the tone of your brand?

KEY PROPS: What 3–5 objects / things represent your brand?

COLOR: What are your brand colors?

PHOTO USE: Where do you plan on using these photos?

DOWNLOADABLE

download your worksheet at www.mikifoto.com/p45

UNDERSTAND YOUR VISUAL MARKETING NEEDS

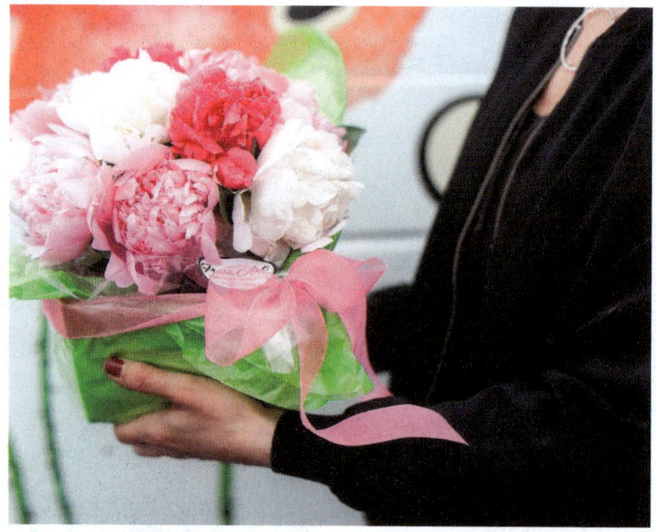

Make a list of all the photos you will need for your online and offline marketing efforts. Take a hard look at your website and have a lengthy conversation with your web designer about what types of photos you should plan for. Discuss sizes and orientations (landscape vs. vertical) of the visuals for every page of your website. For instance, your home page could have a rotating banner header, so you may need three to five images that are horizontal in format and include space for text. Or your "About Me" page might have one to two spaces for photos so you may need both a tight headshot and a wider lifestyle image. It is best to know this information up-front so you can inform your photographer and they can shoot accordingly.

Next, list out your upcoming blog posts, launches, and offerings. Maybe you need to update your business card, print new marketing materials, create a media kit or design a newsletter. Think about what you have planned for your business now and in the future. Share this information with your photographer so that you can brainstorm ideas and create a visual strategy that can deliver content across all platforms.

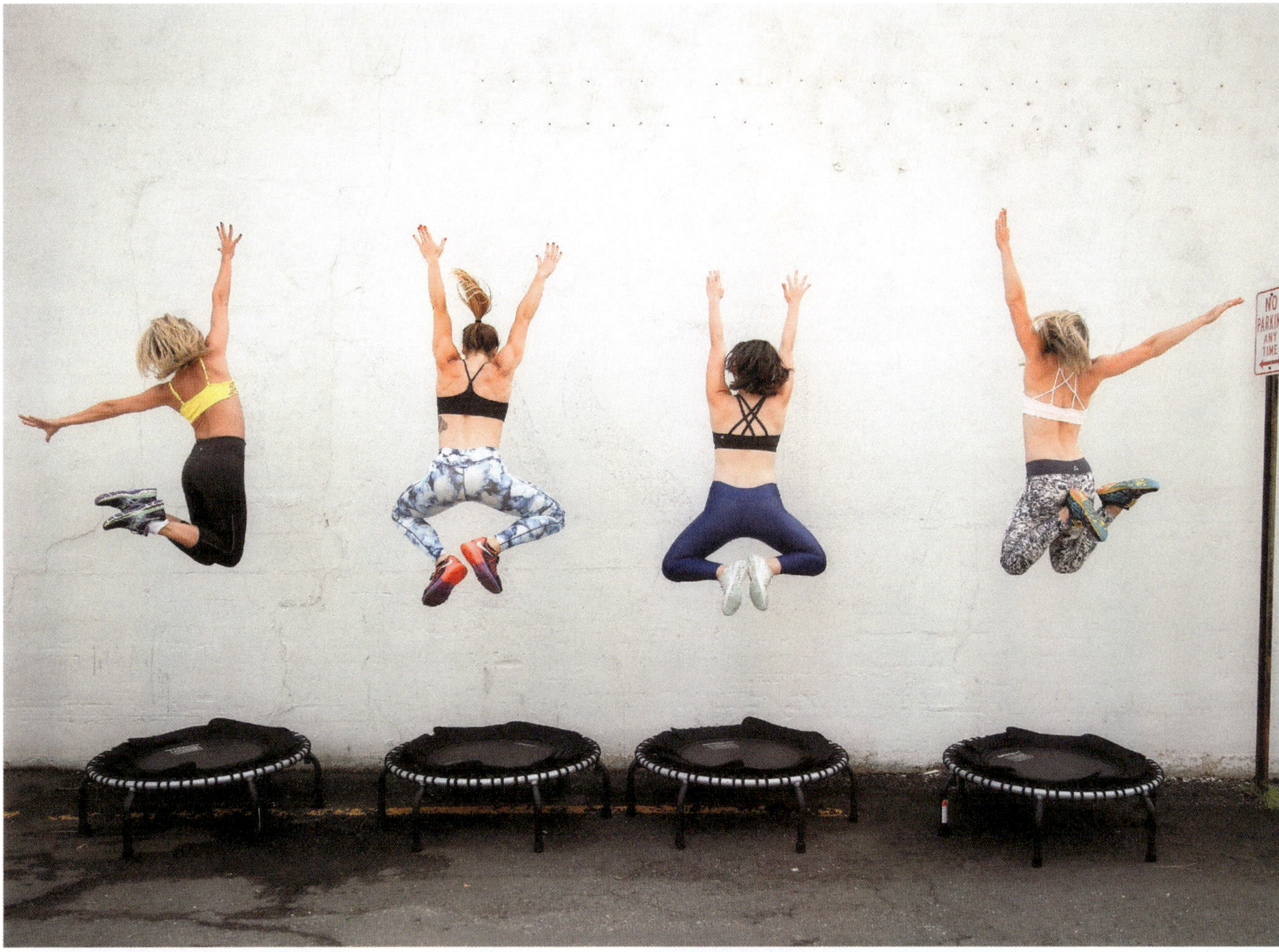
NO
PARKING
ANY
TIME

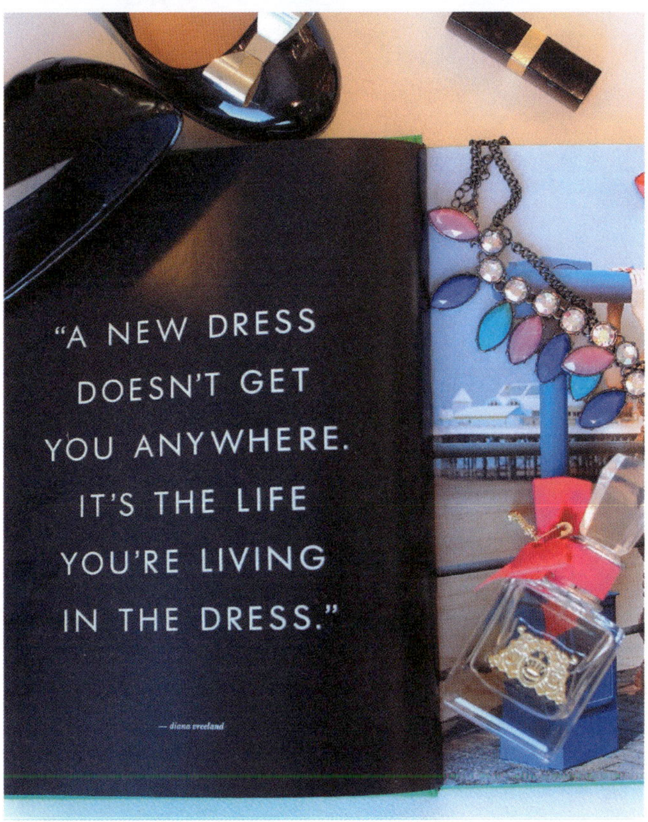
"A NEW DRESS
DOESN'T GET
YOU ANYWHERE.
IT'S THE LIFE
YOU'RE LIVING
IN THE DRESS."
— diana vreeland

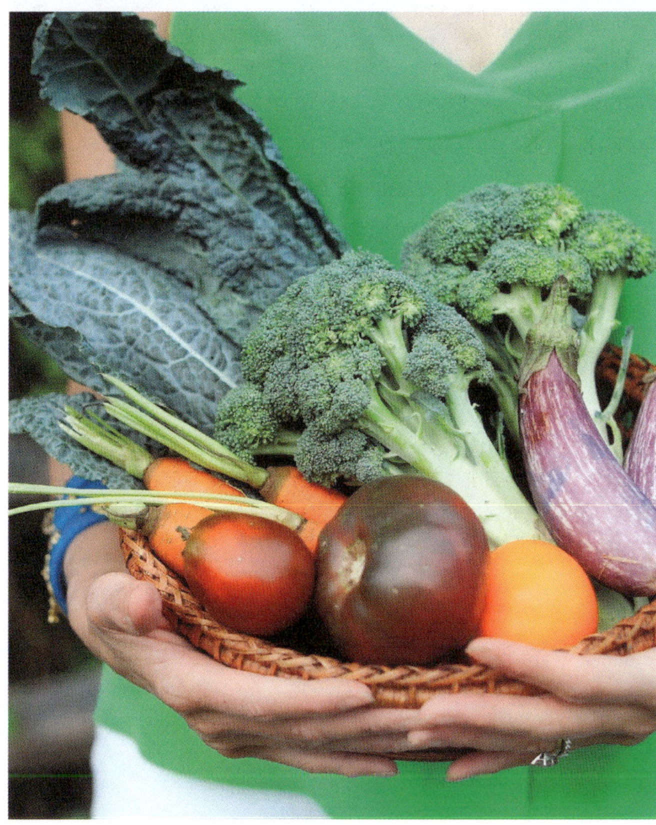

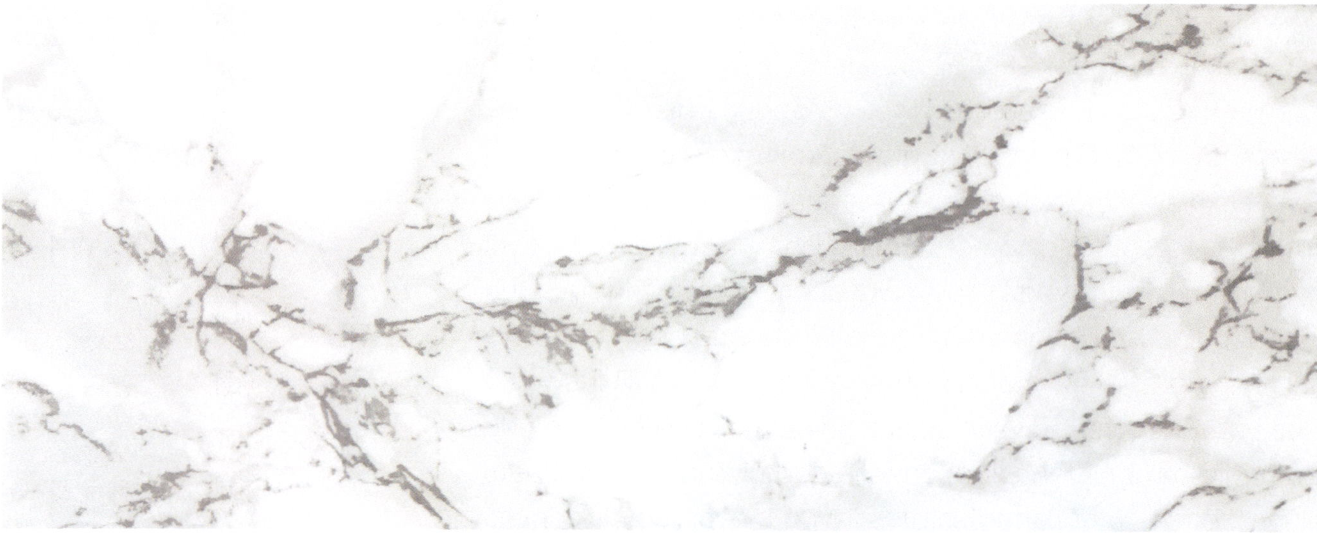

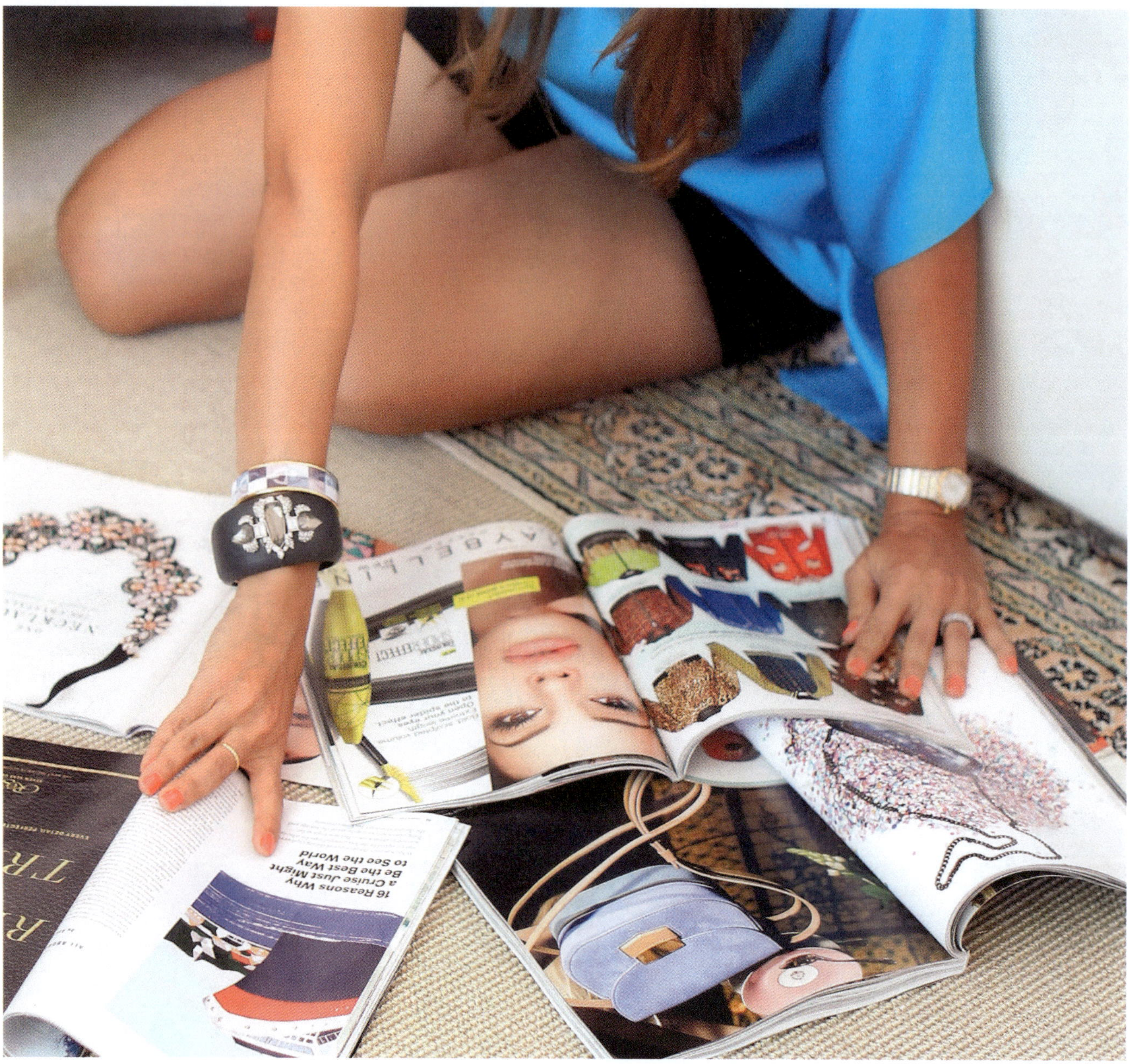
16 Reasons Why
a Cruise Just Might
Be the Best Way
to See the World

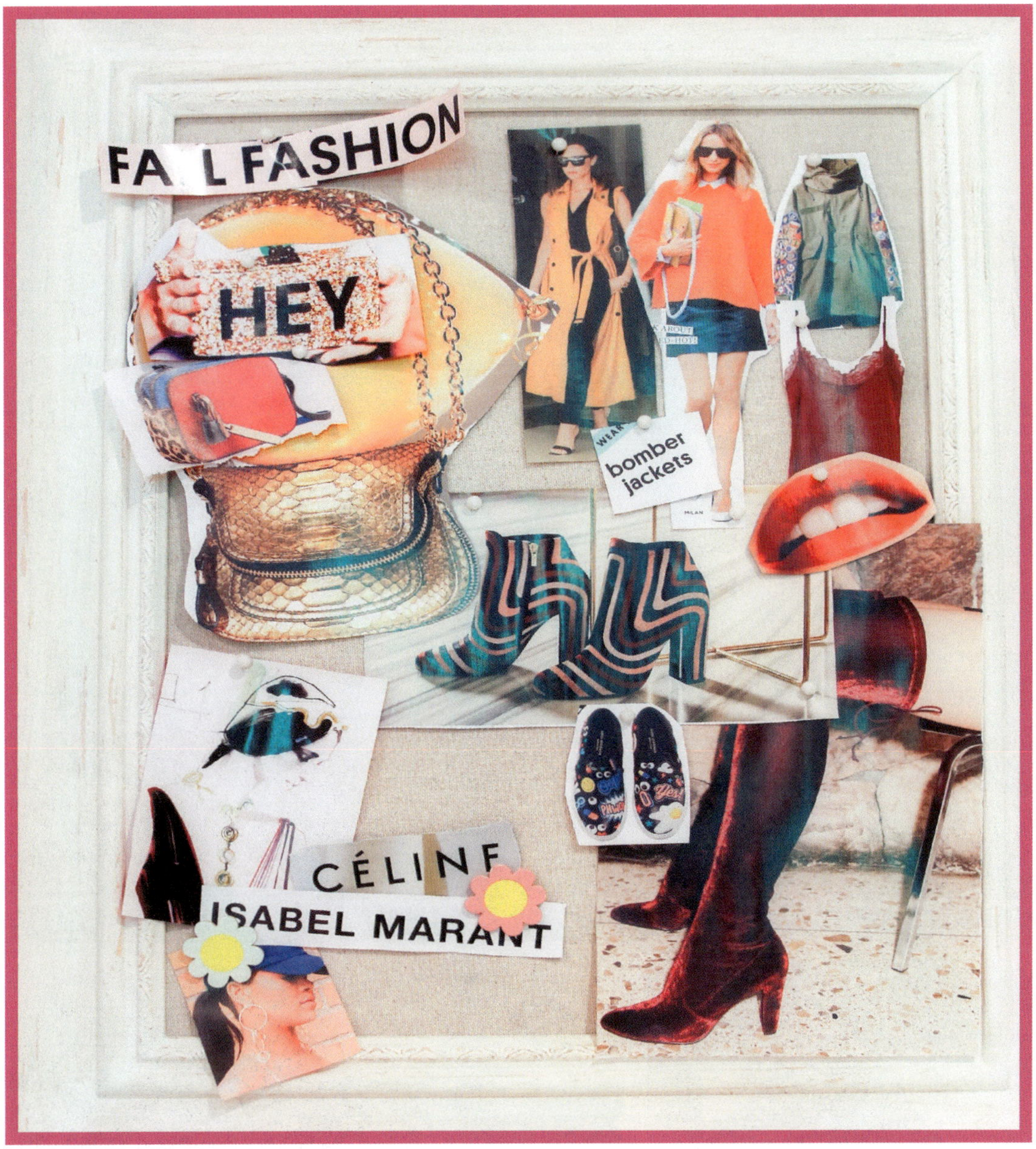

MOOD BOARD

A mood board is your visual starting point. It's your visual road map that will represent the look and feel that you are hoping to capture. It is a collection of images that acts as the inspiration for the creative direction for the photo shoot.

With your brand story in mind, start compiling pictures, either digital via Pinterest or physical via magazines, that fit the vision you have in mind. Think about the mood or feeling you want your audience to have about your brand. Pin pictures, colors, expressions, locations, outfits, moods, environments — anything that stands out to you. Write a description of what you like about each image.

Themes and ideas will emerge from the mood board. An aesthetic and style direction will formulate. Share this with your photographer and later with your hair and makeup artist, your stylist, your copywriter, your web designer — anyone who is involved in the creative process. This will become the visual guide to the brand photo stories that your photographer will capture.

PHOTO STORIES

It's a crowded, noisy world out there. Thousands of businesses and brands are all shouting to get your clients' attention. It's easy to feel frustrated, lost, and invisible. How in the world can your business STAND OUT? Now that we have your brand strategy and mood board, let's create your visual strategy.

Brand photography is a powerful tool that tells stories of the many layers of your business: what you do, what it feels like to work with you, how you are different. We want our visuals to be aspirational and authentic. Strong visuals can help position your brand and you as the go-to expert in your industry and inspire your audience into action — all without saying a single word!

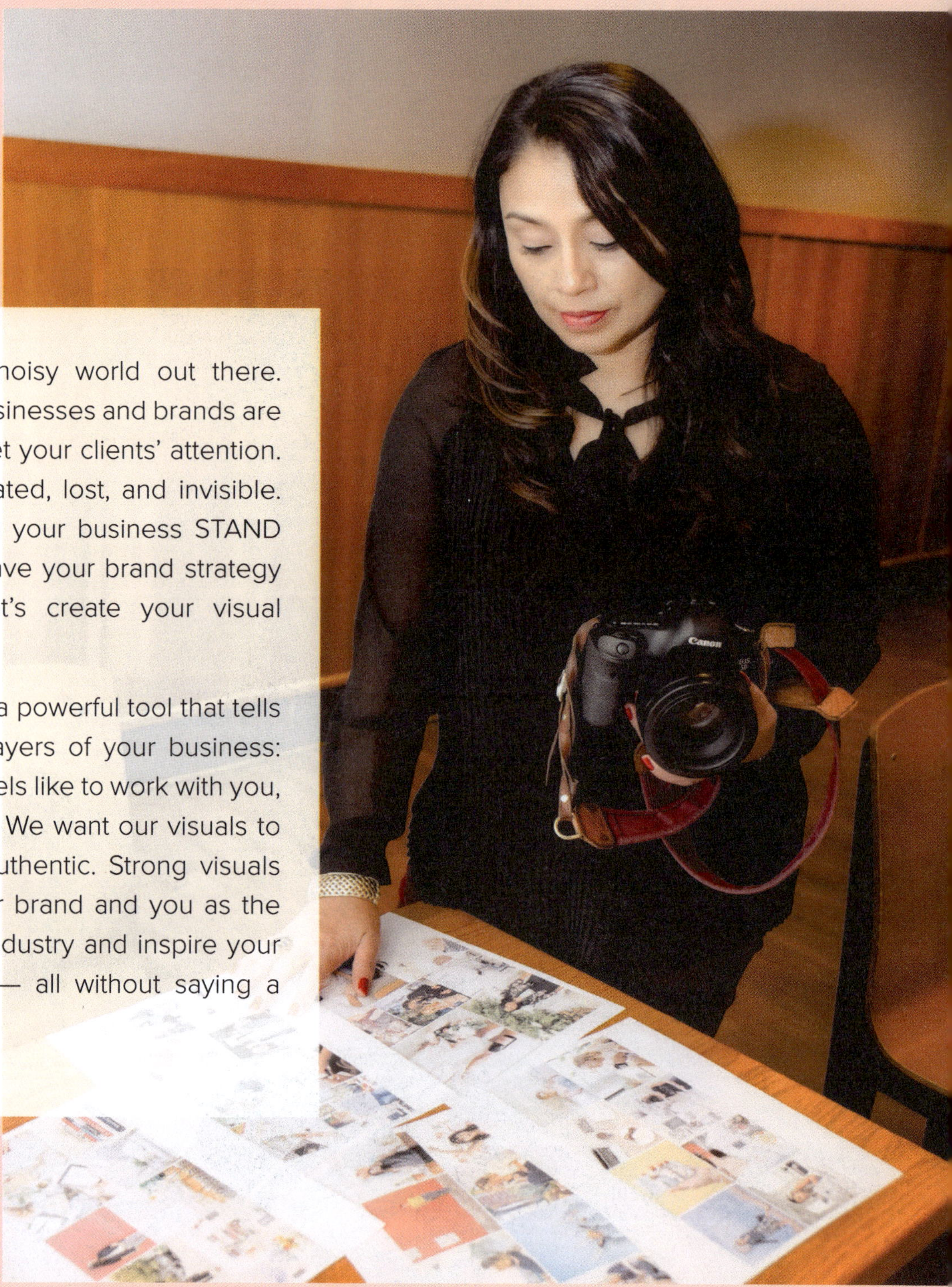

Here are the 11 photo stories you should be communicating to your audience to move your brand from invisible to impact:

YOUR PURPOSE

YOUR PROWESS

YOUR PROCESS

YOUR PRODUCTS OR SERVICES

YOUR PERSONALITY

YOUR PASSION

YOUR PEOPLE

YOUR INSPIRATION

YOUR POINT OF DIFFERENCE

YOUR VISION

YOUR #ALLTHETHINGS

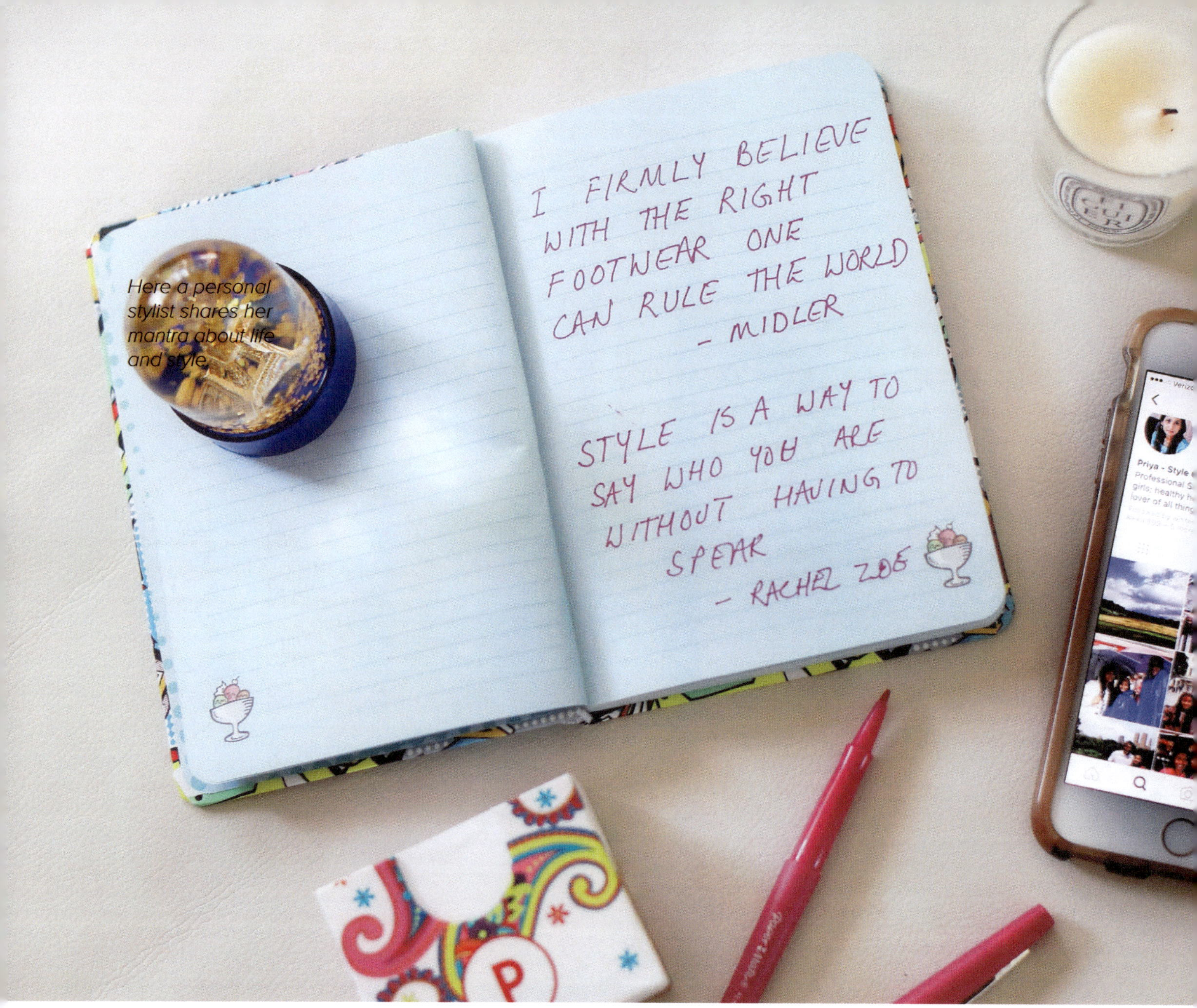

A personal stylist shares her mantra about life and style.

Your Purpose

People hire people, not logos or websites or products or services. They hire you because they believe in your purpose and your values. Connect with your audience by sharing **what matters most to you and why you started your business in the first place.** What movement are you trying to create? This could be conveyed through quotes, books, signs, words, maybe even people. By sharing your why, you will inspire your viewers to take the journey with you.

Your Prowess

It's time to show off how you are the leader in your industry. Share your skills, talent, work experience, awards, press — anything that contributes to the story that you are an expert. This is your opportunity to stand out in your saturated market. **What are you known for?**

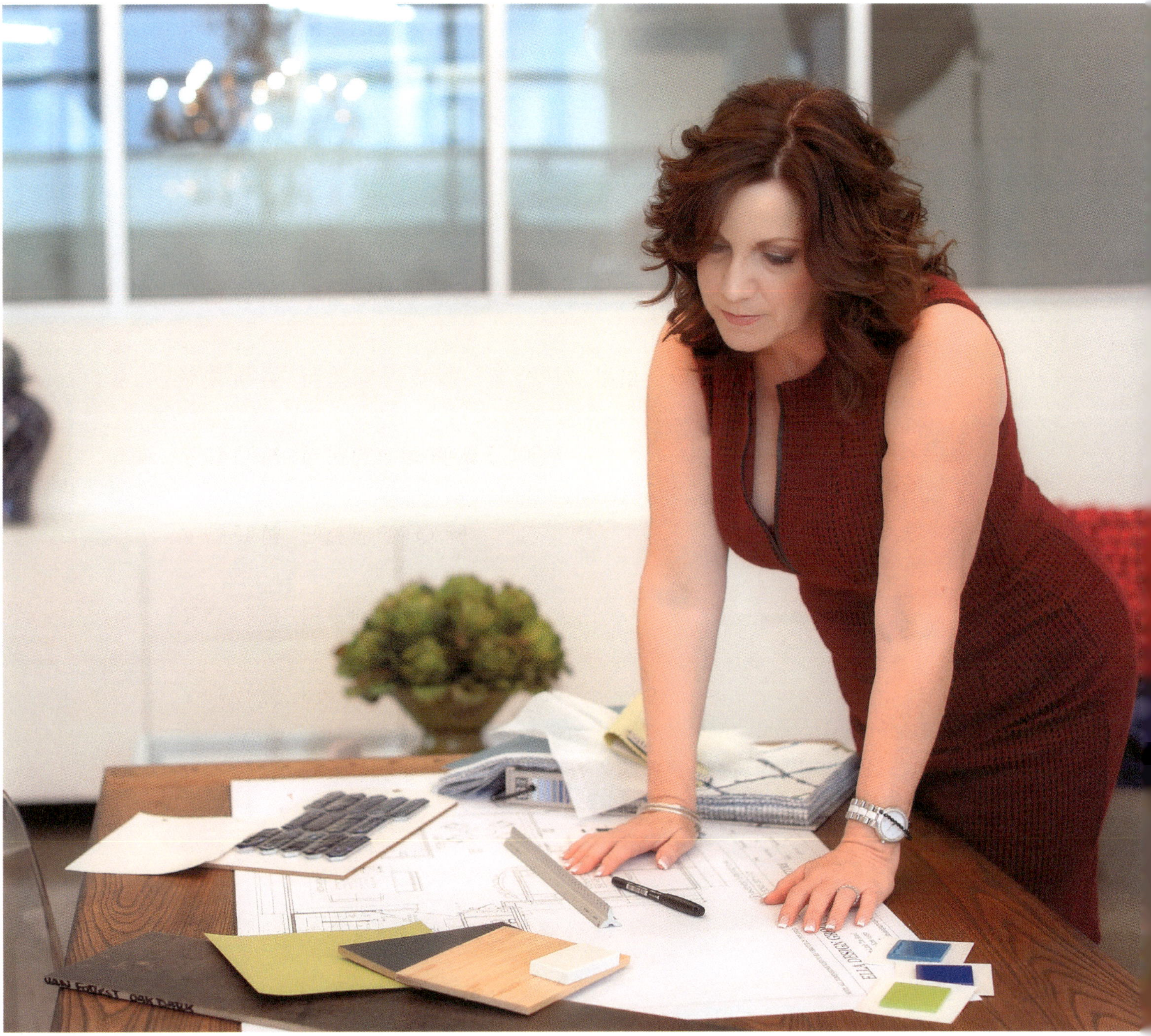

An interior designer shows off her tools and skills for designing residential homes.

Your Process

Take your audience on the journey of your business. **Bring them behind the scenes.** Give them an insider look into your business life. Show them how you work, where you work, and all the steps of your process. This could be a shot of your desk in your home office, the tools (digital or tangible) that you use to create your product, the place where you conduct meetings, or the packaging when delivering the final goods. Answer this question: How do you do your job? When you include the viewer into your story, they become more invested in your brand.

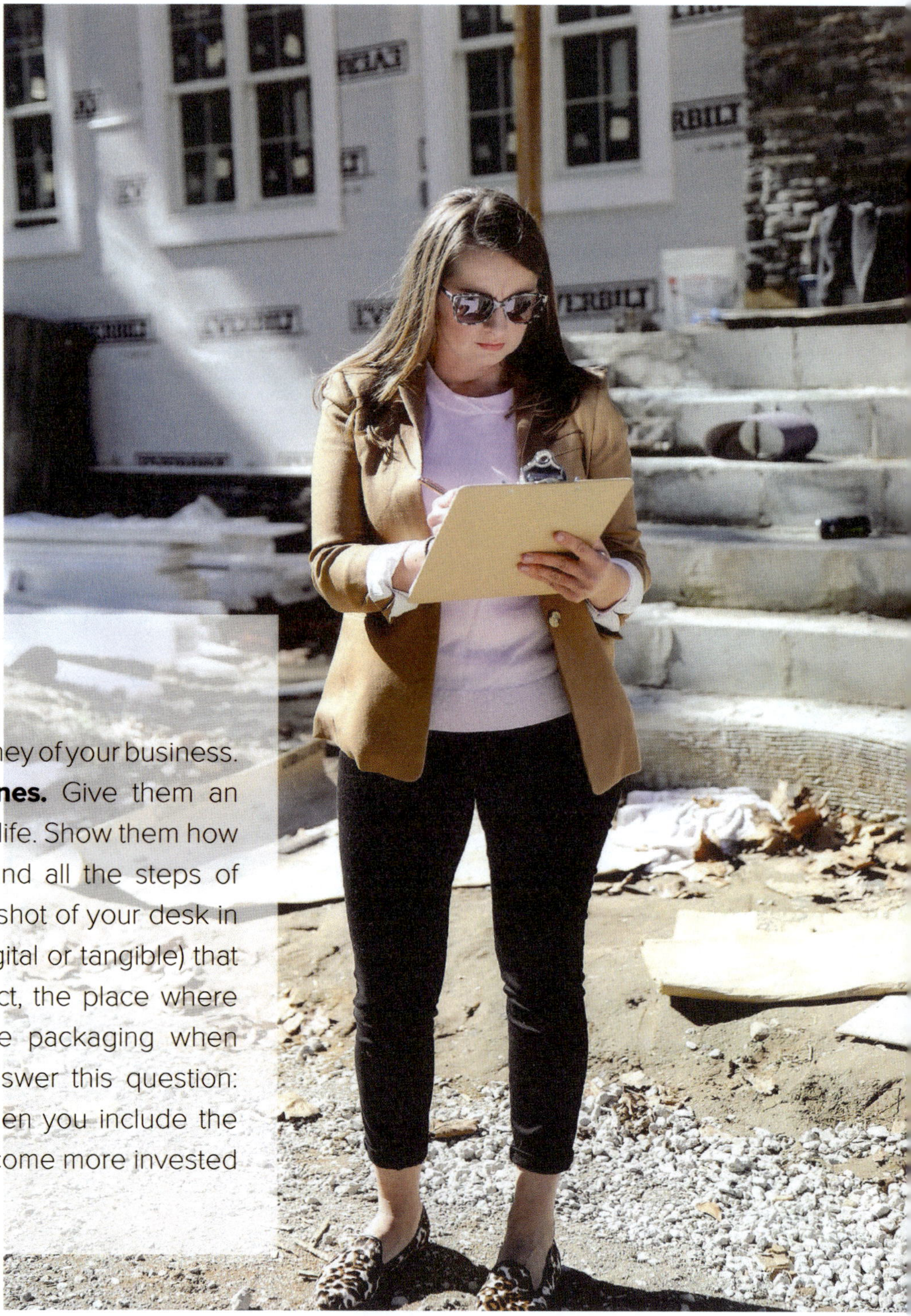

A real estate agent takes us behind the scenes to the construction site of one of her home listings.

Your Products or Services

This is a no-brainer! Of course, you must show the goods and services that you are selling. This could be photos on a website if you are a photographer, a rack of clothes if you are a personal stylist, or the table settings at a party if you are an event planner. But try showing them in a way that allows customers and clients to **envision how they would actually experience it in their life.** What are you selling? How does it fit into their lifestyle? What does the end result look like?

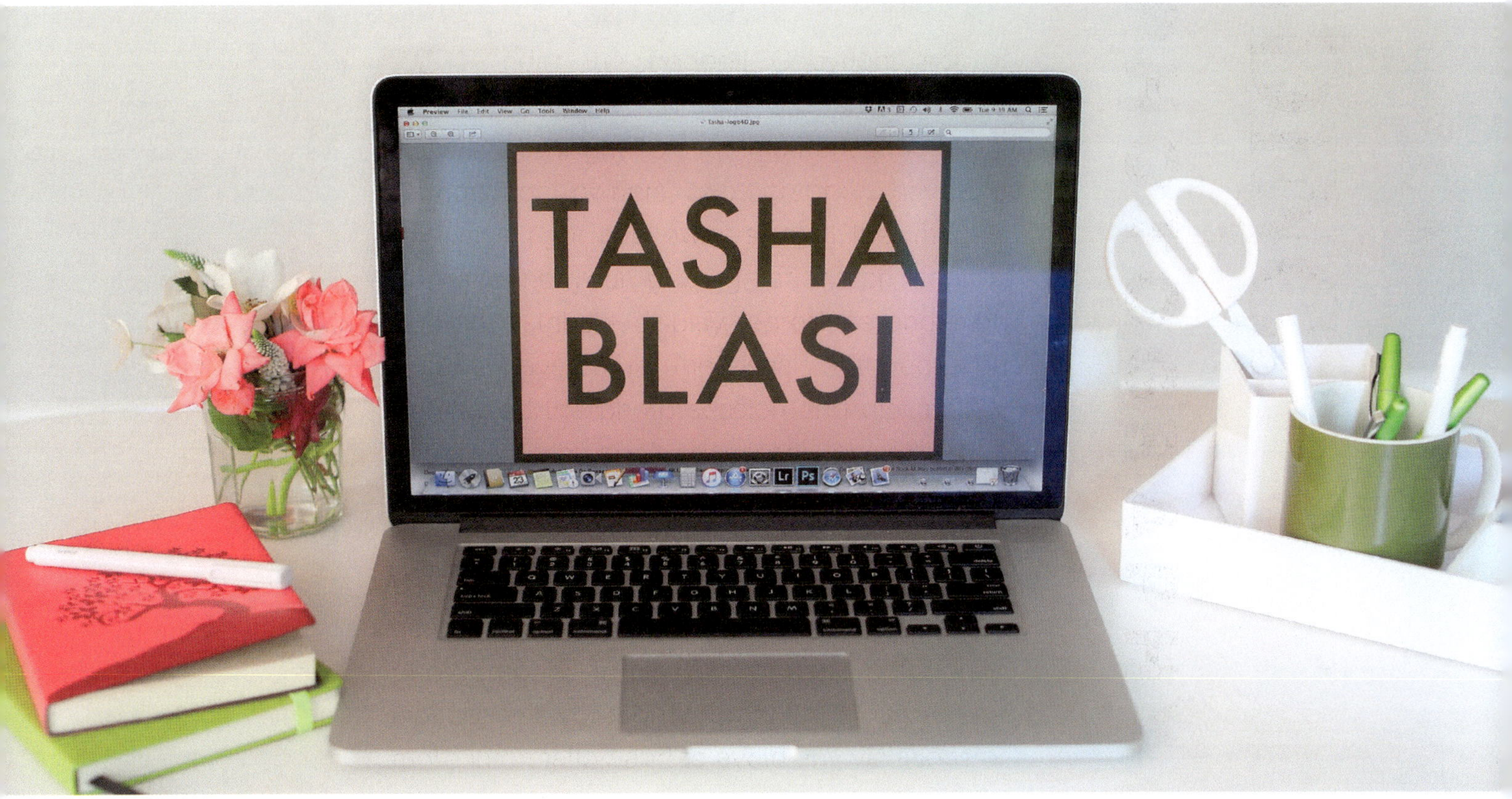

A graphic designer shows her design service through displaying a logo on a laptop at a desk.

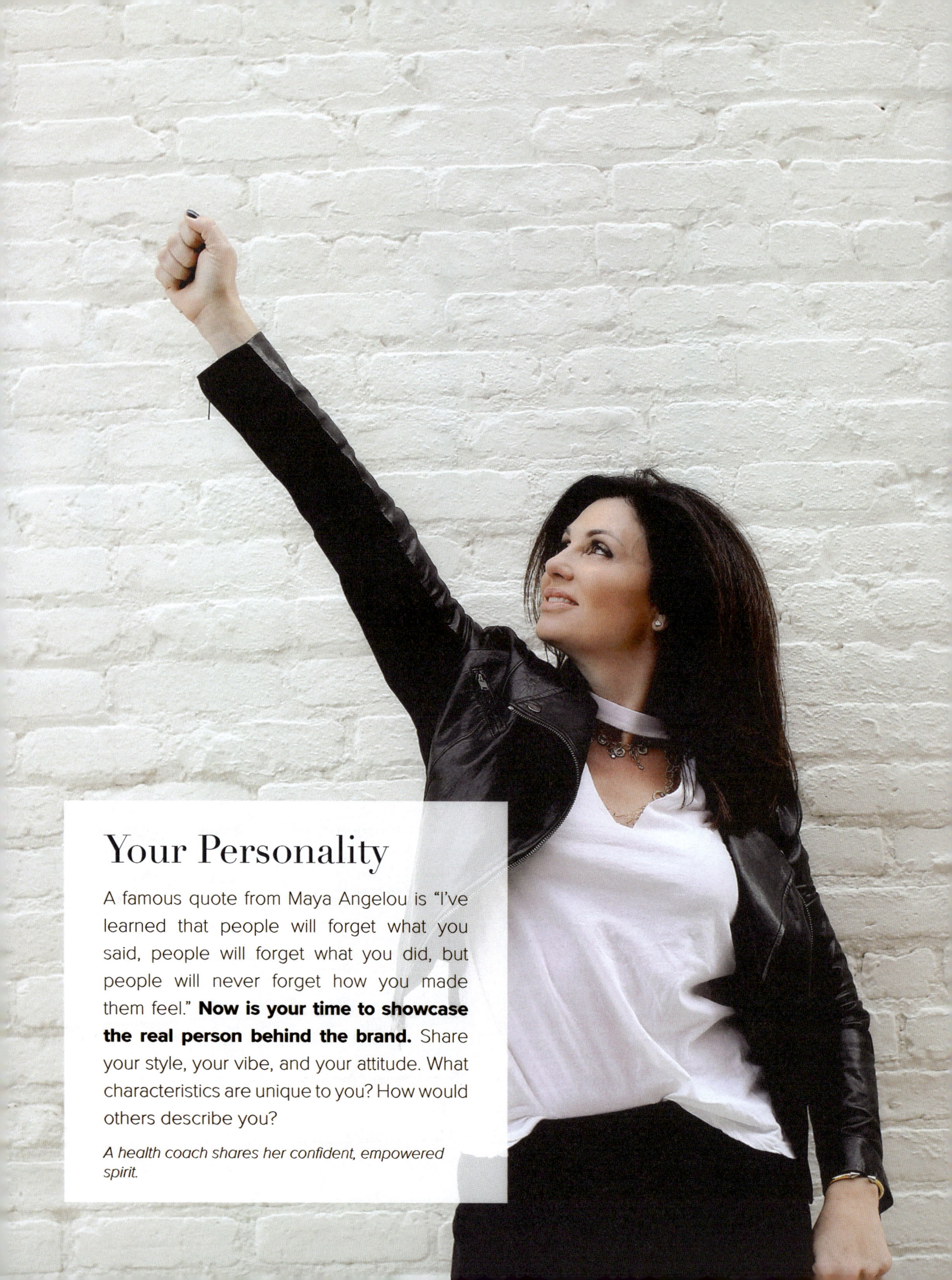

Your Personality

A famous quote from Maya Angelou is "I've learned that people will forget what you said, people will forget what you did, but people will never forget how you made them feel." **Now is your time to showcase the real person behind the brand.** Share your style, your vibe, and your attitude. What characteristics are unique to you? How would others describe you?

A health coach shares her confident, empowered spirit.

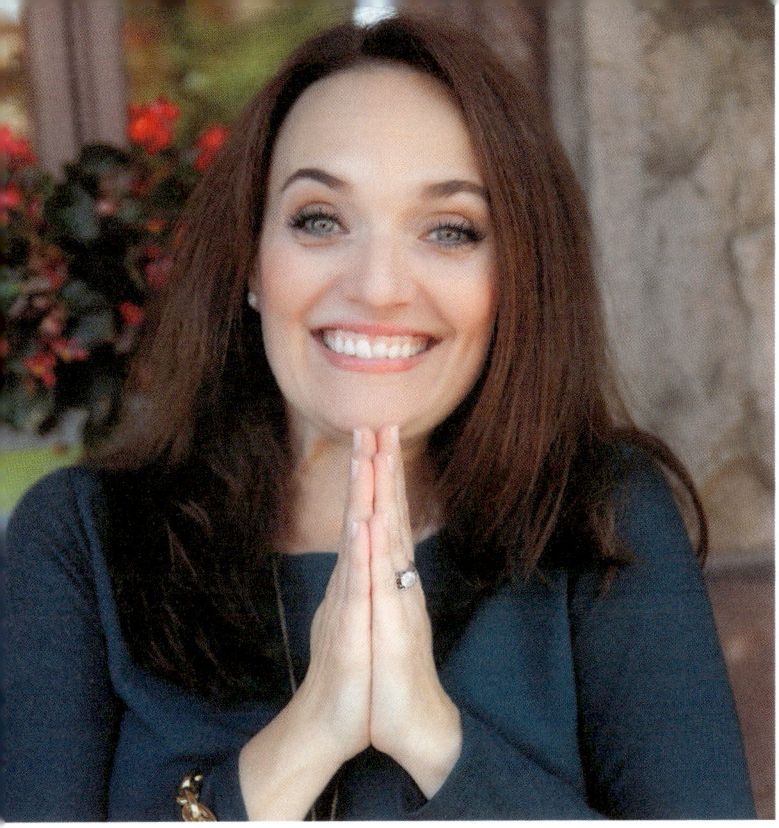

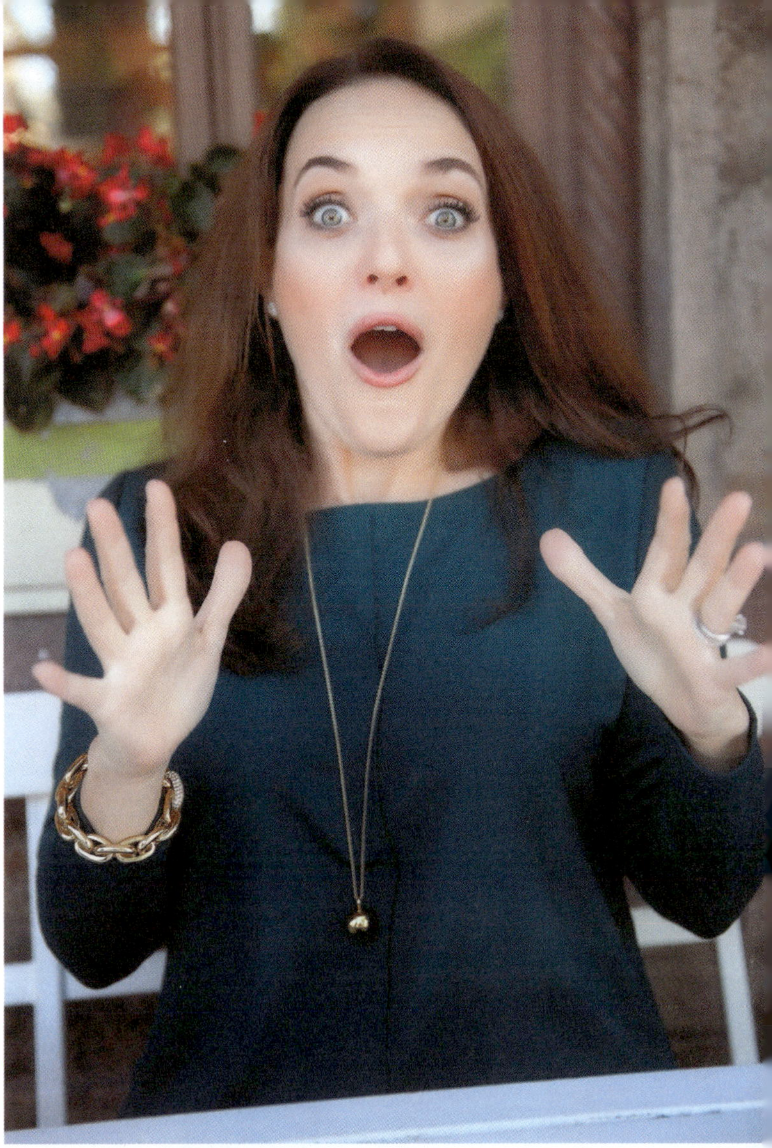

BONUS Tip:

Ask your photographer to capture different moods of you to use in different contexts for your brand, expressions like happiness, frustration, surprise, confidence, anger, sadness, and love. Think about website header photos, launches, and Facebook ads. These photos will help communicate your story better. Plus, they will get attention and build connection. Don't be afraid to put yourself out there!

Emotions to cover:

Happiness
Excitement
Anger
Sadness
Frustration
Confidence
Joy
Love
Suprise
Worry
Peace
Calm
Confusion
Thoughtfulness
Nervousness
Pleading
Embarrassment
Strength

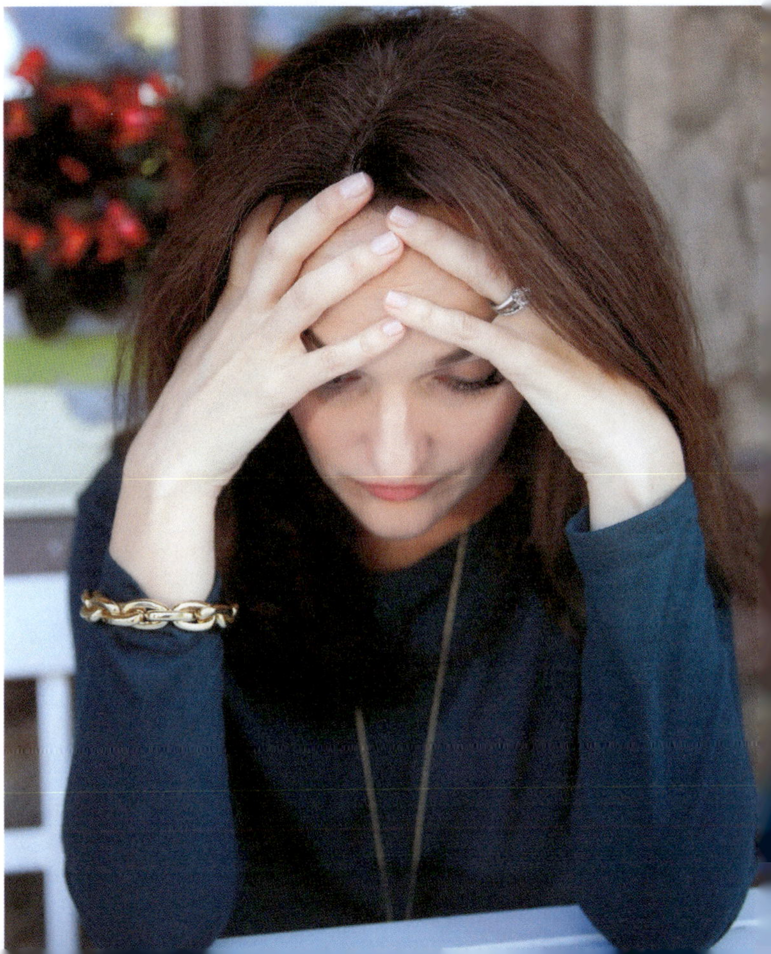

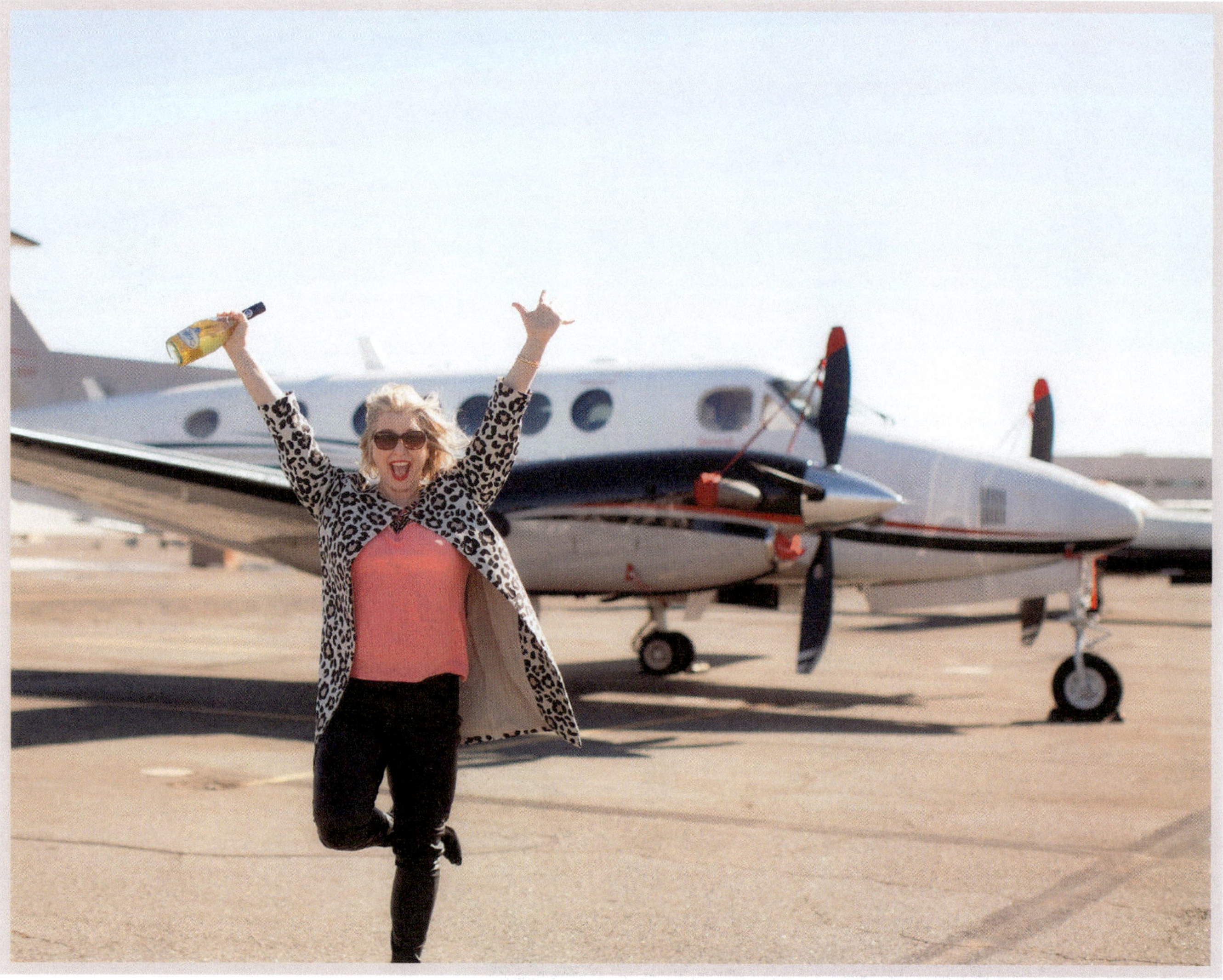

A business coach shares her passion for travel and empowering women globally to be their best selves.

Your Passion

What excites you most about your business? What do you love to do? What can you talk about for hours? What riles you up? Think of experiences, feelings, moods, causes, and objects that communicate your passions. This could be a cover of a book, a colorful cocktail, or your gym sneakers. This could be a sunset or you swirling and twirling. When you **share what lights you up**, you can connect and inspire your audience.

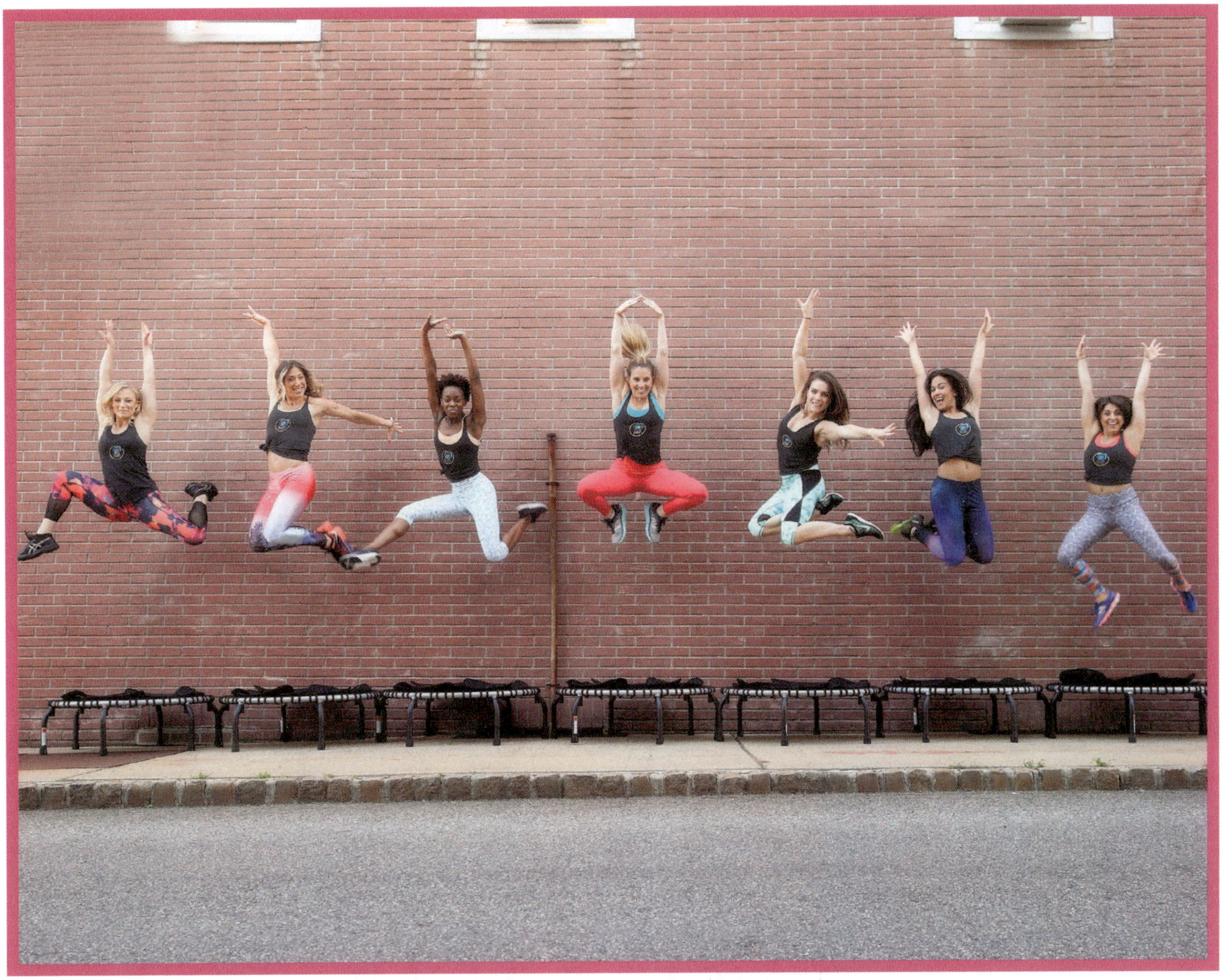

A fitness studio shows not only who is on their team, but also their fun vibe as a community.

Your People

Share more about your clients, your community, and your tribe. Who do you surround yourself with? Who's on your team? What does your ideal client look like? Show photos of the people involved in your business. This could a photo of you working with your clients, brainstorming with your girl squad, or connecting at a networking meeting. This imagery allows your audience to **see the relationships that you are part of**, as well as identify with the people in the photos. Plus, it communicates that you are part of a bigger network.

Your Inspiration

Stand out from the rest by sharing a bit about **where you get your creativity and new ideas from**. How do you keep your creative juices flowing? What rituals help you to think bigger? Where do you go to feel inspired? Show images, rituals, places, practices, objects that impact your creative thinking.

A life coach dives into fashion and design to nurture her creativity.

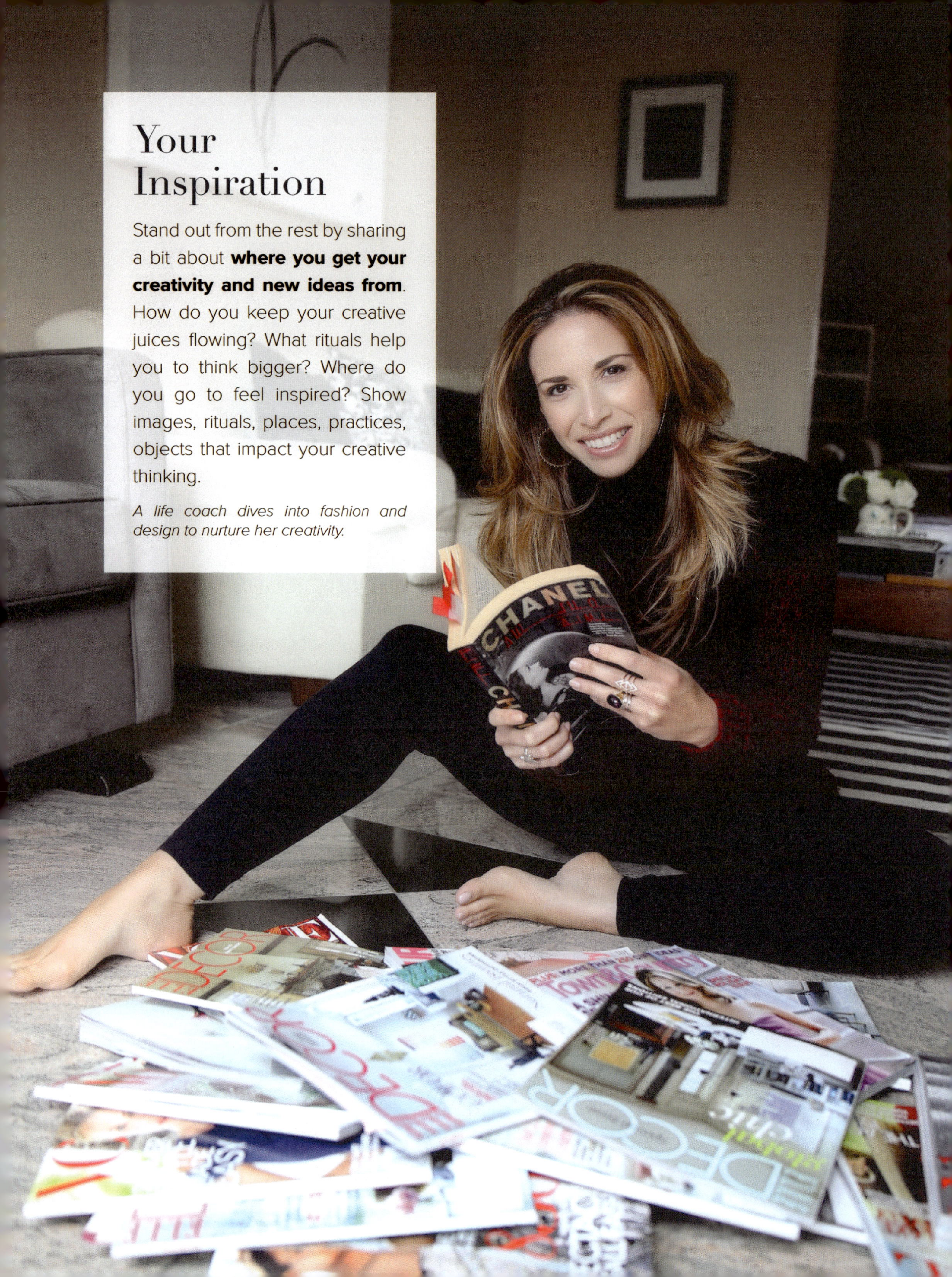

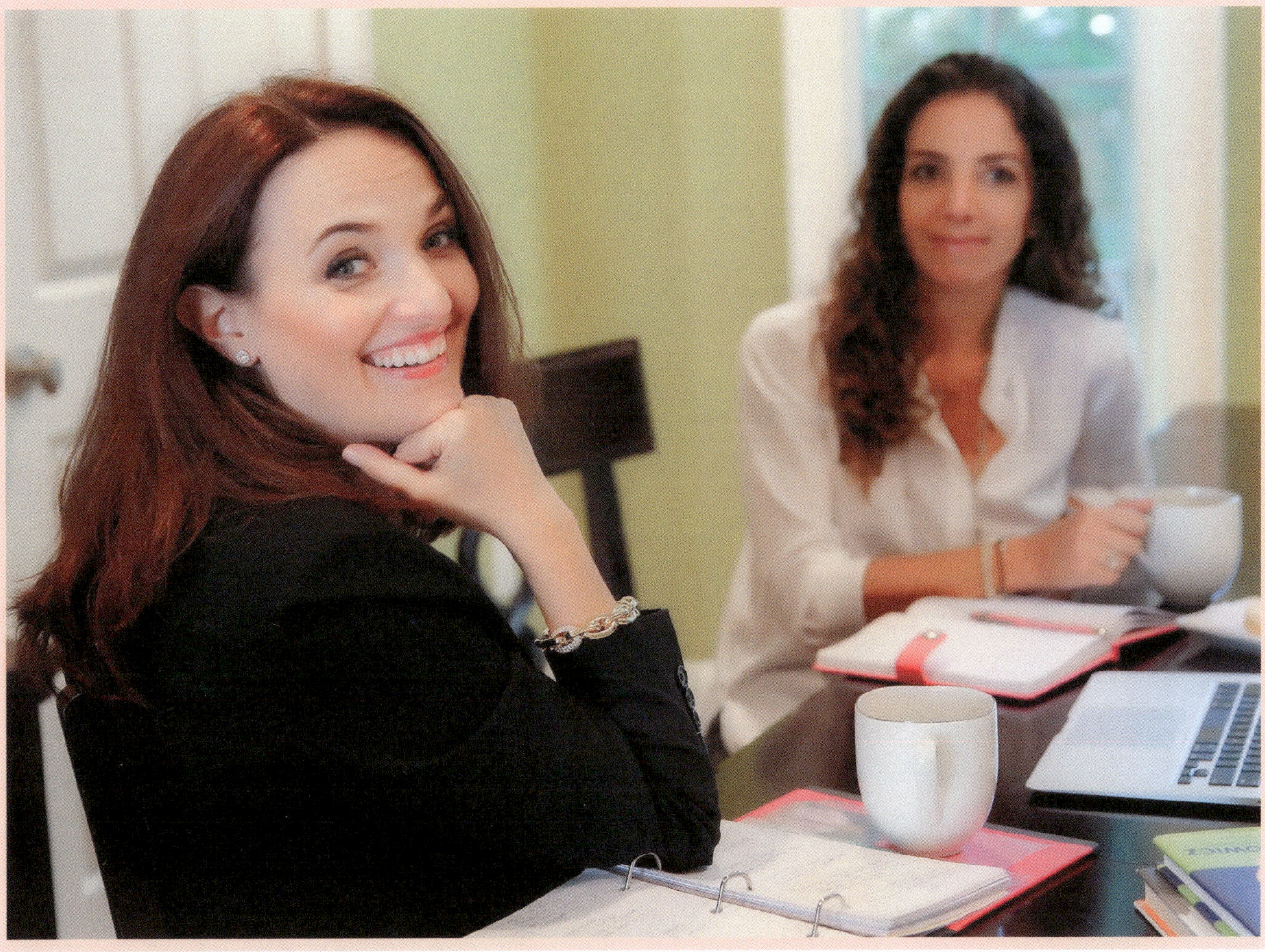

Your Point of Difference

The marketplace is saturated and noisy. How will you stand out from the rest? Take a close look at your business, from your process to your product to your personality, and highlight what you do differently than the competition. How are you specialized? Why do people come to you first? **What distinguishes you from the rest?** There are so many ways to be different. Find your incomparable advantage and showcase this in photos. For example, if you are a personal stylist maybe you also include a service of taking clothes to the tailor. If you are a coach, maybe your point of difference is that you invite clients into your home for an intimate coaching session. If you are a family photographer, maybe it's your energetic personality and "mom experience" of managing multiple kids that sets you apart. Your difference could be the tipping point for someone to hire you, so make sure to make your mark and share it.

A business mentor shares how she invites and works in-person with her clients at her home, in her dining room.

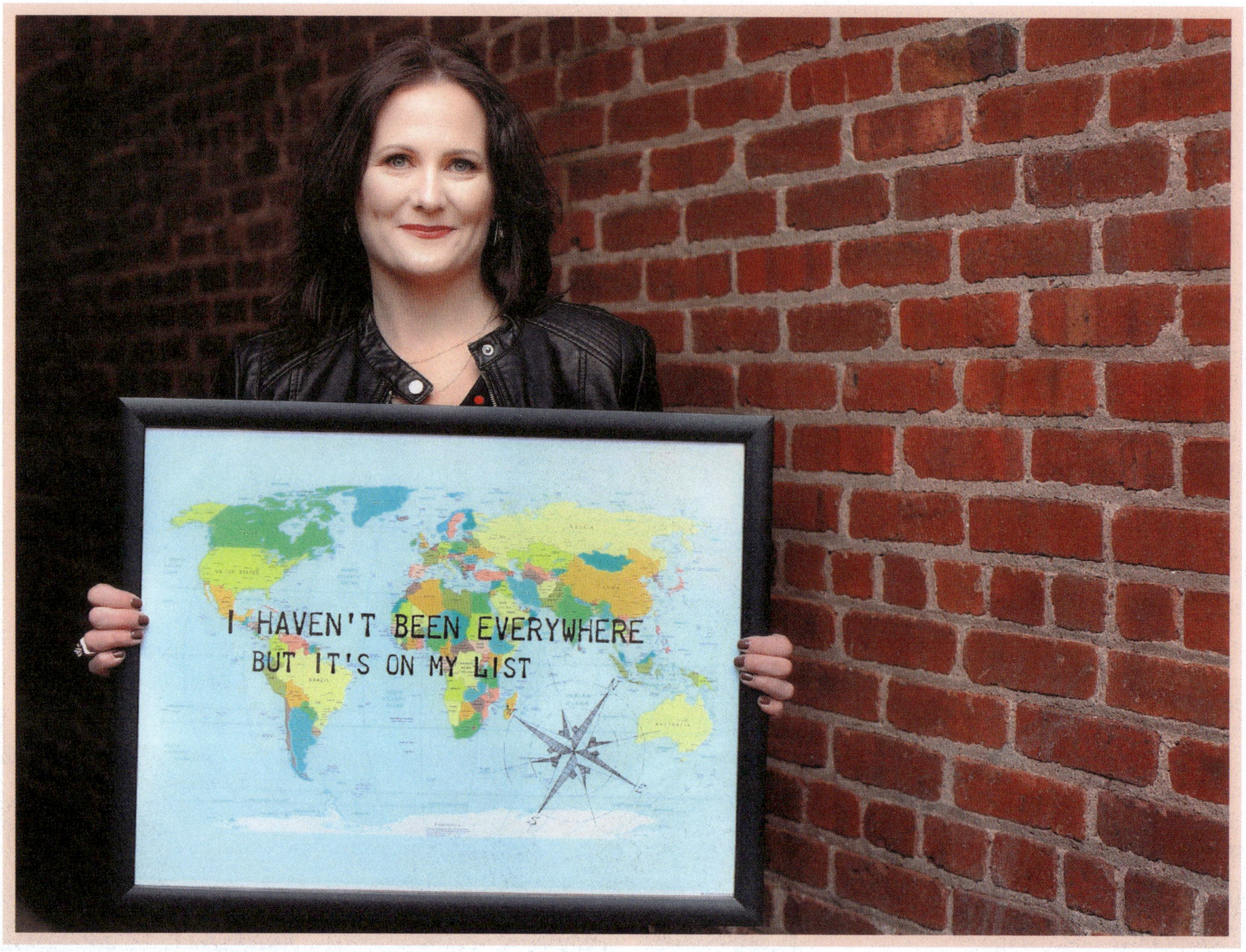

A business strategist shares her dream to travel the world to service her clients.

Your Vision

What's the future forecast for your business? Think about your goals, dreams, and aspirations. Where do you want to be in five years? Ten years? Communicate your vision with your audience through photos. Maybe you want to author a book; take an image of you typing on a laptop. Maybe you dream of speaking on stage; take an image of you with a microphone in hand. Maybe you hope to plan a retreat overseas; take an image of you holding a globe or your passport. Whatever it is, **give your audience a taste of where you hope to take your business.** Not only will you inspire them, but you may surprise yourself by putting things in motion.

Your #ALLTHETHINGS

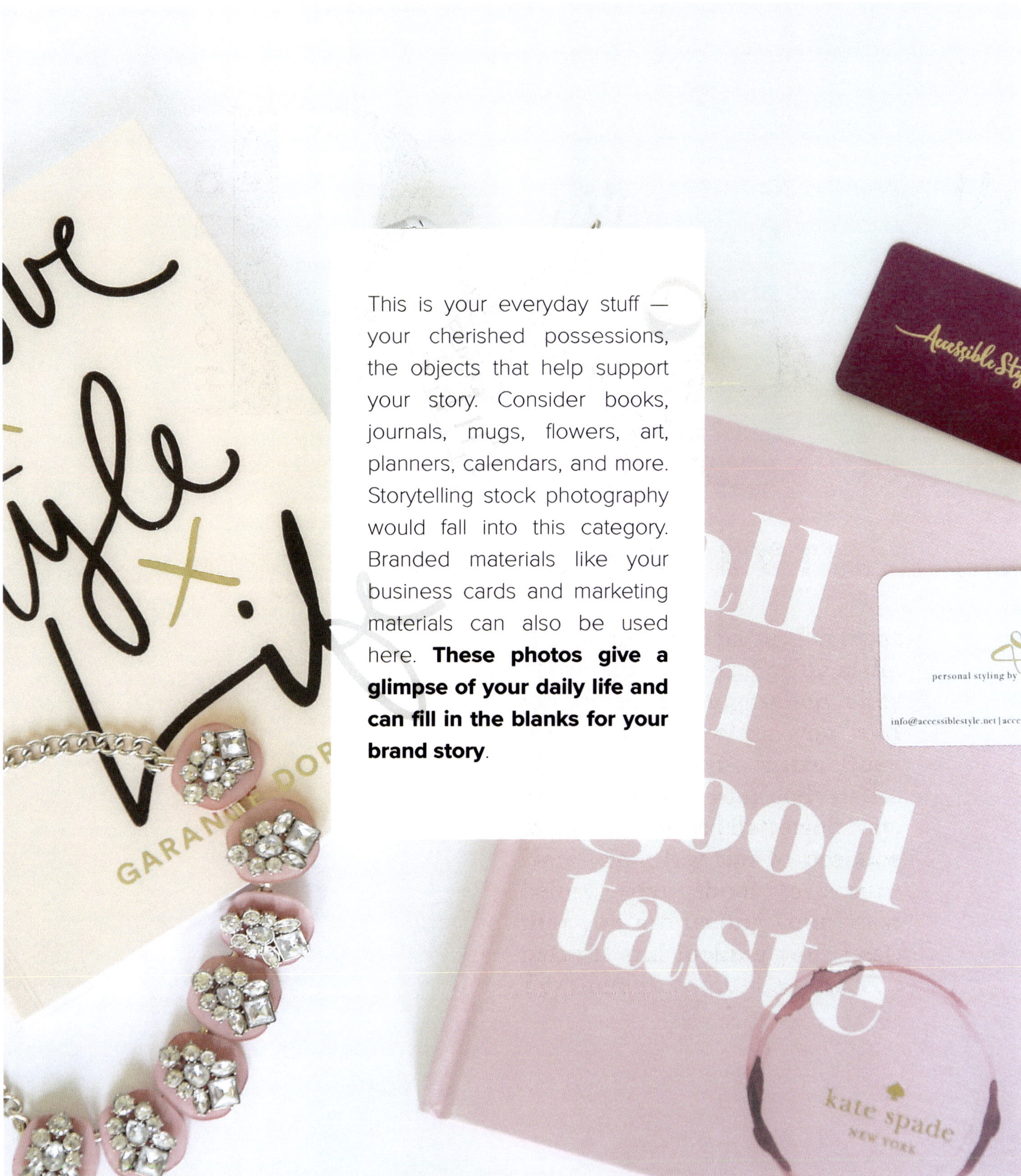

This is your everyday stuff — your cherished possessions, the objects that help support your story. Consider books, journals, mugs, flowers, art, planners, calendars, and more. Storytelling stock photography would fall into this category. Branded materials like your business cards and marketing materials can also be used here. **These photos give a glimpse of your daily life and can fill in the blanks for your brand story**.

A personal stylist tells more of her story by showing her favorite books and accessories.

Now that you know the photo story themes, it's time to start brainstorming ideas for each category. Think outside the box, but make sure everything stays true to your brand. Be creative and strategic. This is your opportunity to really dig deep into your brand story and stand apart from the rest.

YOU HAVE TO TAKE THE TIME TO CLARIFY.

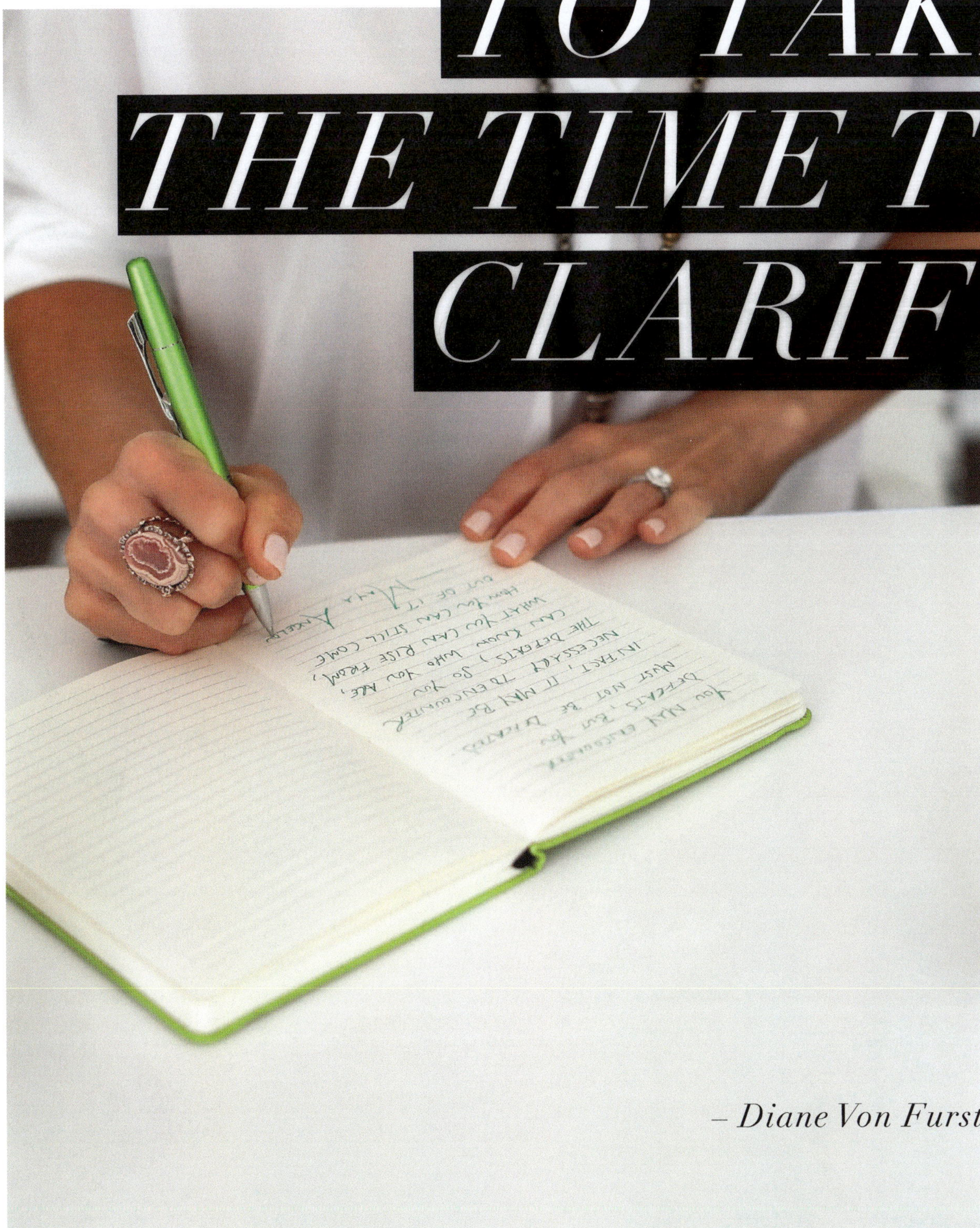

– Diane Von Furstenberg

SHOT LIST

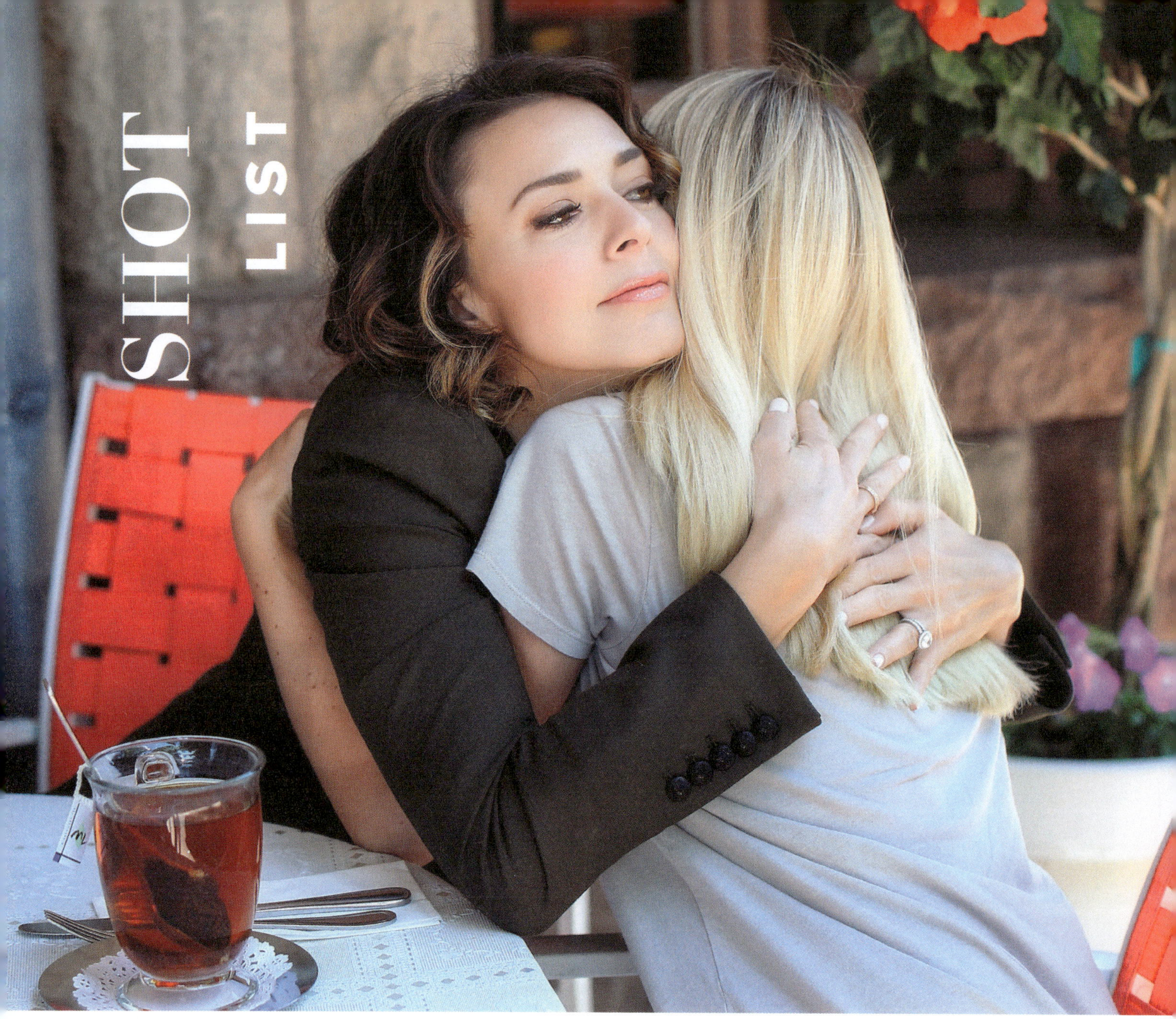

This is your detailed guideline of what stories and scenarios you want to capture at each location. Start by coming up with your dream photo shot list. Remember all those images you drooled over online? Put them down on paper. Also consider the landscape of your website. Think about all the different pages and drop downs, and the kinds of images you will need to help communicate your message. Add these shots to your master list along with notes on the photo orientation and framing (closeups, pull-backs, horizontal shots with empty space for text, vertical tight headshots). Working on a list with your photographer will allow you to feel more organized and confident that all your story ideas will be covered.

I like to write down the specific shot ideas for each location along with the actions, mood/feeling, outfit, and props. Ask your photographer to shoot different angles and orientations so that you have a variety of images to choose from.

Here's a sample shot list for my client Tasha, who is a health coach specializing in helping women struggling with the IVF journey:

Modern Home Office

Working at home on laptop
Talking on phone
Reading book
Writing
Holding clock
To-do list / Goals / Calendar
Creating video
Sitting on chair or couch
At desk
Quote in notebook
Mood: Engaged, Savvy, Warm, Thoughtful
Styling: Casual chic (white blouse/khaki pants)
Close-Ups: To-do list, Quote, Clock
Horizontal: Desk, T at work on laptop

Backyard Boss Mom

Barefoot with kids playing (hula hoop)
Laughing / playful
Drinking coffee
Family connections
Bubbles
Cooking
Multiple expressions
Hugging/loving
Horizontal: T with greenery
Close-Up: Kids' feet
Mood: Joyful, Carefree, Heartfelt
Styling: Fashionable mom (jeans/coral top)

Client Coffee Date

Eating/drinking together
Writing in journal
Showcasing relationship
Communicating high touch/intimacy
Hugging client (empathy)
Holding her hand on table
Laughing together
Solo photos (thoughtful/soulful)
Close-Ups: Holding hands, Words in journal
Mood: Empathy, Warm, Connection
Styling: Coach (printed blouse / black pants)

CLOTHING & ACCESSORIES

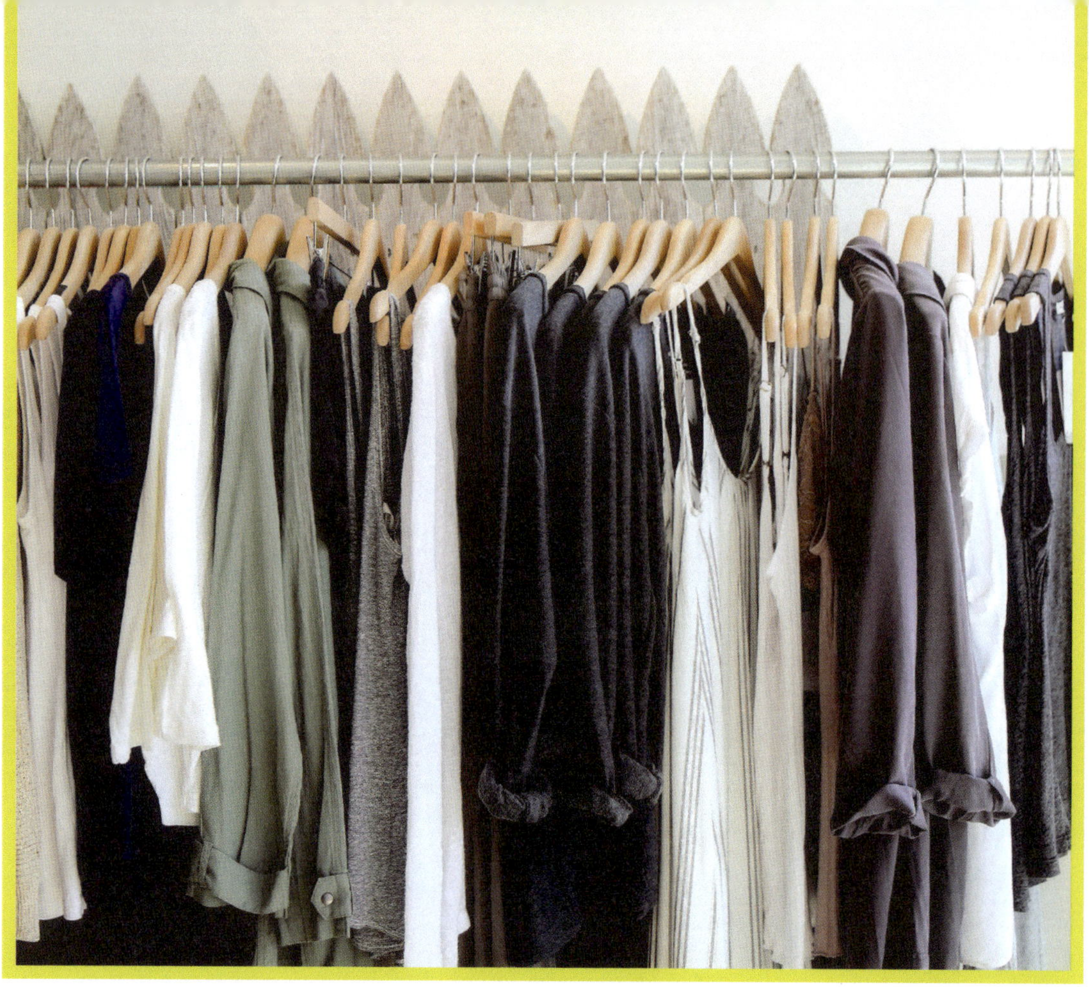

This can sometimes be the most stressful part of the photo shoot. You want to look and feel your absolute best, but not everyone is a fashionista or has a personal stylist on speed dial.

The general styling rule for your shoot is to wear something that reflects your personality, your style, and your brand. It should fit what you do and how you work. It should relate to your audience yet also be a bit aspirational.

Your outfit should communicate confidence and leadership, yet feel authentic and real. This vibe will attract your ideal clients and help build connections.

Pick pieces that flatter your best features and attract your ideal client. For instance, if you are a natural, organic health coach with a casual vibe, then a tight-fitting leopard print dress may not fit your brand and style. Jeans and a colorful t-shirt may be a better fit for your message. Consider your audience.

Every photographer is different in terms of how many outfits they will capture at your shoot. At the shoot, I'd recommend having four different looks planned from head to toe (top, bottom, shoes, and accessories). My clients often bring a small suitcase or garment bag of their outfits with backup pieces and accessories. Be sure to try on everything beforehand multiple times. If you need extra help, consider hiring a stylist. If you prepare and plan ahead of time, then you will feel your most confident.

SOME IDEAS TO ELEVATE YOUR LOOK:

Color Choices

Select colors that flatter and bring attention to your best assets and personality (bonus if they also coordinate with your branding). I tend to like brighter and bolder colors, and I suggest picking one palette (e.g., jewel tones). If you prefer softer and muted shades, consider adding an accessory in a pop of color. Beware of whites and creams because they can look washed out, especially if you have fair skin. If you have a love for prints, go for it! Just be sure that the pattern is subtle and not overpowering.

Dress for Success

There is something about a dress that feels feminine and powerful. I definitely recommend at least one dress (preferably two) in your styling options. Don't be afraid to get dressed up, because this is your time to shine. The camera loves a fitted dress that highlights your body shape. Flowy dresses in soft and silky fabrics allow for movement, flow, and a beautiful twirl.

Neckline Matters

Consider the neckline of the top you're wearing, and avoid blouses or dresses that are too low cut or too fussy (ruffles, for example). Both can be too distracting and take away from the focus on your face and expression. A moderate V-neck or U-neckline is often a safer bet.

Up in Arms

For many women, arms are a trouble spot. One way to slim your arms is to wear a three-quarter-length sleeve. Roll up or bunch up your long sleeves to show some skin. Also consider bringing fitted blazers, cropped jackets, cardigans, vests, or scarves to help. Beware of strapless, off-the-shoulder, or spaghetti-strap tops unless you have toned arms. (In that case, show it off!)

Shoe Fetish

Pick shoes that complement each outfit and make you feel amazing. Heels are your best friend because they elongate your legs, lengthen your body, and change your posture. Try not to wear the same shoes with every outfit. If you are fashion savvy, consider color and print to make a statement. If you plan to wear sandals, make sure you schedule a pedicure before your photo session. On shoot day, bring a pair of flip flops or flats that are easy to walk in as we go from location to location (but don't plan to wear them at the shoot).

Seasonal Disorder

Avoid styles that are too season-specific. For example, you may not want to select a heavy, chunky wool sweater because it would look funny to use that image in your promo for your spring course launch. Also avoid trendy styles, as they may look dated quickly (remember parachute pants?!).

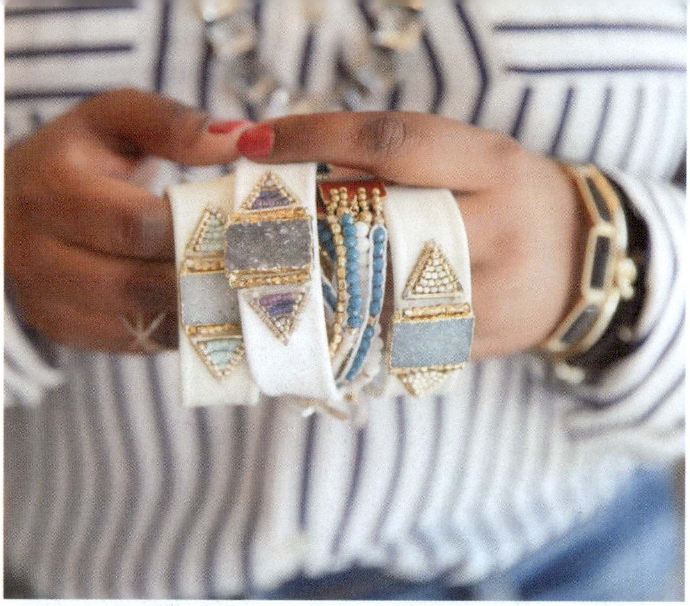

Statement Pieces

Accessories are a great way to style your outfit and upgrade your look. Statement necklaces, stacked bracelets, dangling earrings, a colorful silk scarf, a chunky watch — all can add some visual interest to your photo. Just don't go overboard or wear them all at once.

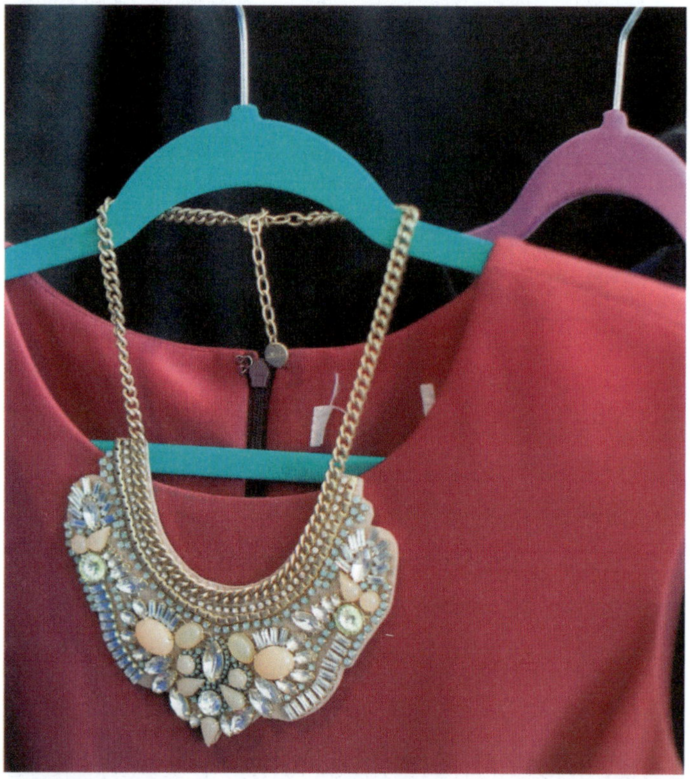

Practice Makes Perfect

If you're trying to decide between a couple of outfit choices, put them on, run, dance, and twirl. See if they feel comfortable and allow you to move. Make sure to try everything on one week AND a few days before the shoot to ensure fit.

Stop and Shop

There are endless options for shopping for your photo shoot. Departments stores like Nordstrom, Bloomingdales, and Macy's have most of everything you need under one roof. For speciality items or unique looks, visit local, smaller boutiques. Also consider second-hand stores (like thredUP) and consignment stores for great style at great prices. Lastly, consider renting clothes from Rent the Runway to create your power outfit.

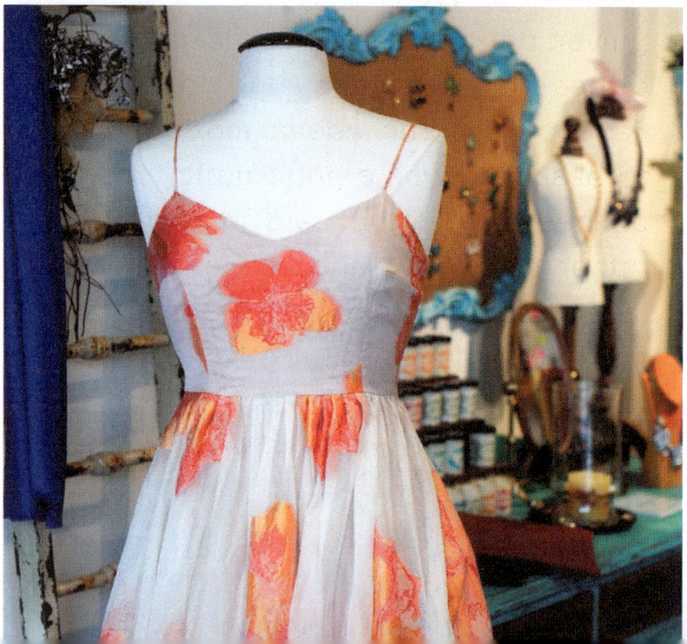

5 Style Hacks for a Great Photo Shoot

1

Do a trial run. Lay out each outfit a few days prior to your shoot and try on each look from head to toe. Walk around in it to make sure you feel comfortable. The camera will sense if you're worried about your outfit.

2

Have a backup outfit. No matter the number of outfit changes you have planned, always add one more. You never know if you will feel bloated or accidentally spill something on the day of your shoot.

3

Make sure clothing is cleaned and pressed ahead of time. Any alterations should be completed a few days prior.

4

Create an easy fashion emergency kit for the day of. Include double-sided tape to create temporary hems or close gaps, anti-static spray to eliminate static cling, and a lint roller to remove dust or particles.

5

Wear heels during your photo shoot. This improves your posture, elongates your legs, and signals your brain to appear more confident. Bring flats for in between outfits and location changes.

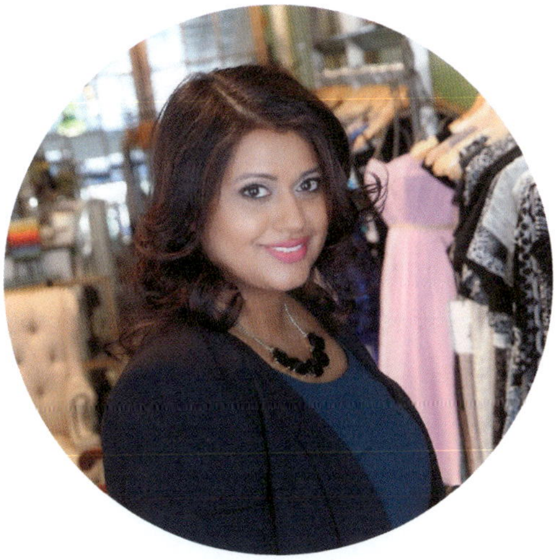

EXPERT ADVICE

from Personal Stylist Neepa Sikdar www.accessiblestyle.net

Top 5 Accessories Every Lady Boss Needs for Her Photo Shoot

1

Keep your outfit simple, and add color and style with a statement necklace. Choose shorter styles to wear with crew and round necks as well as collar shirts. Longer, beaded or tassel styles are great with all necklines, especially V-necks and off-the-shoulder styles. Shorter necklaces draw the attention to you face; longer necklaces add length to your stature.

2

Cuffs are great arm candy! A broad cuff looks great even when peeking out under a long sleeve.

3

Chandelier earrings are a great way to add color and flair to your look. Whether tassels or stones, there are perfect statement earrings for everyone. If you decide to go with a chandelier earring, skip the necklace or keep it very simple and delicate. Shoulder dusting earrings are great with prints, off-the-shoulder looks, and open necklines.

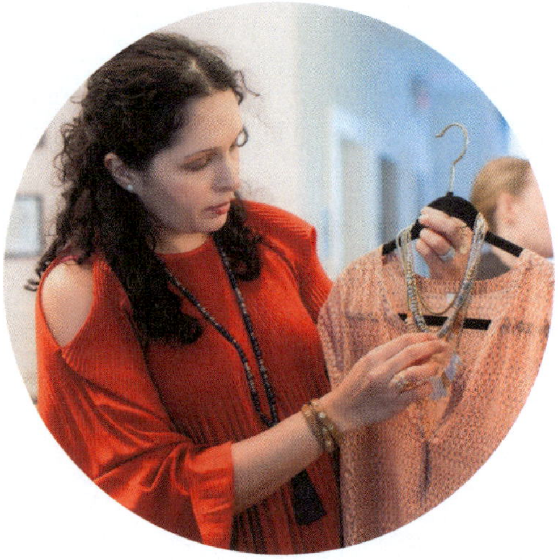

4

While styling your photoshoot, you are guaranteed to have some action shots involving your hands. Whether you are taking notes or grabbing coffee, highlight your fingers with some rings. You can keep it classy or add some drama with colorful, cocktail rings. If you are going with a larger statement ring, pair with statement earrings!

5

Scarves are an often-overlooked accessory. But they are great to add color, fun, and warmth to your story. If you are going for a more crisp and professional look, add a silk scarf that pairs well with your outfit.

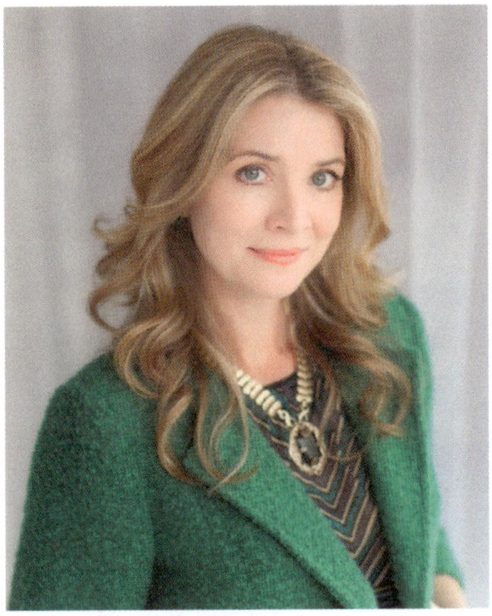
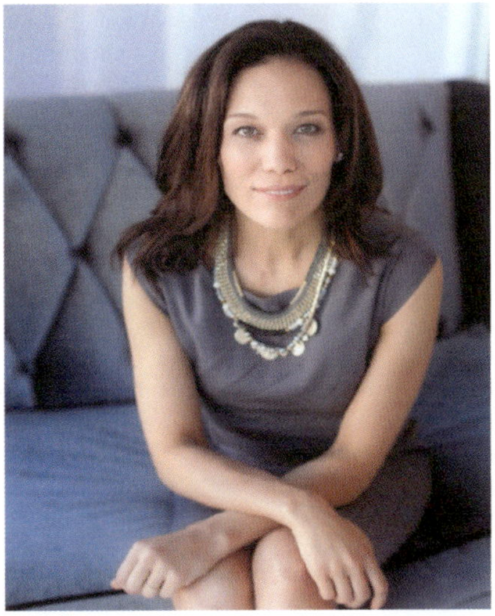
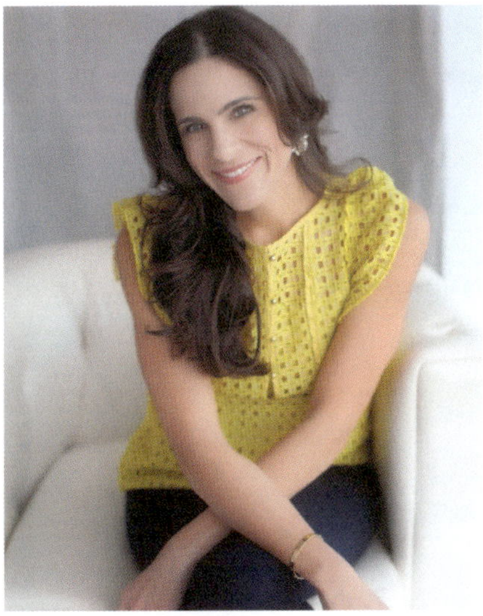
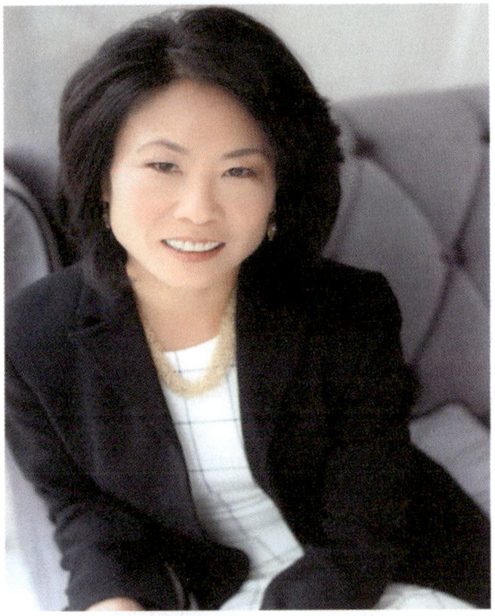
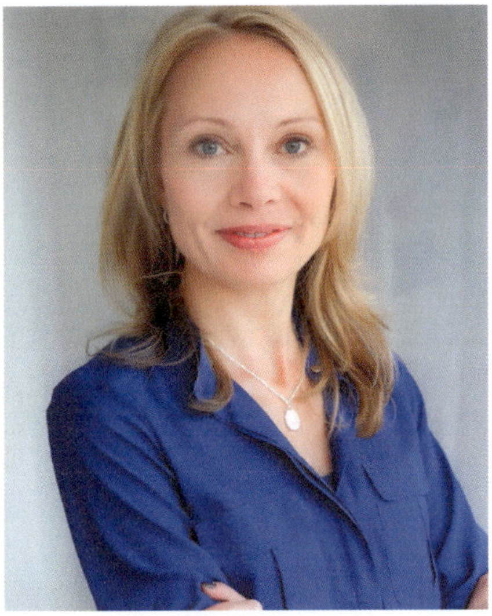
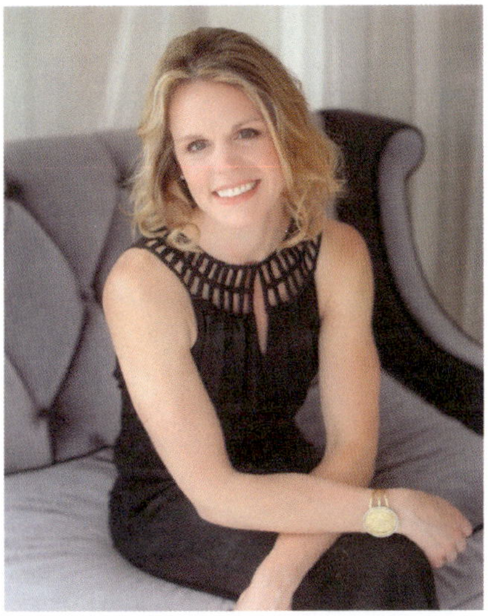
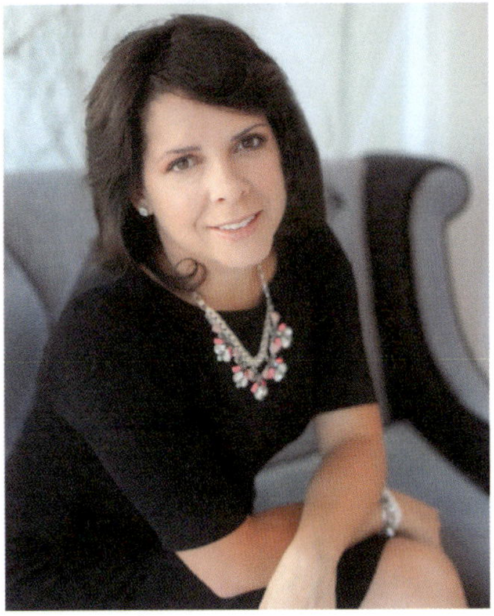
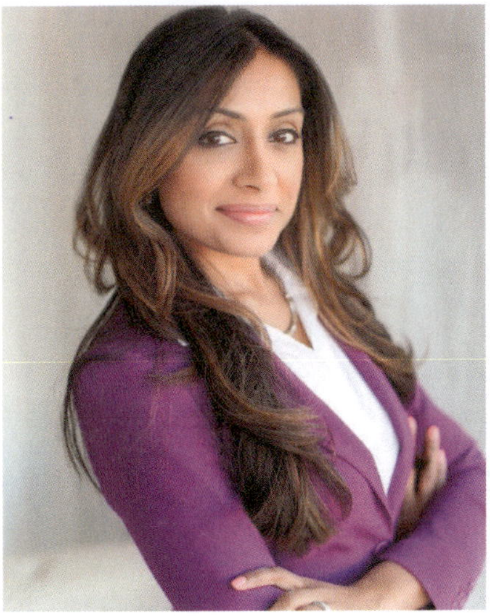
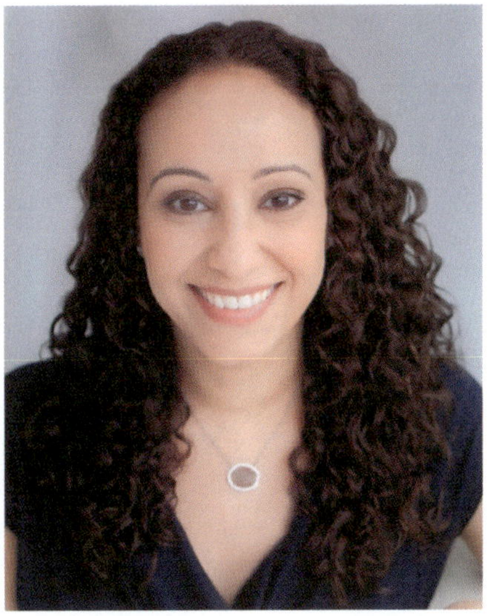

BEAUTY, HAIR, & MAKEUP

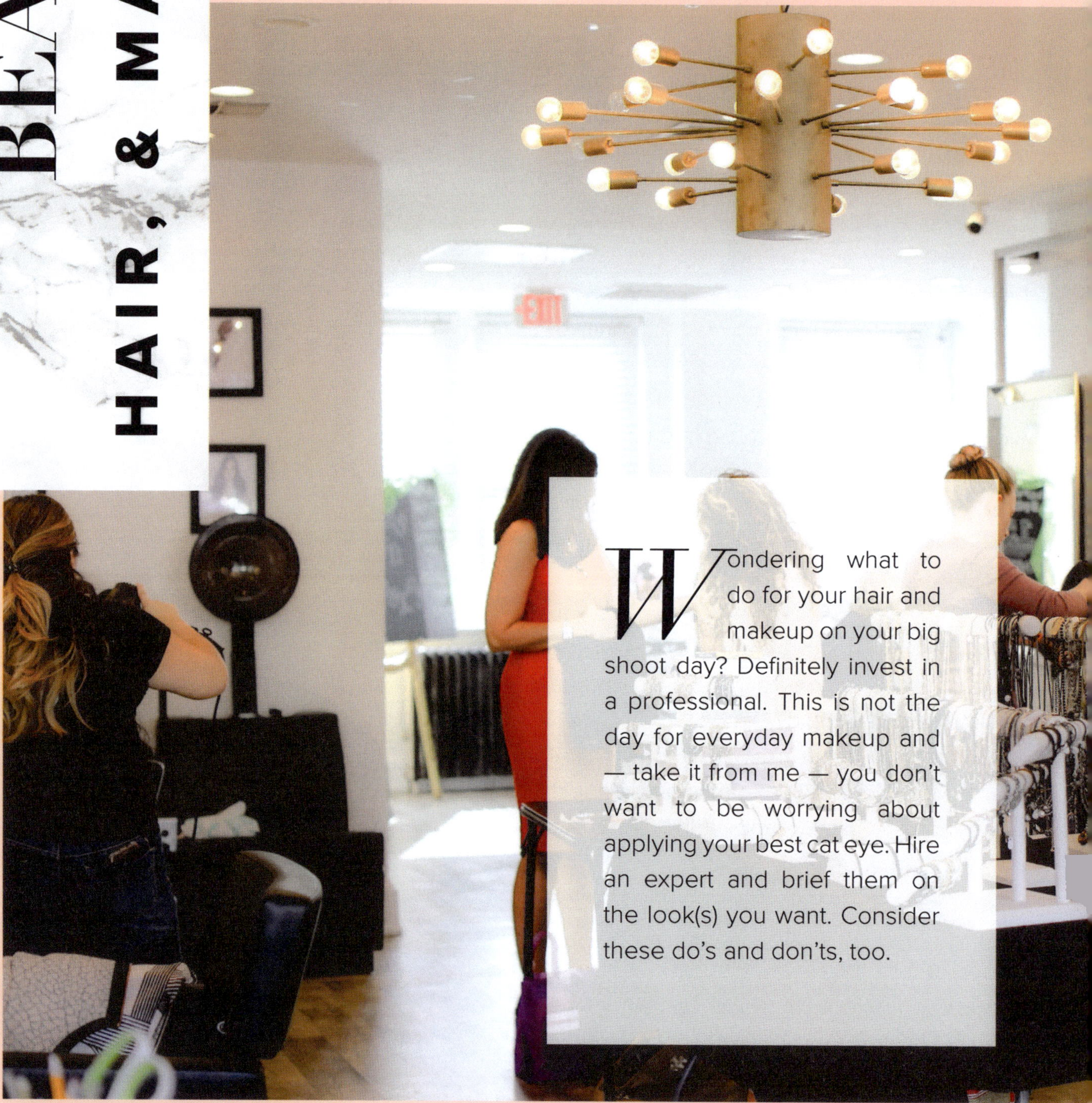

Wondering what to do for your hair and makeup on your big shoot day? Definitely invest in a professional. This is not the day for everyday makeup and — take it from me — you don't want to be worrying about applying your best cat eye. Hire an expert and brief them on the look(s) you want. Consider these do's and don'ts, too.

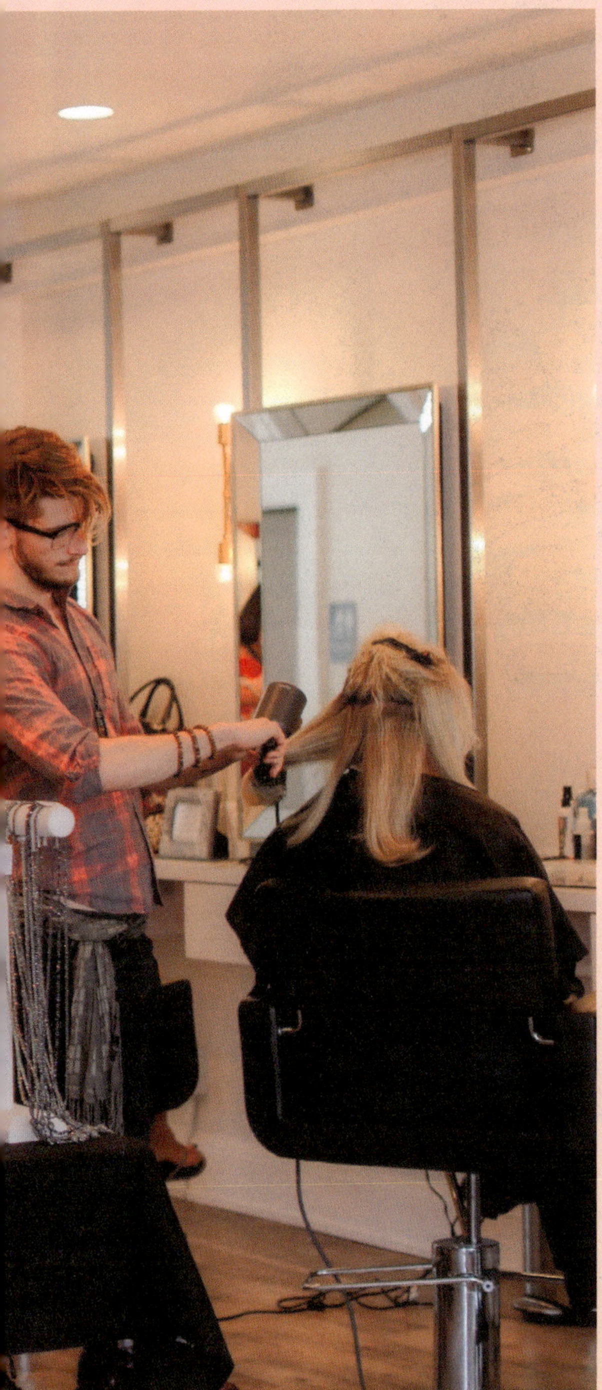

DO'S

- Do ask if hair/makeup is part of your photography package. (If not, do ask for recommendations.)
- Do get your hair colored to cover any grays one to two weeks before the shoot.
- Do bring photos of hair and makeup that you like.
- Do be honest about what you want and feel comfortable with for your hair/makeup.
- Do trust the professionals. Your makeup may look heavier than normal, but it translates differently on camera.
- Do get a manicure and pedicure before the shoot.
- Do get your eyebrows waxed or threaded one week before the shoot.
- Do take extra time moisturizing your lips a week before the shoot so they are smooth and not chapped.
- Do come with clean, dry hair and a clean face on shoot day.
- Do consider using false eyelashes.

DON'TS

- Don't get a new haircut right before your shoot.
- Don't get a facial or do any skin treatments days before your shoot (three to four weeks prior at the latest).
- Don't take chances with a new beauty look on the day of your shoot.
- Don't ask the stylist to do what they think is best. You know yourself and your brand best. Offer some direction.

5 Beauty Tips

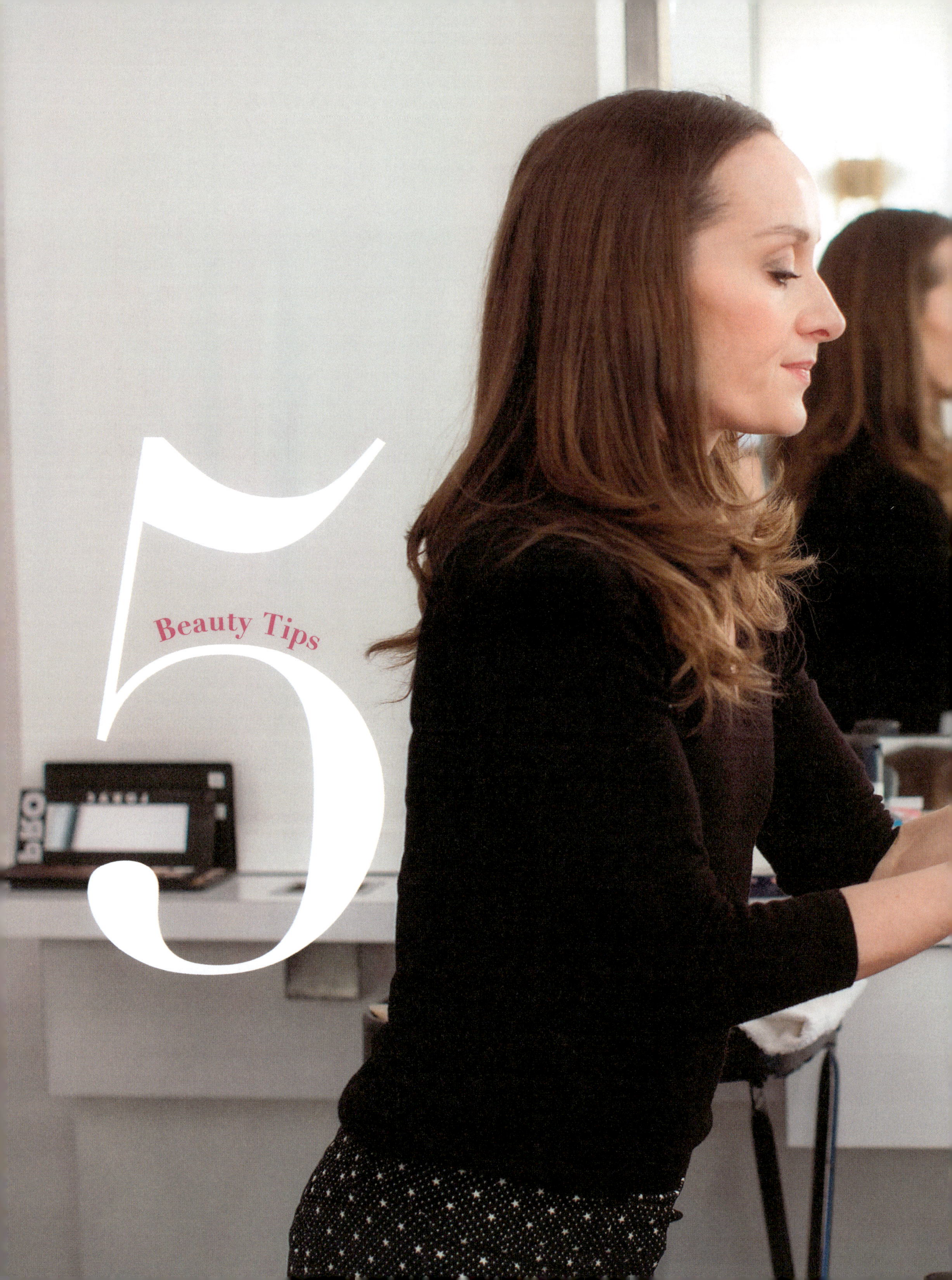

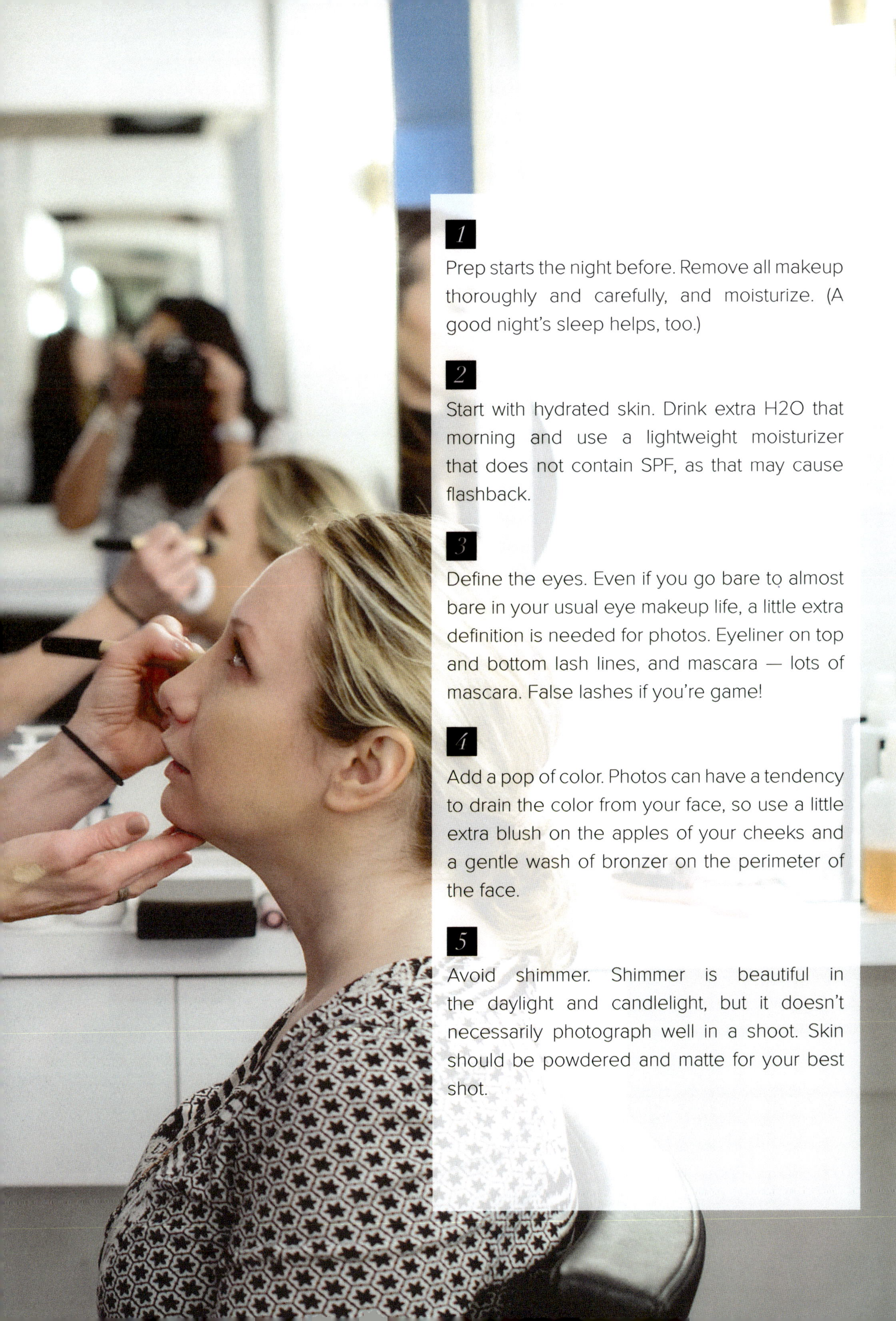

EXPERT ADVICE

from Makeup Artist Lucy Chambers www.lucychambersmakeup.com

1

Prep starts the night before. Remove all makeup thoroughly and carefully, and moisturize. (A good night's sleep helps, too.)

2

Start with hydrated skin. Drink extra H2O that morning and use a lightweight moisturizer that does not contain SPF, as that may cause flashback.

3

Define the eyes. Even if you go bare to almost bare in your usual eye makeup life, a little extra definition is needed for photos. Eyeliner on top and bottom lash lines, and mascara — lots of mascara. False lashes if you're game!

4

Add a pop of color. Photos can have a tendency to drain the color from your face, so use a little extra blush on the apples of your cheeks and a gentle wash of bronzer on the perimeter of the face.

5

Avoid shimmer. Shimmer is beautiful in the daylight and candlelight, but it doesn't necessarily photograph well in a shoot. Skin should be powdered and matte for your best shot.

5 Hair Tips

1

Seek referrals for an artist that works with photography clients. Trust your photographer's referral if they have one. They know what looks best in their photos.

2

Consultation, consultation, consultation! It's so important to develop communication and discuss your comfort zone and desires for the overall look! Think about doing this in person and possibly scheduling a trial.

3

Provide two to three photos that you love of yourself for the artist to build visual reference of your "best self" and develop a clear communication of your hair goals (even if the photo is a special occasion and not the same look you desire for a branding shoot). Bring inspiration photos of hair and makeup you are drawn to (even if you have not worn it before).

4

When deciding a hairstyle, think effortless. Of course, effortless hair takes effort. Every woman's style should complement and frame their face.

5

Waves in hair can make a look feel special and effortless at the same time. If straight and sleek are more your style, just make sure your stylist adds slightly more volume to help create framing from every different angle you will be photographed from.

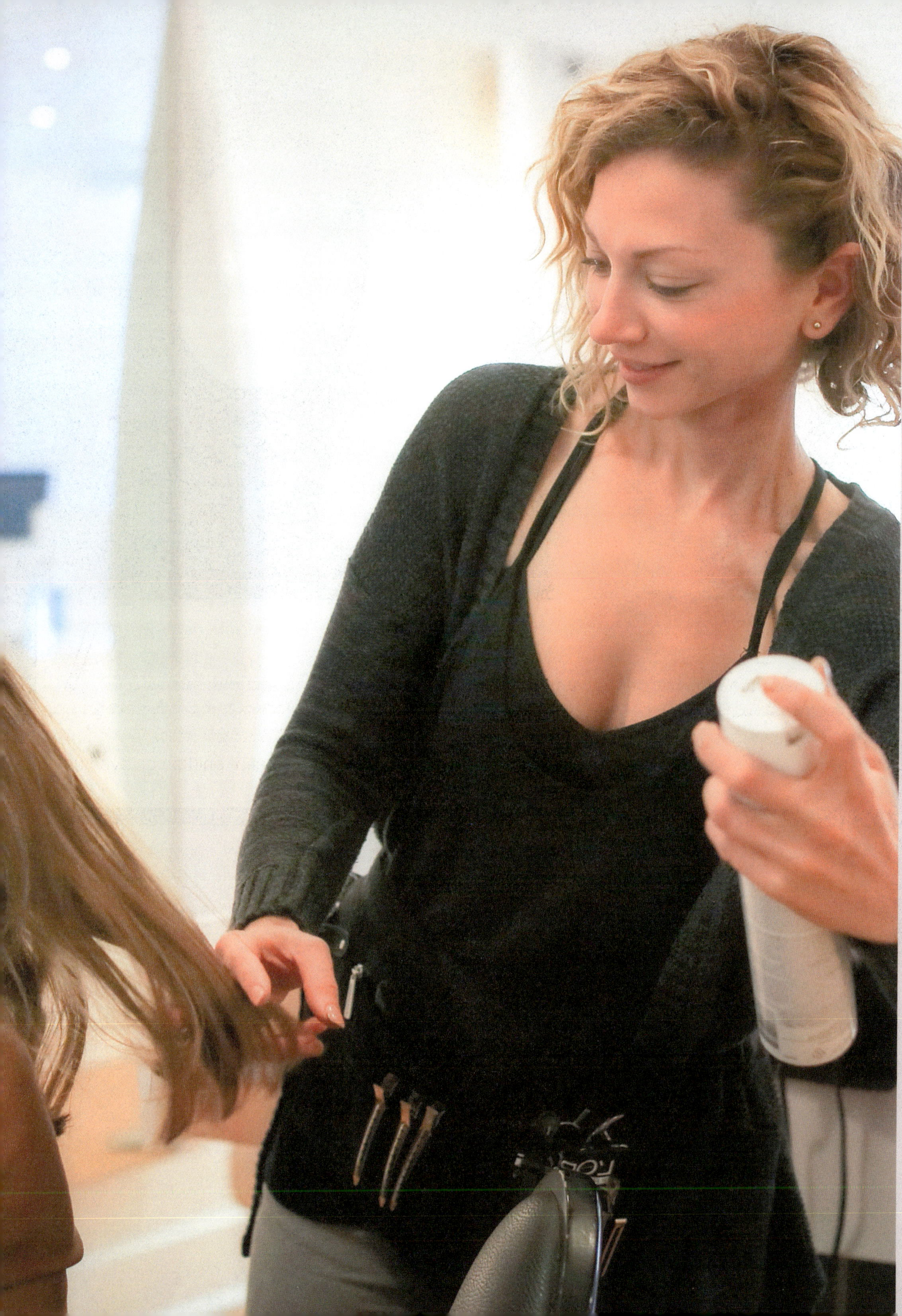

EXPERT ADVICE

from Hair Stylist Kelly DeSario *www.reelstylebeauty.com*

LOCATION

Where to shoot? What locations, places, and backdrops should we use? Should we be indoors or outdoors, or both? To answer these questions, I always advise my clients to first think about their brand story. Consider where you work, how you work, and the vibe of your business.

Think about the message you are trying to communicate, and brainstorm places that connect to that story. Think about your ideal client and the locations that they frequent. Think about the places that inspire you and your work.

Still looking for a unique space? Check out Airbnb for renting homes and apartments with character. Also visit Breather if you live in select big cities like New York, San Francisco, and Boston. This resource rents beautiful, professional work spaces that can make for an amazing backdrop. And if you live in a smaller or rural town, there are still location options. You may need to be creative or look a little harder, but they are definitely out there.

- Coffee Shop
- Bookstore
- Museum
- Downtown/Urban
- Natural/Park
- Restaurant
- Office
- Hotel
- Boutique
- Farmers' Market
- Flea Market
- Winery
- Garden
- Corporate Lobby
- Workout Studio
- Library
- Rooftop
- Beach
- Amusement Park
- Airport
- Store
- Train Station
- Street/Sidewalk
- Spa
- Florist
- Your Home
- Work Site
- Theatre
- A Client's Home
- Colored Walls
- Garage Doors
- Art Gallery
- Marina
- Staircases
- Parking Lots
- Playground
- Stadium
- Farm
- Pool
- Woods
- Mountains
- Lake
- Arboretum
- Hiking Trail
- College Campus
- Candy Store
- Bakery
- Bar

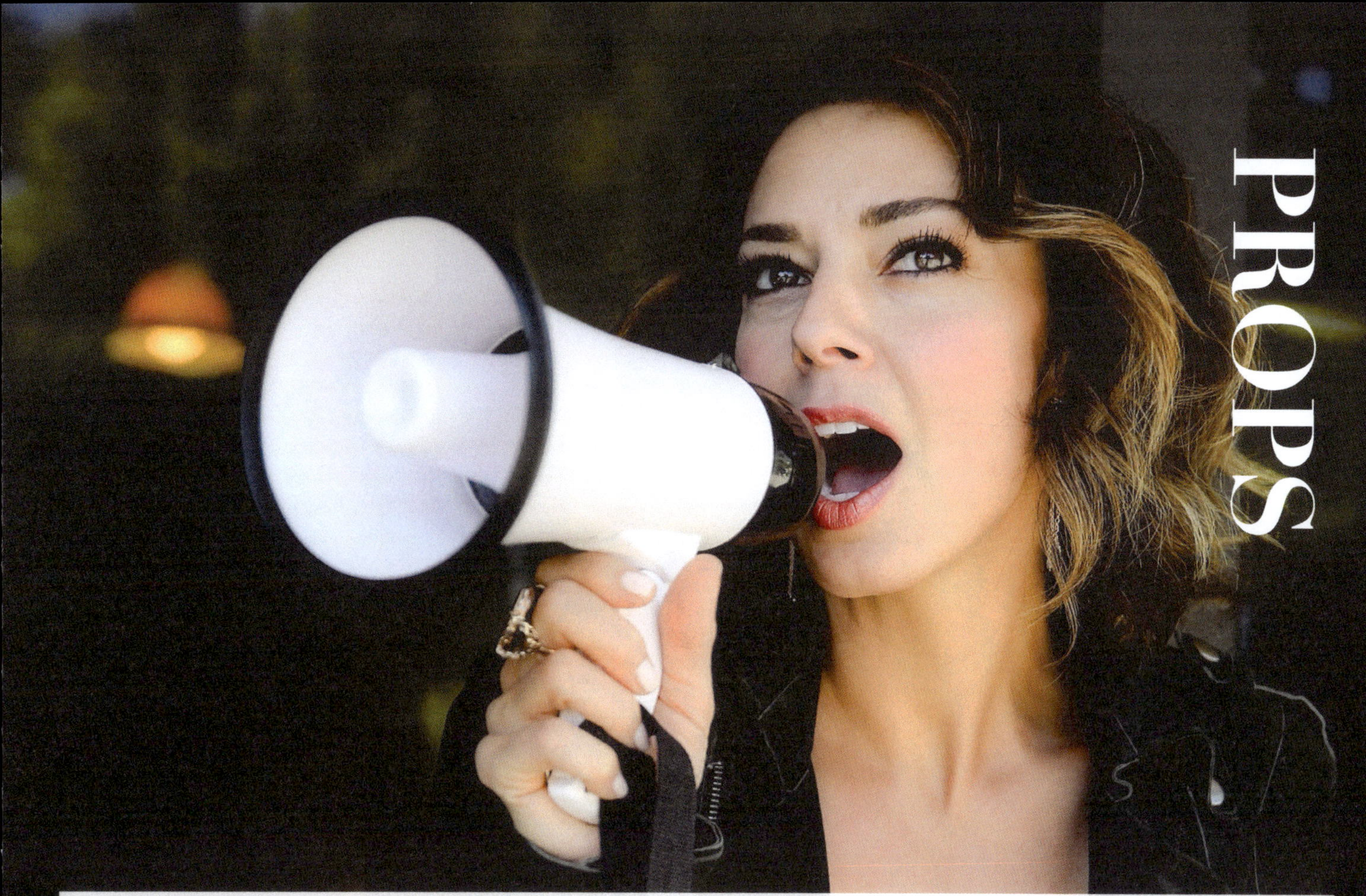

PROPS

Props are objects that add variety, support your branding message, and help round out your story. They can communicate your personality, your values, and your work style. *Consider selecting props that your ideal customer uses and understands. Consider incorporating tools that are essential to your business and represent your industry. Consider all the things you can't live or work without.* Props can also help you act more "natural" in front of the camera since you have something to interact with.

- Laptop
- iPad
- iPhone
- Coffee Mugs
- Keyboard
- Books
- Magazines
- Journals
- Planner
- Calendar
- Desk Accessories
- Cards
- Artwork/Signs
- Stationery
- Flowers
- Confetti
- Branded Materials *cards,logos, etc.*
- Wine Glass
- Champagne Flutes
- Cookies/Macarons
- Balloons
- Accessories *Jewelry*
- Cosmetics
- Candles
- Press Clippings
- Awards
- Quotes on Paper
- Pens/Pencils
- Fruit
- Newspaper
- Sunglasses
- Passport
- Globe
- Maps
- Camera
- Photos
- Microphone
- Notebook
- Megaphone
- Bike
- Ice Cream/Sweets
- Hats
- Fruit
- Cupcakes
- Clipboards
- Binoculars
- Work materials and tools of the trade *e.g., worksheets, swatches, color chips, paint brushes*

Top-5 Winning Props for Your Photo Shoot

1

Book with a title that communicates your brand story

2

Mug with a saying that reflects your values or mindset

3

Laptop or phone (pull up your website or Instagram)

4

Calendar or planner with handwritten notes or to-do list

5

Branded business card or promotional items

Bonus tip: Consider props in your brand color to reinforce your brand look. Bring out all your branded collateral: business cards, post-cards, brochures, packaging, signs, etc.

FEELING CAMERA CONFIDENT

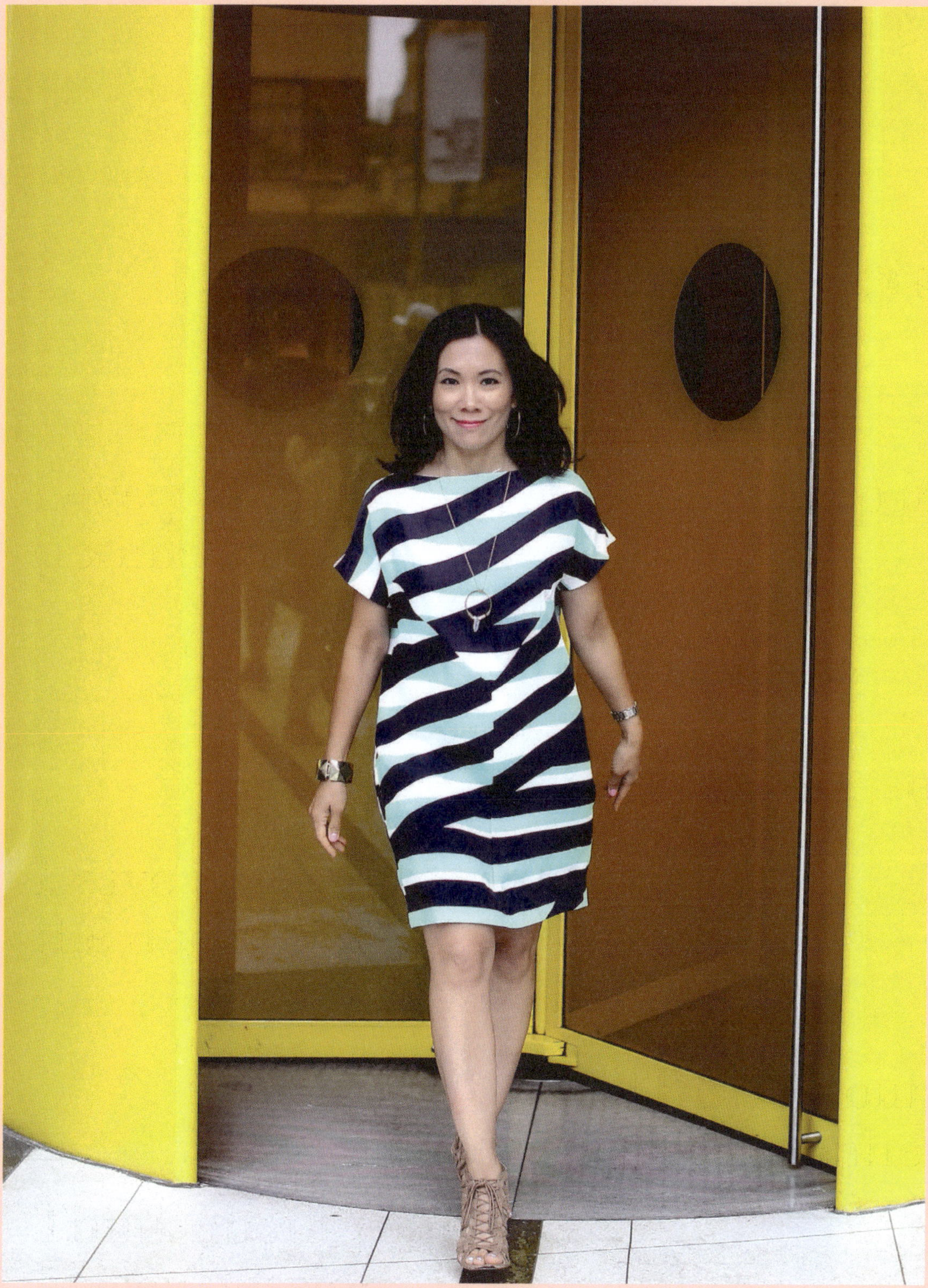

Being in front of the camera is indeed stressful and nerve-wracking. We want to look and feel natural, but the focus of the lens can often turn us into stiff robots. What is the trick to being yourself and showing your spark? After doing hundreds of brand photo shoots and capturing all types of personalities, I have discovered the secrets to boosting your confidence so you shine in front of the camera.

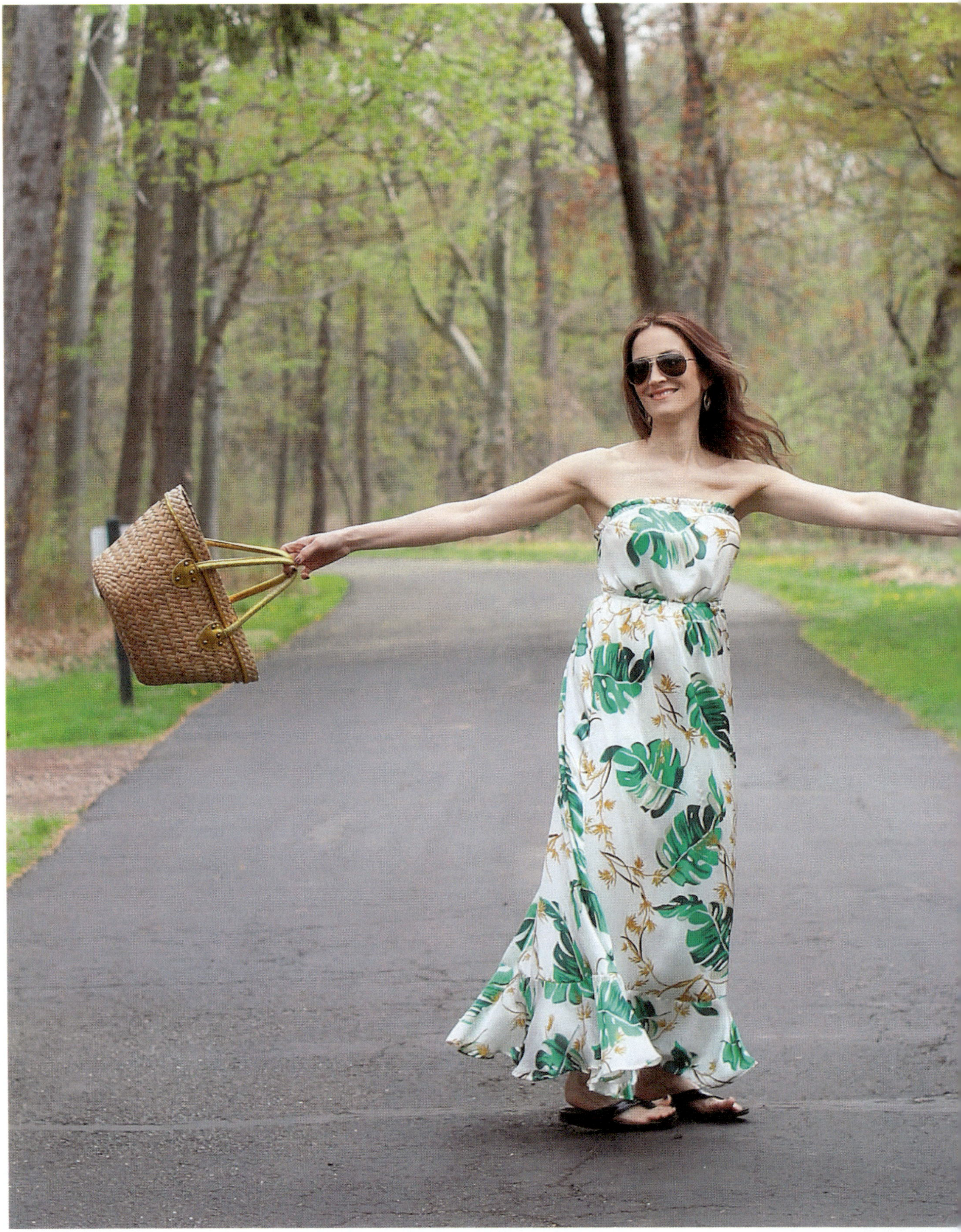

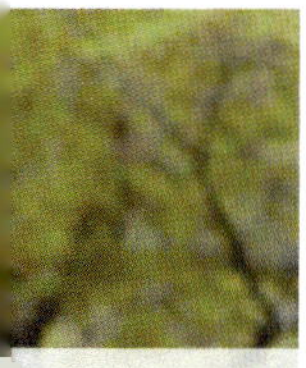

HOW TO SHOW YOUR SPARK

Give yourself permission.

Yes, you deserve this photo shoot! You are a rock star with a message that will inspire others. Quiet those inner demons that are telling you otherwise. One effective way is to write out all those doubts. Then put away that paper and be bold enough to start sharing your story.

Leave perfection at the door.

Nobody wants perfect. They want the real, authentic you! It's okay to be silly and goofy, especially on shoot day. It's these moments that reveal the natural expressions that feel most like you and will connect with your audience.

Think about your bigger mission.

Remember the people you serve and why you do this work in the first place. These photos are a tool for your bigger movement!

Come prepared.

Make sure you do the necessary work on your brand story, your visual strategy, your outfits, and your props way ahead of schedule. It's no fun running around the day before your big shoot.

Strut your stuff.

Put on your outfits and make sure everything fits well. Dance, twirl, sit, walk — move to make sure you feel comfortable. Look in the mirror and practice smiling, laughing, and all different expressions. This may feel silly, but it helps your face feel prepared and relaxed.

TRUST your photographer.

Take a moment, close your eyes, and breathe. You hired them for a reason. Let them be the expert here and guide you through the process. Try not to micromanage and ask to see every photo after the camera clicks. This will hurt the creative process and the rapport with your photographer. Have some fun!

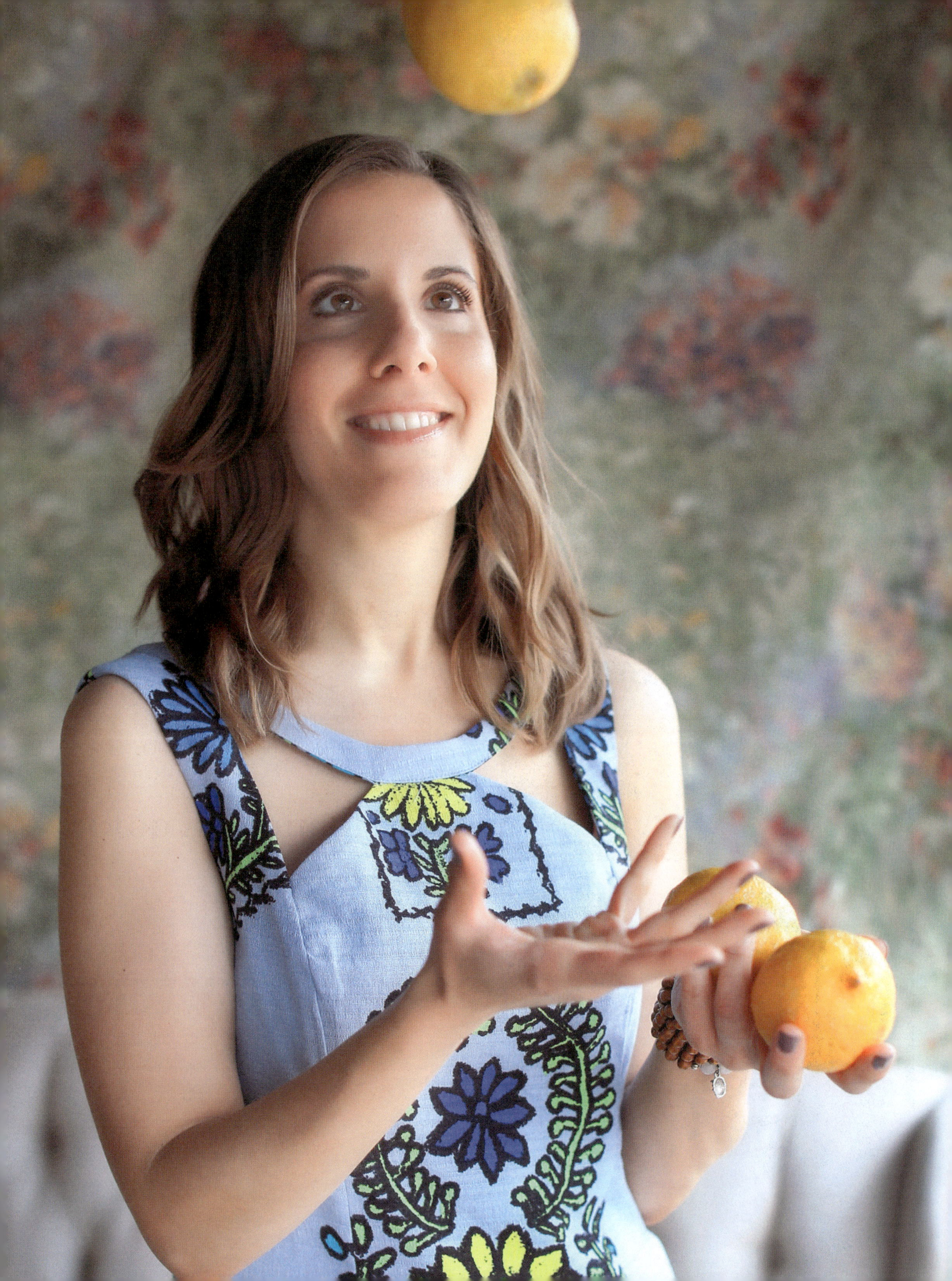

10 Tips for How to Feel Your Best on Shoot Day

Be sure you follow these tips for seven to 10 days leading up to your shoot.

1

Hydrate. Be sure to drink several cups of room-temperature water each day to promote the cleansing of toxins, to improve digestion, and to increase energy.

2

Eat an anti-inflammatory diet. Certain foods and drinks, such as dairy, gluten, sugar, alcohol, and caffeine, cause inflammation in the body. Inflammation can cause several skin issues like acne, eczema, and psoriasis. Stick to dark leafy greens, vegetables, grass-fed meat, healthy fats, and minimal fruit.

3

Get your zzz's. The term "beauty sleep" holds truth. When you have a full night of sleep, you not only feel well rested, but your stress is reduced, your skin is clearer, and you minimize those dark under-eye circles.

4

Reduce stress. Stress can make you appear worn down. Be sure to prioritize self-care, such as an Epsom salt bath, lavender oil self-massage, body brushing, pedicure, or whatever you love!

5

Detox with lemon. Fresh lemon juice helps to promote detox in the body. Start your day with water and fresh-squeezed lemon juice, or incorporate it into your meals.

6

Balance gut health. Nobody wants a bloated belly during a photo shoot. Make sure your gut bacteria is balanced by taking a daily probiotic.

7

Naturally whiten teeth. Many tooth-whitening strips and kits contain toxic ingredients. You can create your own paste at home by mixing a bit of baking soda and water. Lemon juice also does the trick. Just be careful not to do it too often, as the acid may strip some tooth enamel.

8

Tone arms. Show off those lady guns! A great way to tone up your arms is by doing push-ups, lifting light weights, or even doing yoga. A little each day goes a long way.

9

Moisturize. One of my favorite ways to moisturize is with old-fashioned Jojoba oil. Massage it into your face and around your eyes to maintain young, healthy-looking skin.

10

Have fun! Most importantly, this is your time to shine, so have a great time!

from Health Coach Claudia Petrilli www.claudiapetrilli.com

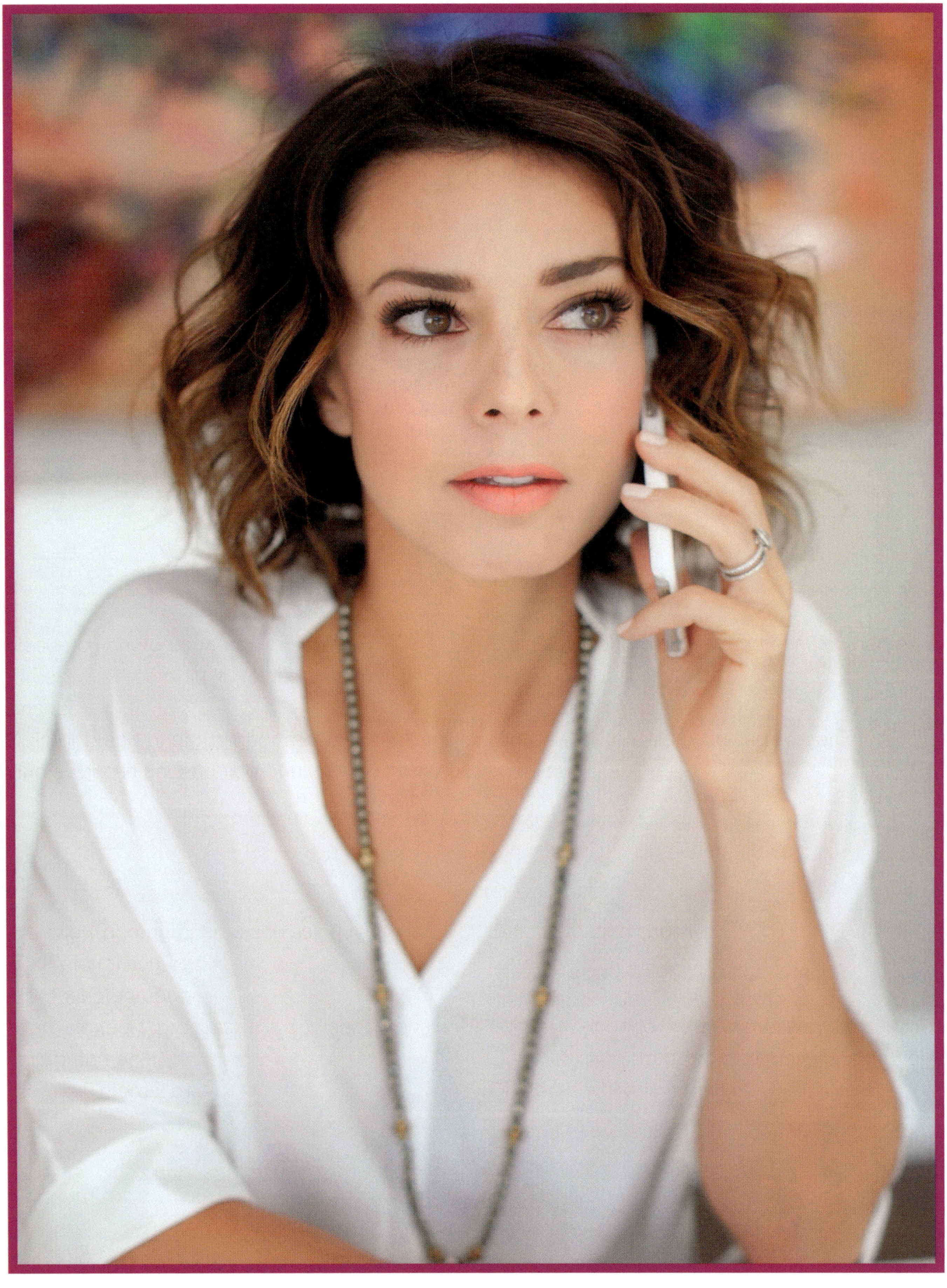

PHOTO SHOOT

COUNTDOWN

06

This section offers a general overview of the time line leading up to a brand photography shoot. Every client, every photographer, and every shoot are different, so timing may vary. It's best to plan and discuss this with your creative team.

Months

4 Months Prior to Shoot Date

Research photographers.

Create a "dream shot" folder of brand photo images.

Ask for brand photographer recommendations and advice in Facebook groups.

3 Months Prior to Shoot Date

Interview photographers and ask questions.

Call referral sources.

Book photographer.

Start strategic process. Fill out questionnaire and brand brief.

Create Pinterest board.

2 Months Prior to Shoot Date

Brainstorm photo stories and confirm themes.

List props/locations/outfits.

Book hair/makeup.

Hire stylist or start putting together outfits yourself.

1 Month Prior to Shoot Date

Start preparing shot list.

Confirm locations, props, and outfits.

Start shopping for props/outfits.

Get hair cut or colored if necessary.

Get teeth whitened professionally or start your DIY teeth whitening routine.

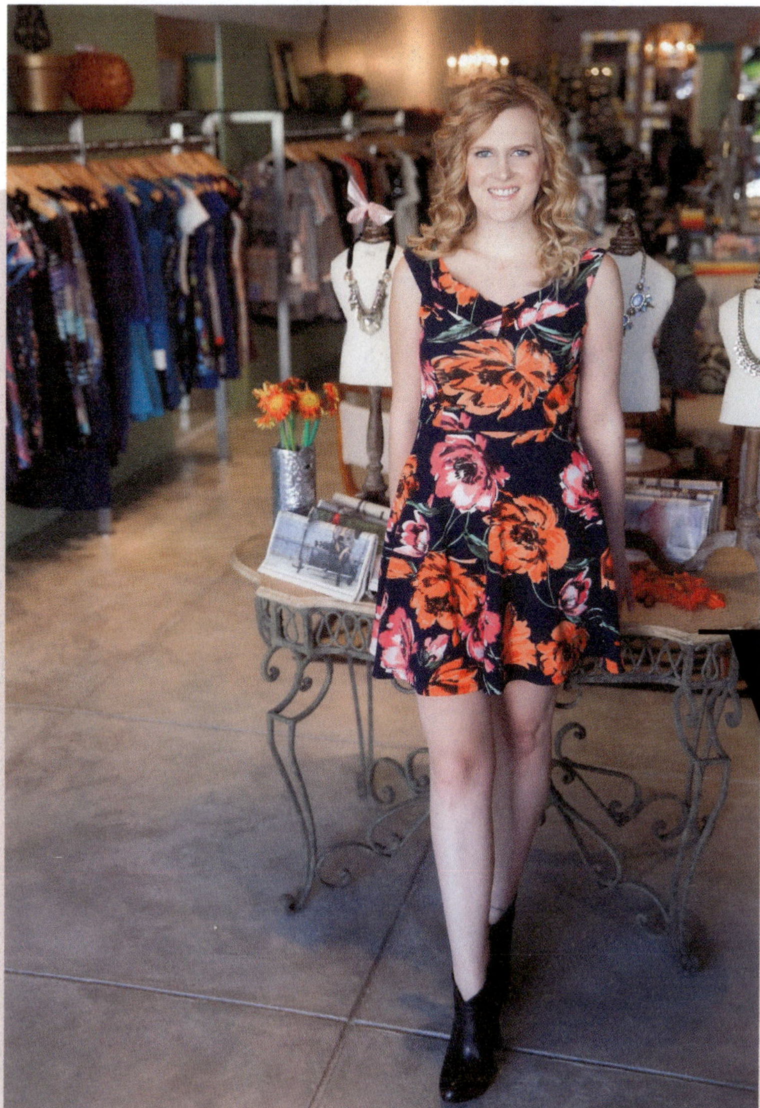

WeeKs

3 Weeks Prior to Shoot Date

Continue collecting props.
Considering a facial? Do it now.
Considering Botox? Do it now.

2 Weeks Prior to Shoot Date

Confirm shot list.
Try on all your outfits.
Touch up hair color.

1 Week Prior to Shoot Date

Get eyebrows groomed.
Start hydrating and moisturizing.
Write away all doubts.

Days

3 Days Prior to Shoot Date

Steam/iron all outfits.

Interested in spray tan? Do it now.

Confirm final details with photographer, hair, makeup.

Organize all outfits, accessories, undergarments for each shot (put in separate garment bags).

Put all props in a laundry basket.

2 Days Prior to Shoot Date

Get manicure/pedicure.

Feeling stressed? Get massage.

1 Day Prior to Shoot Date

Prep all your outfits and put them in the car.

Prep all your props and put them in the car.

Pack water, snacks, and flip flops.

Shave body parts.

Moisturize.

Sleep well.

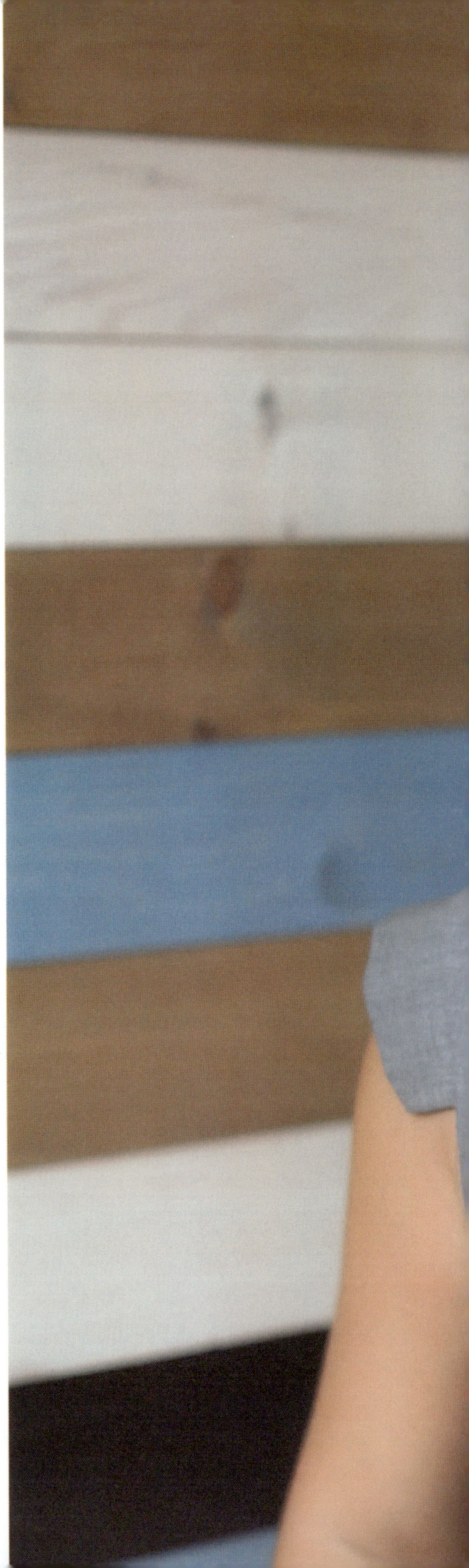

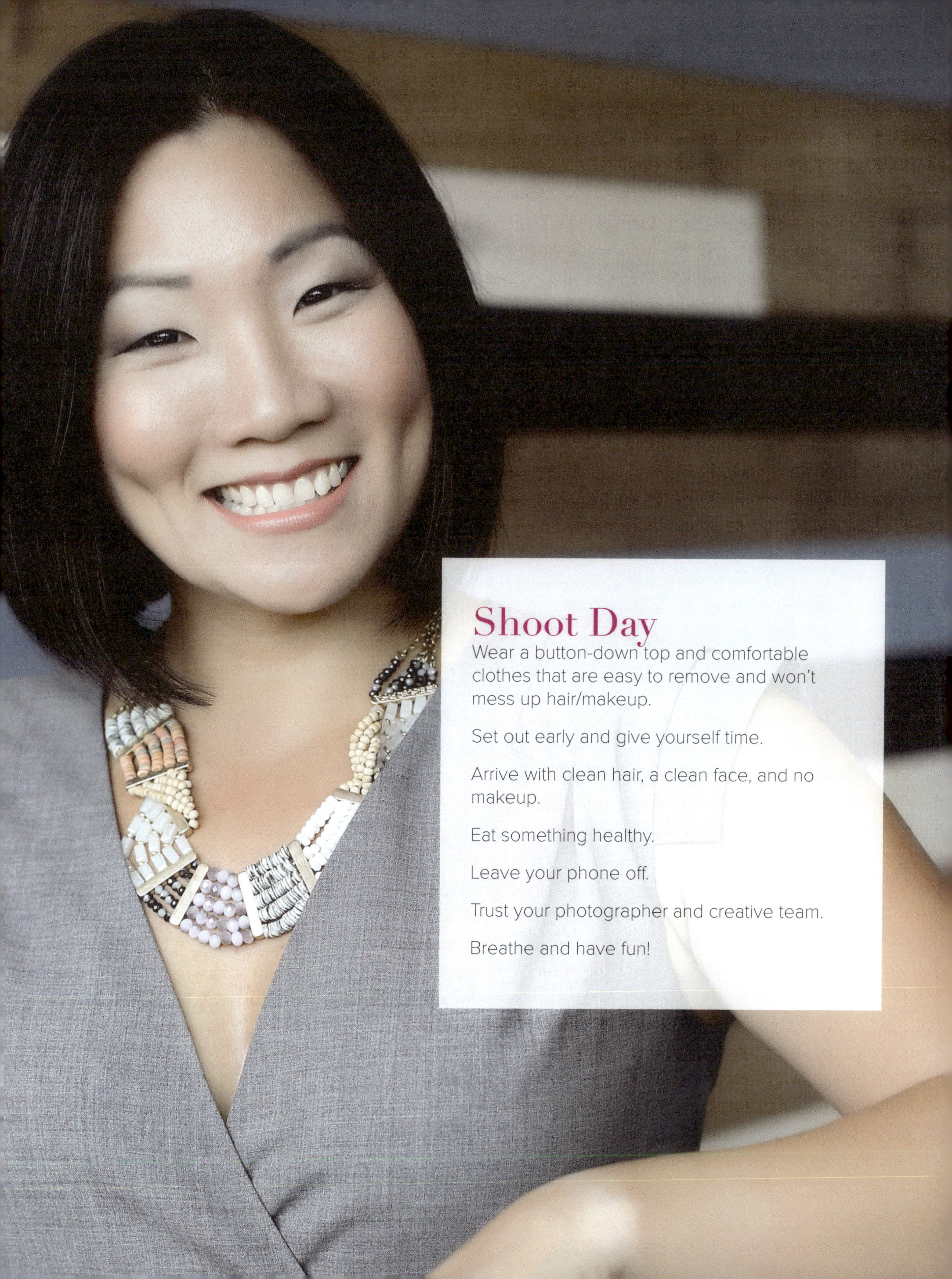

Shoot Day

Wear a button-down top and comfortable clothes that are easy to remove and won't mess up hair/makeup.

Set out early and give yourself time.

Arrive with clean hair, a clean face, and no makeup.

Eat something healthy.

Leave your phone off.

Trust your photographer and creative team.

Breathe and have fun!

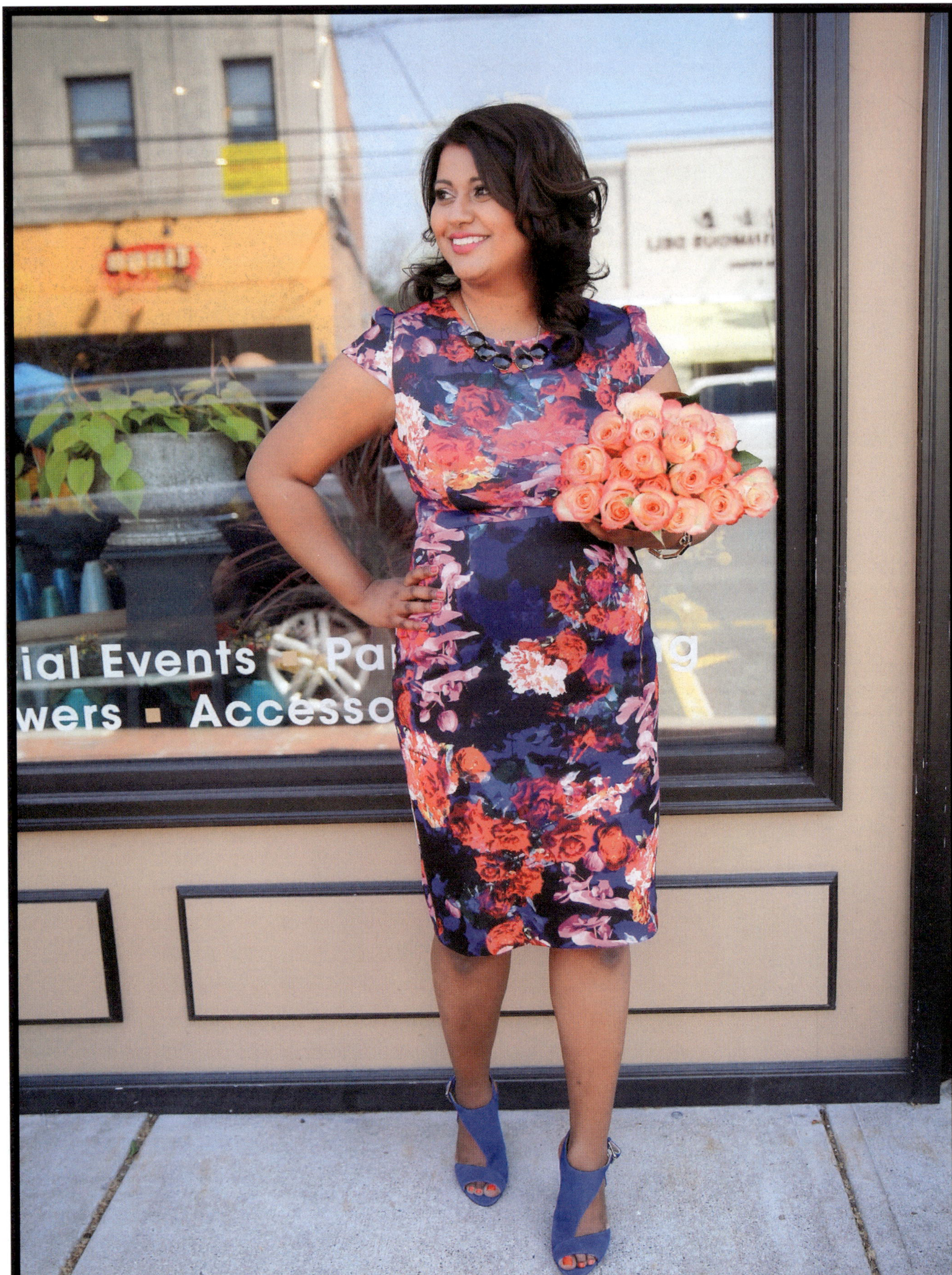
ial Events ▪ Pa
wers ▪ Accesso

HOW DO I Pose NATURALLY?

07

It's tough to feel natural in front of the camera lens. Posing is the job of your photographer. They should be directing you and giving you specific instructions on how to move your body in the most natural and flattering way. Here are a few tips to practice before your shoot to assure that you are feeling your most natural and looking your best. Try them in front of a mirror.

1

Always watch your posture. Stand up straight and stretch out your neck, as if a string is being pulled from the top of your head. Suck in your abdominals.

2

Pull back your shoulders but make sure they are relaxed. Never be hunched!

5

A slight tilt of the head does wonders. (Now try tilting the other way, too.)

6

Watch your hands. When we are nervous, we clench them into fists. Make sure your hands are relaxed and loose.

9

Think of a secret or something naughty. This spark will be revealed in your eyes and smile.

3

Stick your chin out and down.

4

Bend your elbows slightly. Never leave them heavy and lifeless at your sides.

7

Always position your chin and face toward the light source. Light is your friend!

8

Are your eyes sensitive or twitching? Close your eyes and open them right before the click of the camera.

10

Breathe. Laugh. Shake your face. This will loosen your expression and make you look more natural.

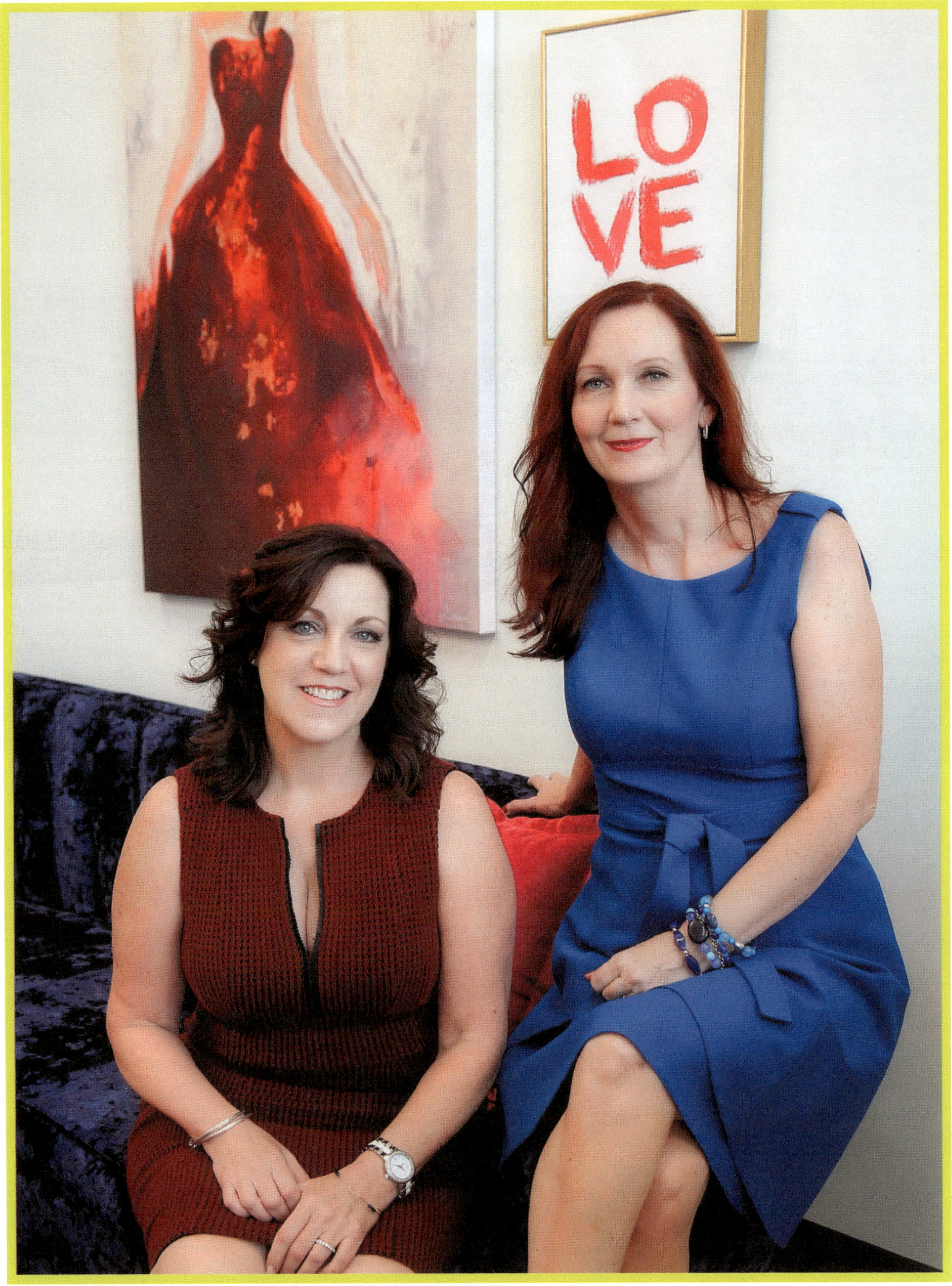
LOVE

08

PHOTO usage GUIDELINES

HOW TO SELECT THE RIGHT PHOTOS FOR YOUR BRAND

The shoot is finished! Your photographer has uploaded your images into a gallery, and they're ready for you to review and select. It's time to build your brand photography library. Before you pick 15 similar-looking headshots, think about the story you want to tell. You want a robust collection of visuals that you can use ongoing for multiple purposes.

How do you choose the right images for your business?

First, revisit the list you made before the shoot of all your online and offline visual marketing needs. Consider all the image content you will need for your current and future marketing plans (your website, blogs, printed marketing collateral, etc.). Select visuals with these needs in mind.

Next, think about the 11 photo stories listed in Chapter 5. Make sure you pick photos that can communicate all of these themes. This list will build strong connections with your audience.

1. Your purpose
2. Your prowess
3. Your process
4. Your products or services
5. Your personality
6. Your passion
7. Your people
8. Your inspiration
9. Your point of difference
10. Your vision
11. Your #allthethings

Lastly, when selecting your images, focus on variety. Variety will add depth and differentiation to your brand. You want to include headshots, lifestyle images, environmental portraits, stock photos, and behind-the-scene stories. You want images with space, tight shots, and both vertical and horizontal formats. You want to feature different outfits, locations, and expressions. The goal when selecting your photos is to have many separate stories but all supporting a cohesive and consistent overall message.

WHERE TO USE THE PHOTOS

Congrats! You made your selections, and your photographer has sent you the edited files. Before you start posting images, make a backup copy of your finished branding photos on a jump drive. Also create a folder in cloud storage like Dropbox so that you can access your images at all times. This will be a time saver when you want to post an image on the go across all your marketing platforms.

Now is the time to start telling your story! Your brand photos are a powerful tool to connect with your audience and share your message. Make sure you are intentional and strategic with the photos that you choose to use. Consider the story you are trying to tell. Consider the platform you are using and how the photos can best serve that space. Beware of posting randomly, too often, or not often enough.

Here are a few examples of what your photos can do for you:

- Attract viewers, share who you are, and what you do (website)
- Announce news like a course or product launch (sales page)
- Educate with tips or how-tos (blog)
- Showcase your process or behind the scenes (Instagram)
- Inspire with stories, quotes, and advice (Facebook)

The options are really endless for where you can showcase your brand photography from upcoming launches, courses, books, presentations, and social media. Consider the content, and pair it with images that are relevant and appropriate and that add value. Don't just post pretty pictures blindly. Photo placement should be thoughtful and strategic. Remember: Photos can act as storytellers, allowing your viewer to visualize your message, idea, product, or service. They can bring your concepts to life and communicate your content more clearly.

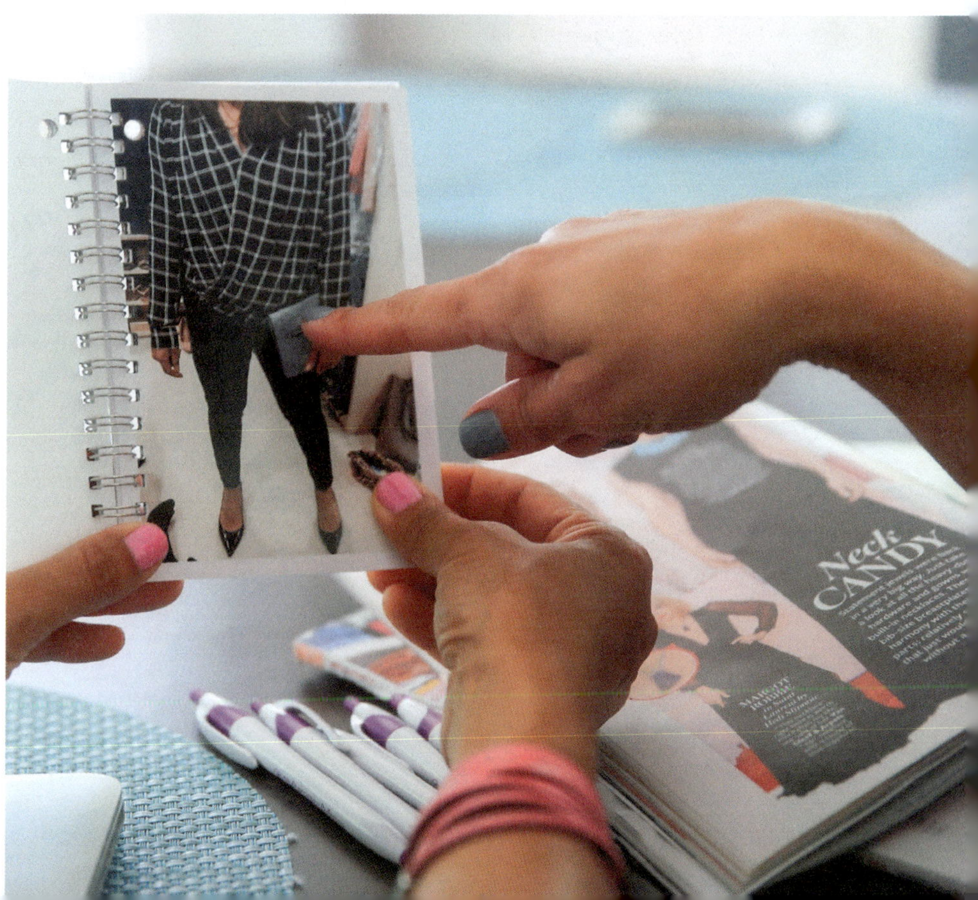

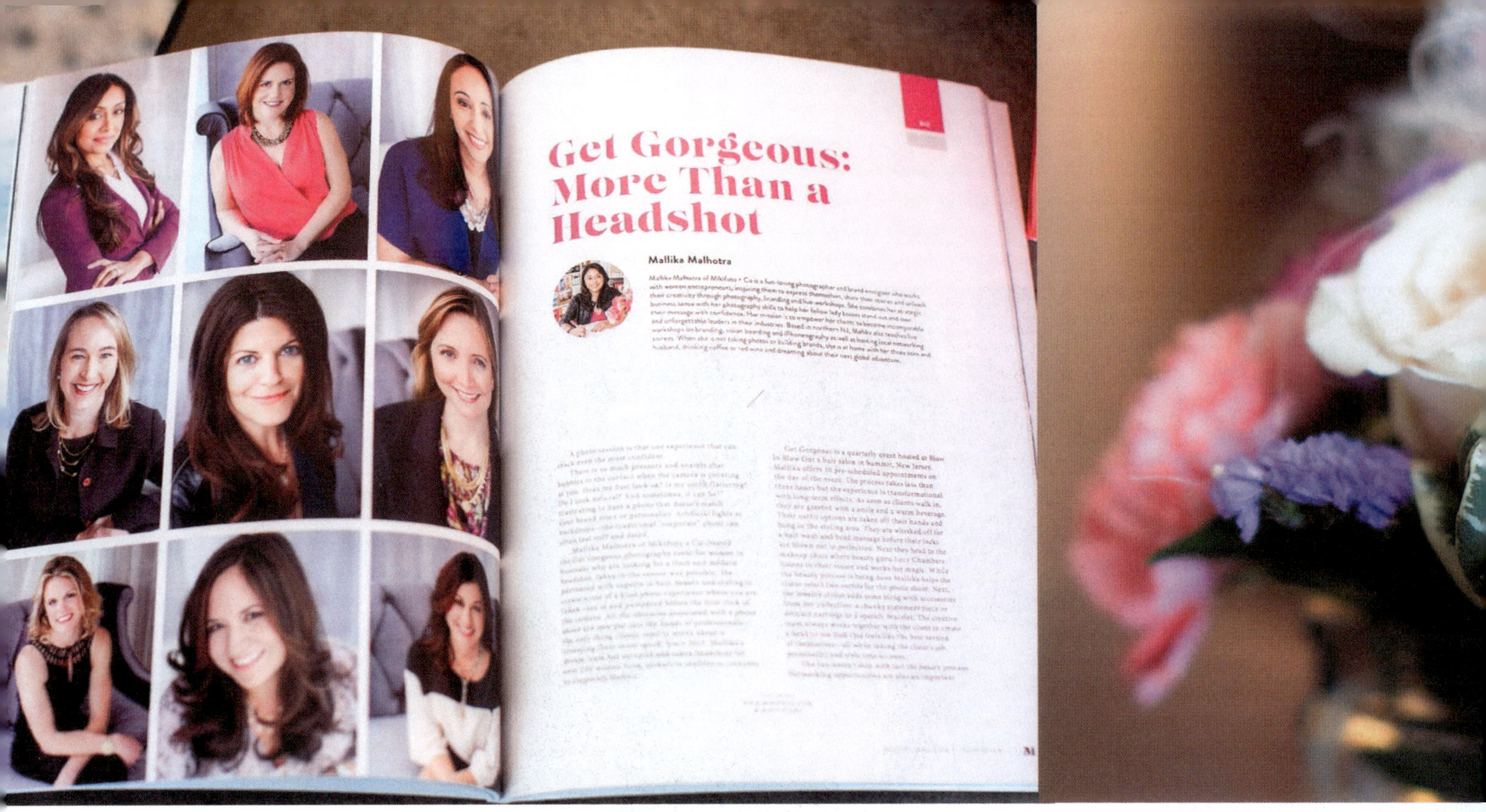

Here are a list of marketing ideas for you to consider:

- Website (all pages)
- Blog
- Media Kit
- Speaker Bios
- Social Media (Instagram, Facebook, Twitter, Pinterest, LinkedIn)
- Sales Pages
- Newsletters
- Online Courses and Presentations
- Digital Products (ebooks, e-magazines)
- Email Signature
- Opt-Ins
- Advertising
- Facebook Ads
- Print (books, magazines)
- Press
- Business Cards
- Postcards
- Marketing Collateral (brochures, signage)
- Thank-You Cards
- Packaging
- Photo Art

BONUS tip:
Beware of adding extra filters to or further editing your finished brand photos. Your photographer may not approve of this step and may feel that the integrity of their work is compromised. Most photographers prefer that you post and share the photos in the exact finished format that they provided to you. Make sure to have this conversation before the photo shoot takes place to manage expectations.

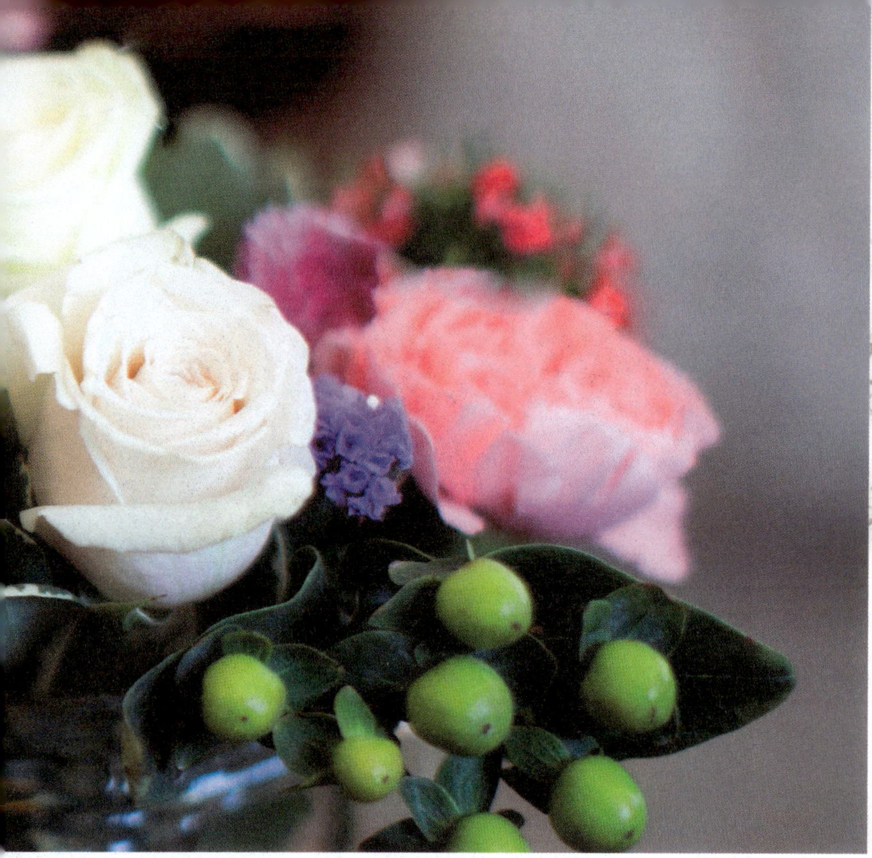

UNDERSTANDING
COPYRIGHT & PHOTOGRAPHY

Under the Federal Copyright Act of 1976, photographs are protected by copyright from the moment of creation. As copyright owners, photographers have the exclusive right and ownership of the images. This means your photographer can control, publish, distribute, display, reproduce, and even receive payment for the visuals. Although you purchased the photo session and digital files, you (the client) don't necessarily own the right to the photographs. Since I am a photographer and not a lawyer, I don't know all the legalities. But it is important to understand the photo usage and copyright rules because every photographer treats this process differently. Do consult your photographer or lawyer for more information and to avoid any violations or infringements.

CAN I SPRINKLE IN OTHER PHOTOS?

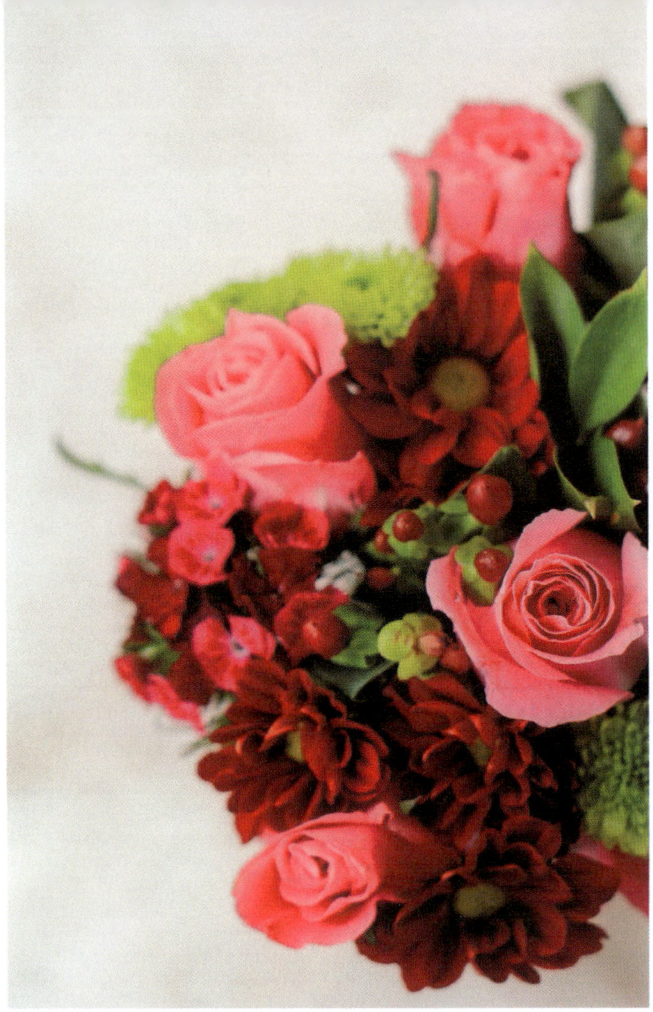

A nice way to keep your brand current is to balance your professional brand photos with your own DIY photos. It's tough to hire a photographer every time you need a photo for your website, your blog, or a social media post. Instead, you can take visuals with your smartphone, point and shoot, or DSLR. We now have the technology to take good images ourselves. And let's be honest, sometimes the best camera is the one always with you. ***This DIY approach adds an authentic, "real" nature to your brand while also sharing photo stories of what is actually going on right now with your business.*** Consider sharing content that inspires, educates, shares news, and reveals the behind the scenes.

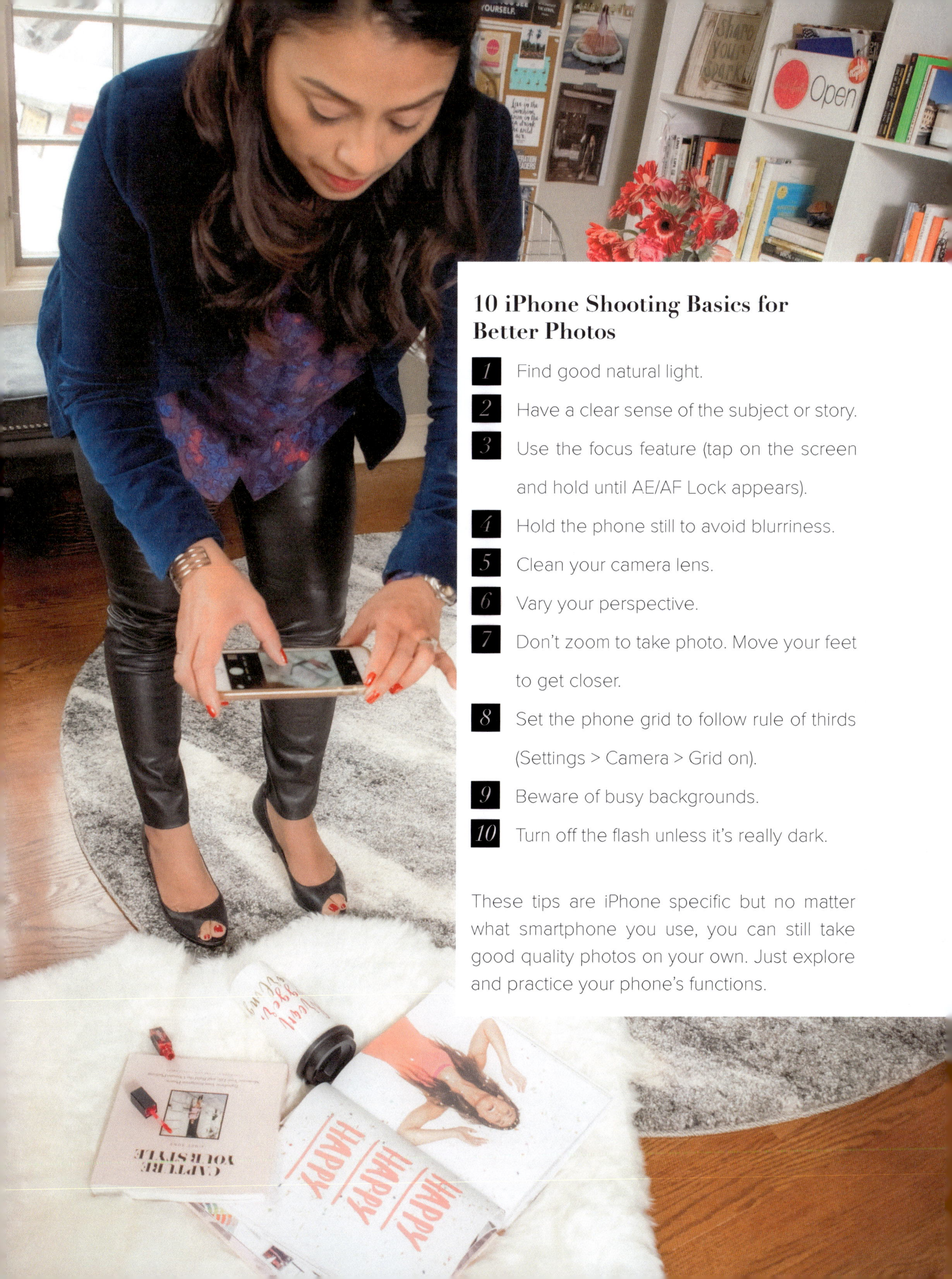

10 iPhone Shooting Basics for Better Photos

1. Find good natural light.
2. Have a clear sense of the subject or story.
3. Use the focus feature (tap on the screen and hold until AE/AF Lock appears).
4. Hold the phone still to avoid blurriness.
5. Clean your camera lens.
6. Vary your perspective.
7. Don't zoom to take photo. Move your feet to get closer.
8. Set the phone grid to follow rule of thirds (Settings > Camera > Grid on).
9. Beware of busy backgrounds.
10. Turn off the flash unless it's really dark.

These tips are iPhone specific but no matter what smartphone you use, you can still take good quality photos on your own. Just explore and practice your phone's functions.

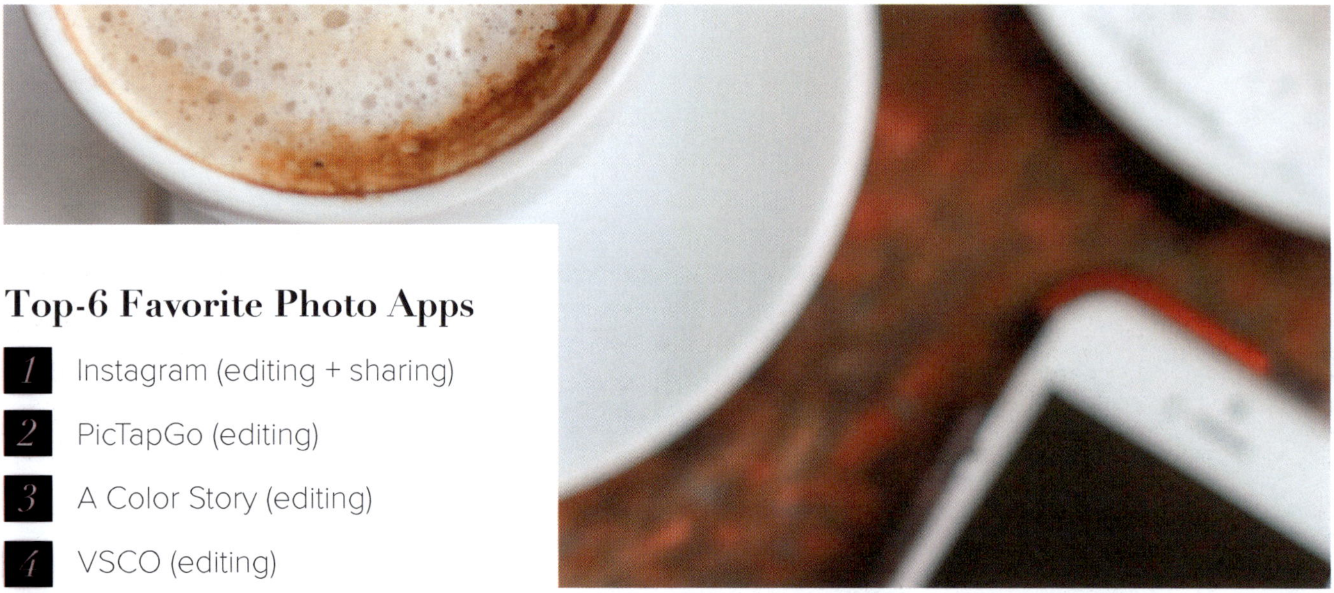

Top-6 Favorite Photo Apps

1. Instagram (editing + sharing)
2. PicTapGo (editing)
3. A Color Story (editing)
4. VSCO (editing)
5. Over (adding text)
6. Moldiv (creating collages)

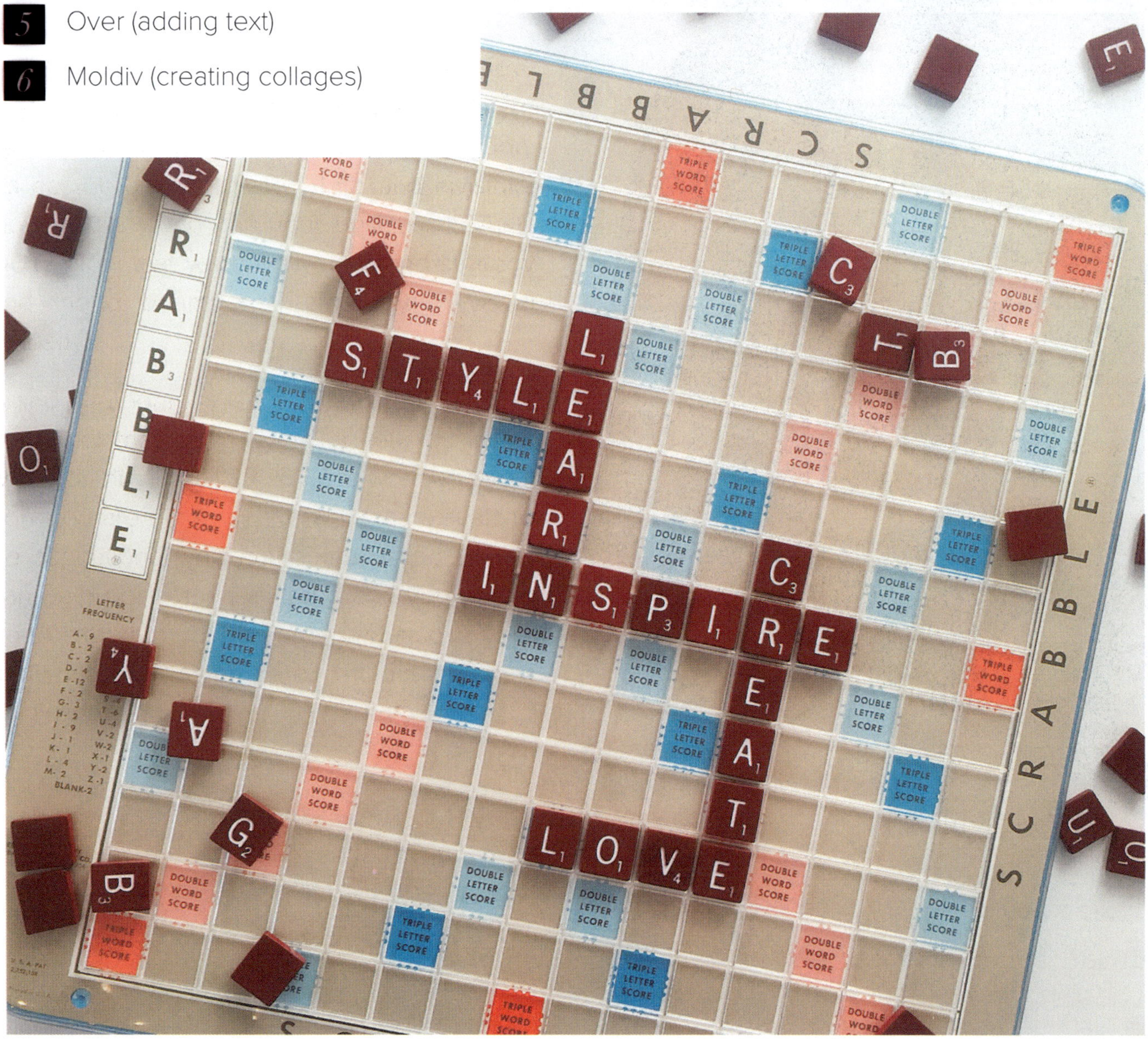

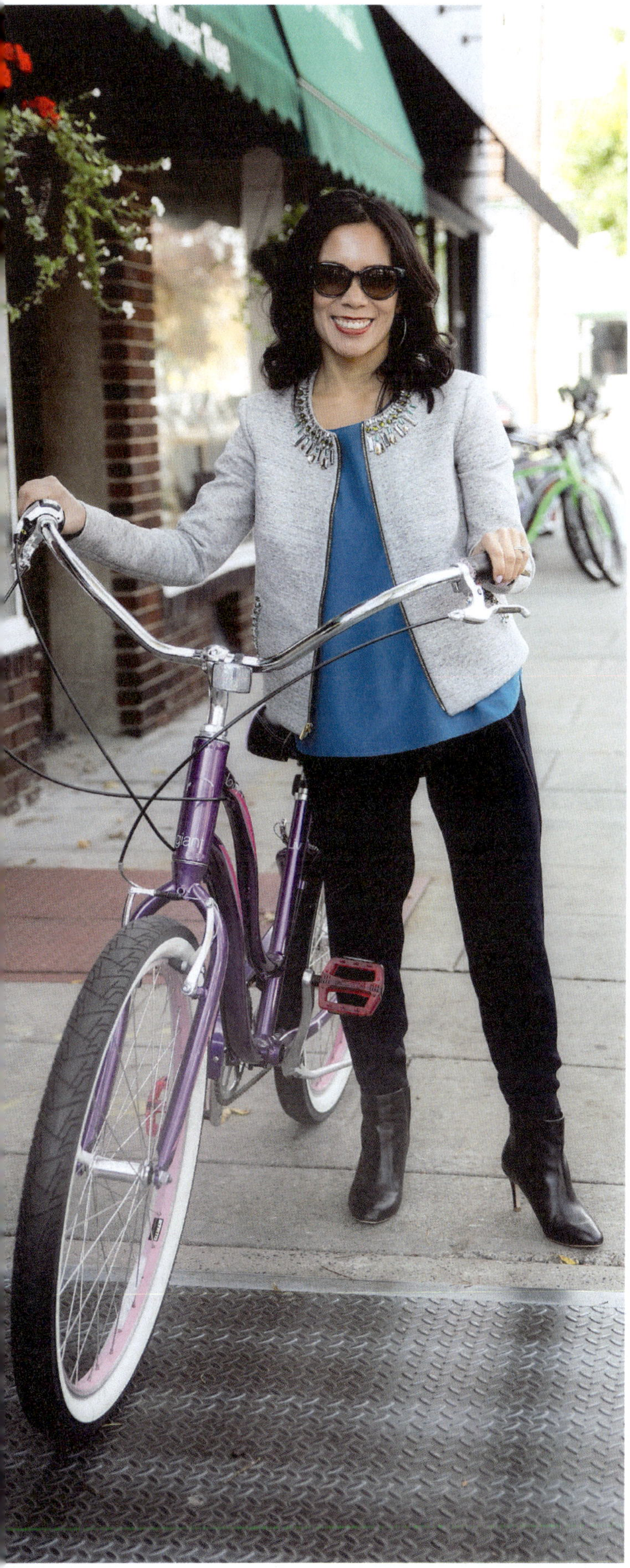

Another idea to augment your brand library is stock photography. Some sources are free, like Unsplash or Death to the Stock Photo. This option is helpful if you don't have the time or energy to style and shoot something on your own. However, if you choose this path, just be aware that others are also using the same visuals and there is risk of having your brand look generic.

Lifestyle stock photography can also be purchased at affordable prices or in a subscription format from sources including The Bloguettes, Haute Chocolate and Turquoise and Palm. If you decide to purchase styled stock photos, make sure the aesthetic and look match your brand. It should feel cohesive. But again, remember that others may be using the same visuals as you are.

A third option, if you have a larger budget, is to consider hiring a photographer who can customize stock photography for your brand. They will create still-life and lifestyle type images that include your products and your brand specific themes and color. The benefit here is that images will be unique and made for your business only.

BONUS tip:

Interested in converting your brand photos into a graphics? Add words or embellishments with apps like Over or Canva. These tools can easily create visual content that can attract and engage your audience across all your marketing and social media platforms.

HOW OFTEN SHOULD I CHANGE MY PHOTO?

I think it's best to update your professional brand photos every two-plus years. In our entrepreneurial worlds, much can change in our businesses in a short period of time. If you are experiencing growth or a shift in your brand, you may need new images to tell that story. For example, in my own business, I shifted from family photography to brand photography. Once I made this pivot, I knew it was time to invest in new images that would support my new positioning. Further, you want to make sure that you still look like the person in your photos. There is something suspicious and untrustworthy about meeting someone in person who looks nothing like their brand images. If you have a physical transformation of some kind, like weight loss or a change in hair color or style, you may want to consider a photo update.

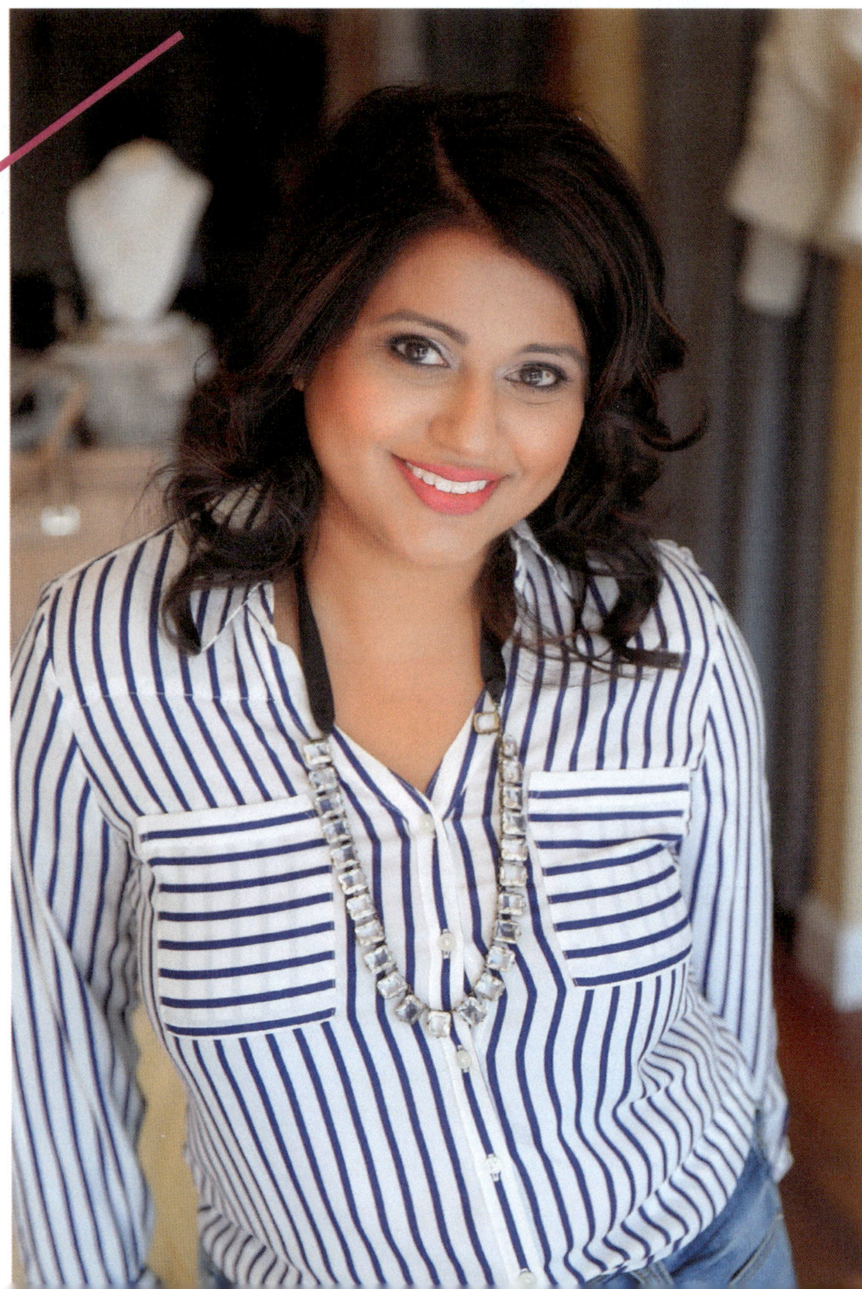

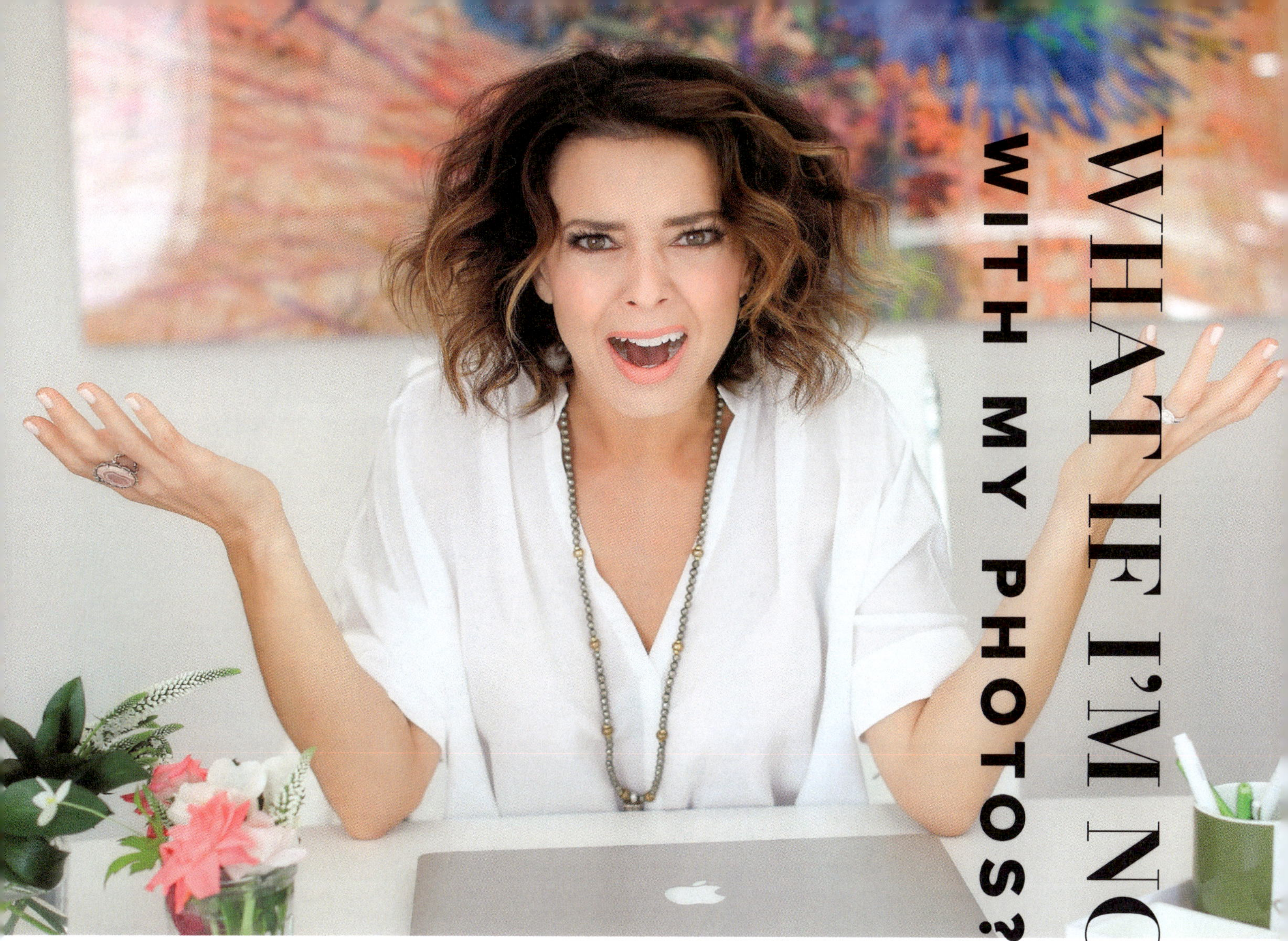

WHAT IF I'M NOT HAPPY WITH MY PHOTOS?

Hopefully, this guide will help avoid any sticky situations like this. Strategy and preparation with your photographer can really help minimize any disappointment with the images. But things do happen, and I am so sorry if this is the case for you. First, I suggest taking some time to write down what you don't like about the photos and why you feel disappointed. Make sure your "inner critic" isn't coming out to sabotage you. Then have a live conversation with your photographer, either in person or over the phone, to explain your thoughts. Be clear on what you feel went wrong. Give direction on what you feel like is missing. Be open to hearing what the photographer has to say. Maybe they can help you see the photos in a different way? Maybe they can go back to the photo shoot images to find more options for you? If after this conversation you are still unhappy, then you can consider asking for a re-shoot or a partial refund. Every photographer is different in how they handle these situations, but most of us want our clients to be happy with the images.

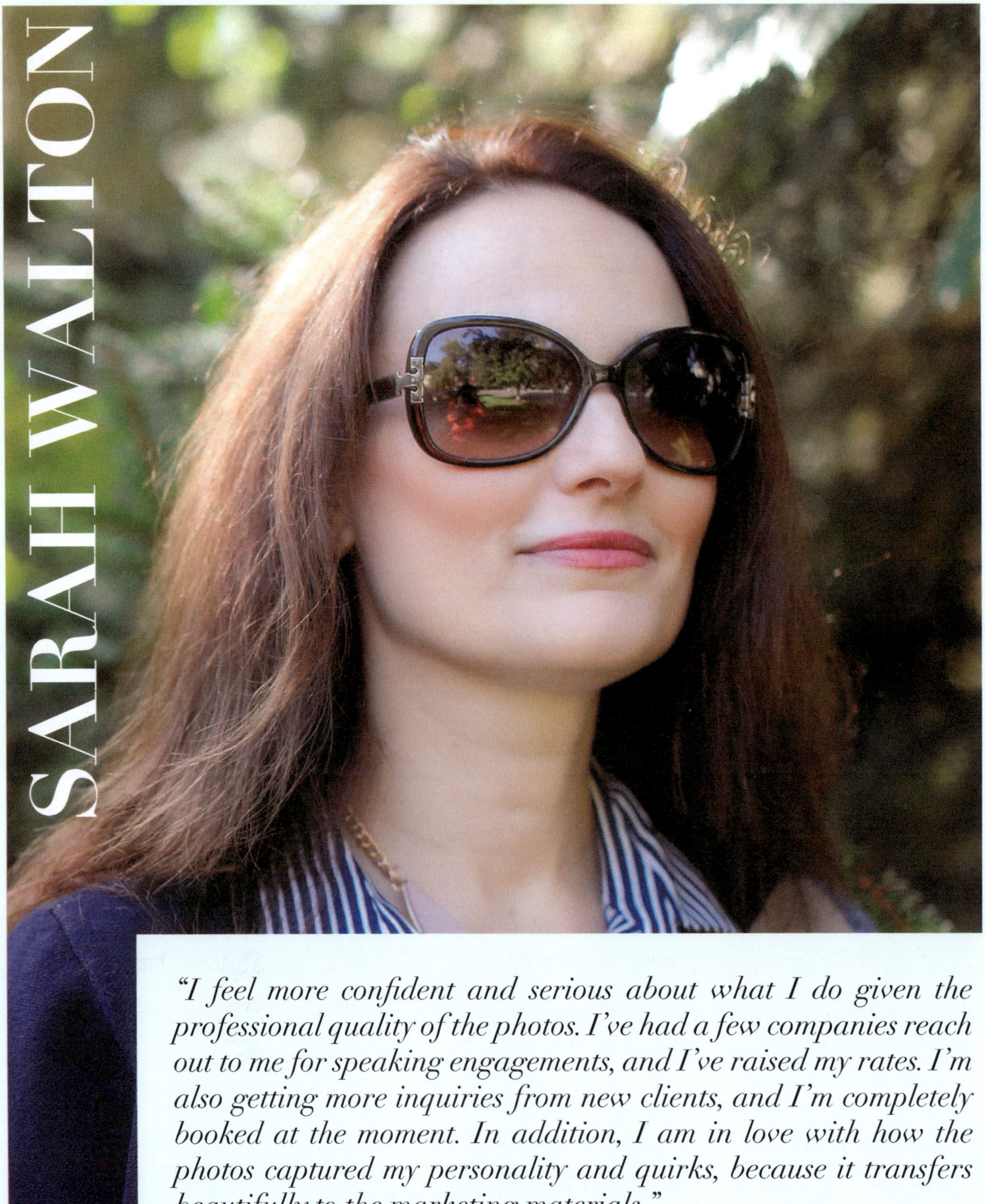

SARAH WALTON

"I feel more confident and serious about what I do given the professional quality of the photos. I've had a few companies reach out to me for speaking engagements, and I've raised my rates. I'm also getting more inquiries from new clients, and I'm completely booked at the moment. In addition, I am in love with how the photos captured my personality and quirks, because it transfers beautifully to the marketing materials."

CASE *Study* *09*

WANT TO TAKE A LOOK AT THE ENTIRE BRAND PHOTOGRAPHY PROCESS THROUGH A REAL-LIFE EXAMPLE?

Meet my client Sarah Walton (www.sarahwalton.com). She is a speaker, author, and business mentor in New Jersey. She is on a mission to help women find the work they really love to do and live life to their highest potential. She hired me for brand photography to develop a more visible brand and to create a customized photo library of images that she could use for all of her marketing needs including, the launch of her first online course, The Money Mindset.

BRAND BRIEF

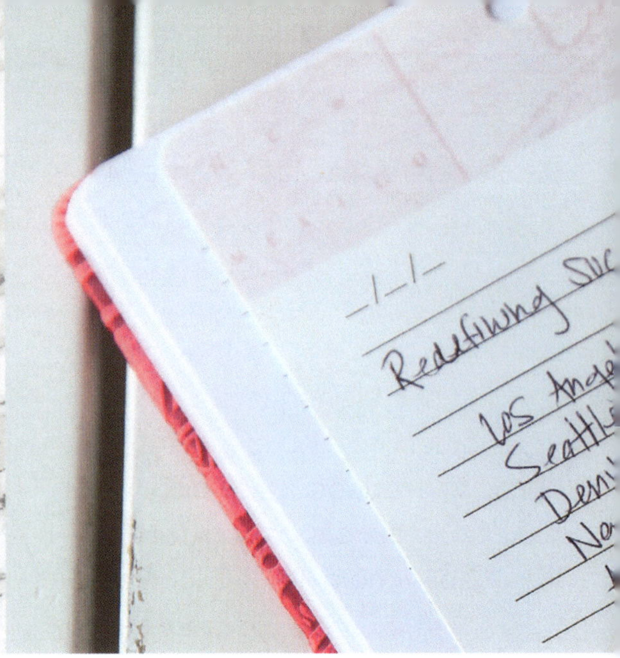

Brand Name: Sarah Walton
Website: www.sarahwalton.com
Social Media Handles: @thesarahwalton
facebook: www.facebook.com/sarahwaltonpage/

Product/Service: What are you selling?
When I Grow Up Consulting, My Speaking, and The Money Mindset Course

Intention: What do you want the brand photos to do for you?
Make my brand instantly recognizable and inviting.

Values: List three to five values that you believe in.
Hard work, generosity, kindness, and integrity.

Client: Who is your ideal customer?
A woman in her 30s who has let a dream or two slip through her fingers. She is hard-working, loves her friends and family, has an incredible work ethic, believes in self-growth, and has a talent she knows she can be sharing with the world.

Problem: What are they struggling with?
How to get their dreams and ideas out of their heads and out into the world. She's probably also scared that she won't be able to make a real living doing what she loves.

End Result: What problem are you solving?
Showing these women that they can create their dream business and company and support themselves and their families doing it.

Personality: What are you and your brand like?
Warm, loving, and inspiring.

Mood: How do you want your client to feel?
Absolutely cared for, respected, loved, and fired up.

Style: What is the look/feel of your brand?
Soft but powerful.

Message: What is your one key story that you want your client to know/learn?
I know so many women are feeling stuck and trapped today. Reeling from the stress of having to be perfect, of "having it all" by giving up on what they want most. I want to put a stop

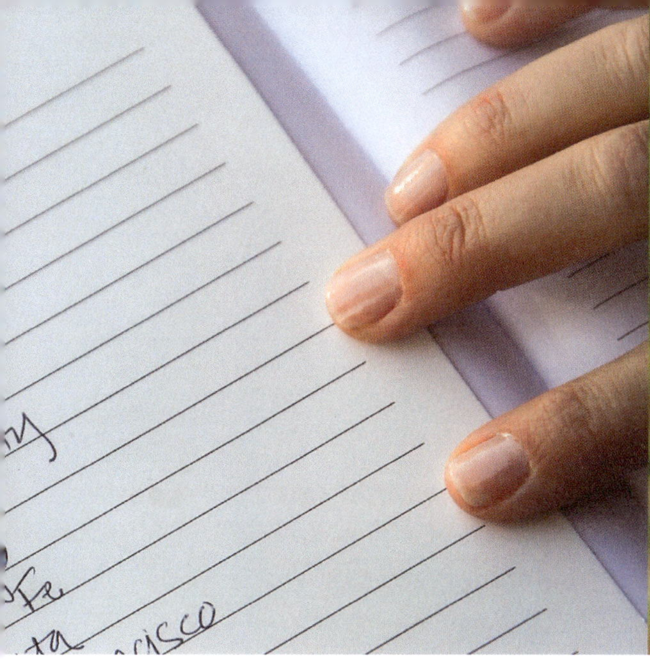

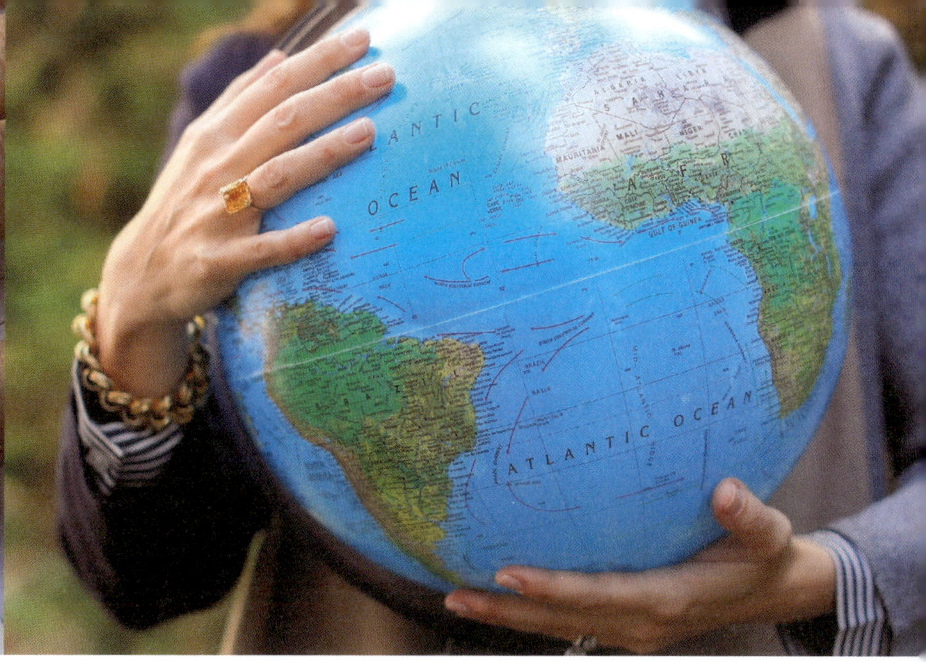

to that. We can take care of our dreams and our goals, while making sure we have the time, energy, and love to be with our families at the same time.

Expertise: **What do you specialize in and want your brand to be known for?**
I want my brand to be known for causing results, for showing women how to live their best lives, and for giving them the confidence, tools, and support to get it done.

Process: **How do you work with your clients?**
I work in one-on-one sessions, in masterminds, and through my video course.

Differentiator: **What is your point of difference and how do you stand out?**
I've been through the trenches. I don't just say the pretty words, or make people feel good with ideas and platitudes. I've been down in the dumps. I've cried in the middle of the night because I missed my kids, hated my job, but felt trapped because my family needed the money. I GET it. I've lived it. And I'm here to make sure no other woman has to go through it alone.

Vision: **What is your future goal for your business?**
I will be on stages all over the country, and abroad, inspiring women to go for it — to plan out what they really want, run the financial numbers behind their business ideas, and turn those goals into reality. I will offer the When I Grow Up Consulting package as a virtual course, in addition to my one-on-one coaching. I'll also be offering different courses on influence, confidence, charging what we're worth, and stamping out our fears.

Key words: **What are three to five words that describe the tone of your brand?**
Loving, kind, inspiring, real, and challenging.

Key props: **What three to five objects/things represent your brand?**
A journal, flowers, and laughter.

Color: **What are your brand colors?**
Pink, green, and black and white.

Photo Use: **Where do you plan on using these photos?**
On Facebook, Instagram, brochures, ads, my website, and at my conferences and retreats.

PINTEREST BOARD

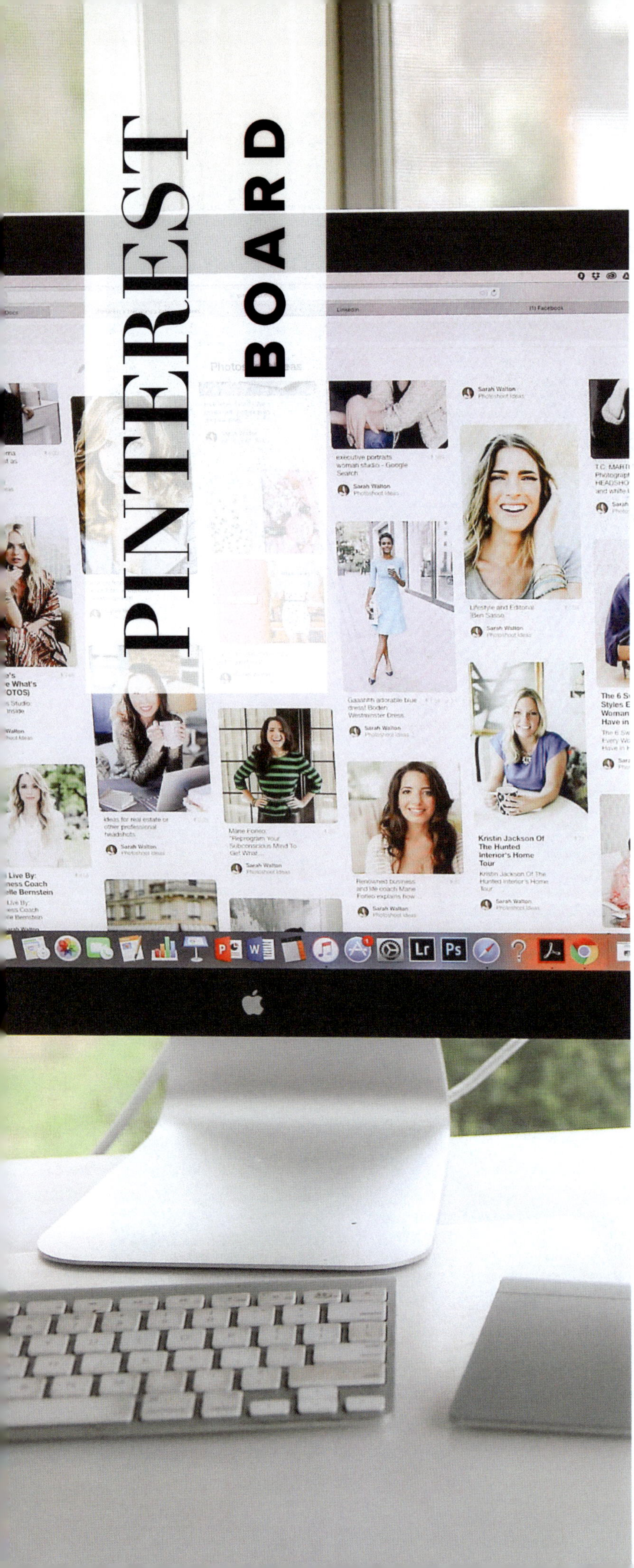

1 Boss Mom (Working at Desk + Couch)

- Working at home on laptop
- Talking on phone
- Reading book
- Writing – pens/ pencils
- Mockup of $ course on laptop
- Desk w/flowers + books + kid pics
- To-do list, goals, calendar
- Fave books (Huffington + kids books too)
- Handwritten quotes in journal
- Coffee mug

Style Direction: Colorful, Casual Chic

2 Biz Bestie (Client Session in Dining Room)

- Working together with notebooks/ laptop
- Open books (books you give), magazines
- Vision board
- Coffee + macarons
- Laughing, writing, deep convo
- Working, brainstorming
- One-to-one connection
- Creative, workshoppy

Style Direction: Professional, Classy Creative

3 Extracurricular Fun (Reading on Couch + Flower Arranging in Kitchen)

- Reading on couch w/ coffee
- Writing/reflecting w/ journal + tea
- *Style Direction: Cozy, Warm*
- Flower arranging on kitchen island/table – flower stems, vases, scissors, ribbons

Style Direction: Colorful, Casual Chic

4 Making a World of Difference (Outdoors/ Backyard)

- Nature backdrop
- Jetsetter globe/map/passport
- Travel mags/books (Fodors)
- Sunglasses
- Where in the world is Sarah?
- Globe in hands

Style Direction: Smart, Professional, Feminine, Powerful

5 Money Maven (Office)

- $ bills in hands
- Cash, cards, coins spilling out of wallet
- Bank statement + love notes
- At desk with newspaper
- With laptop open to $ mockup
- Holding finance/money books

Style Direction: Smart, Professional, Feminine, Powerful

6 Speaker Sarah (Front Entry)

- Blank wall with headset
- Sitting with microphone
- Speaking/laughing/inspiring

Style Direction: Colorful, Feminine, Powerful

7 Coffee Date (Cafe Angelique)

- Sitting outside at pretty table with a coffee/journal/book
- Meeting with client over lunch

Style Direction: Feminine, Soft

PROPS:

Laptop
Cell Phone
Journal
Books/Mags
Desk Accessories (pens/ pencils)
Planner/Calendar
Macarons
Coffee Mugs
Flowers
Vision Board
Planner
Calendar
Vases
Scissors

THINGS TO HAVE READY AT SHOOT:

Write quotes in notebook
Write a to-do list
Mock calendar with important dates highlighted
All branded materials
Step & Repeat (up night before)
Globe (hard and inflatable)
Passport
Maps
Sunglasses
Travel Books/Mags
Bills/$/Coins
Wallet
Newspaper
Glasses
Step & Repeat
Microphone/Headset
Branded Marketing Materials (biz cards, collateral, notebooks, etc.)

SHOOT SCHEDULE + SHOT LIST

8:00–10 **Hair/Makeup/Review Outfits**

9:15 **Mallika arrives**

9:30–10 **Photograph stock/desk shots**

10–10:20 **Making a World of Difference (Outdoors Backyard)**

Nature backdrop
Jetsetter: globe/map/passport
Travel mags/books (Fodors)
Sunglasses
Where in the world is Sarah?
Globe in hands

Style Direction: Smart, Professional, Feminine, Powerful

10:30–10:50 **Money Maven (Office or Kitchen)**

$ bills in hands
Cash, cards, coins spilling out of wallet
Bank statement + love notes
At desk with newspaper
With laptop open to $ mockup
Holding finance/money books
Sitting on chair barefoot with shoes

Style Direction: Smart, Professional, Feminine, Powerful

11–11:20 **Speaker Sarah (Front Entry)**

Step & Repeat backdrop
Headset
Speaking/laughing/inspiring
Microphone seated shot

Style Direction: Colorful, Feminine, Powerful

11:30–11:50 Biz Bestie (Client Session in Dining Room)

Working together with notebooks/laptop
Books/magazines
Vision board
Coffee and macarons
Laughing, writing, deep convo
Working, brainstorming
One-to-one connection
Creative, workshoppy

Style Direction: Professional, Classy Creative

12–12:30 Extracurricular Fun (Reading on Couch + Flower Arranging in Kitchen)

Reading on couch w/ coffee
Writing/reflecting w/ journal + tea

Style Direction: Cozy, Warm

Flower arranging on kitchen island/table

Flower stems, vases, scissors, ribbons

Style Direction: Colorful, Casual Chic

1–1:30 Coffee Date (Cafe Angelique)

Sitting outside at pretty table with a coffee/journal/book
Lunching with client

Style Direction: Feminine, Soft

2:00 THAT'S A WRAP!

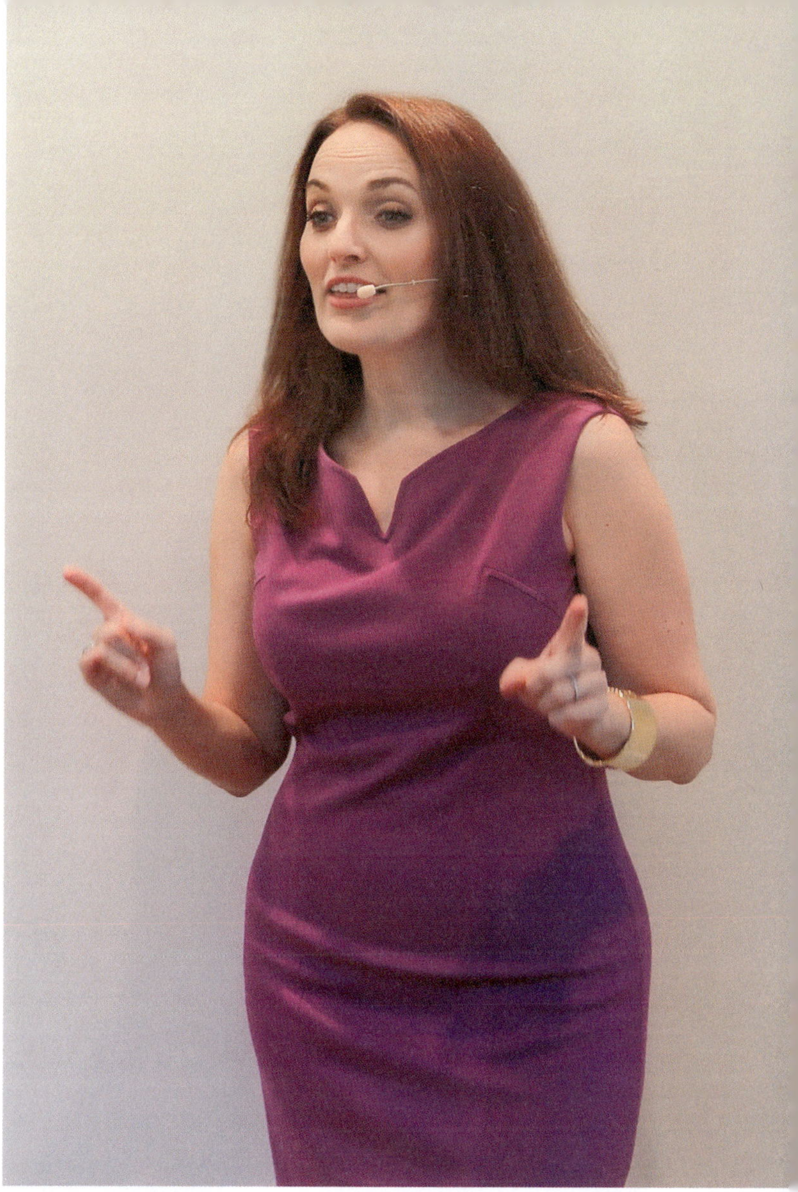

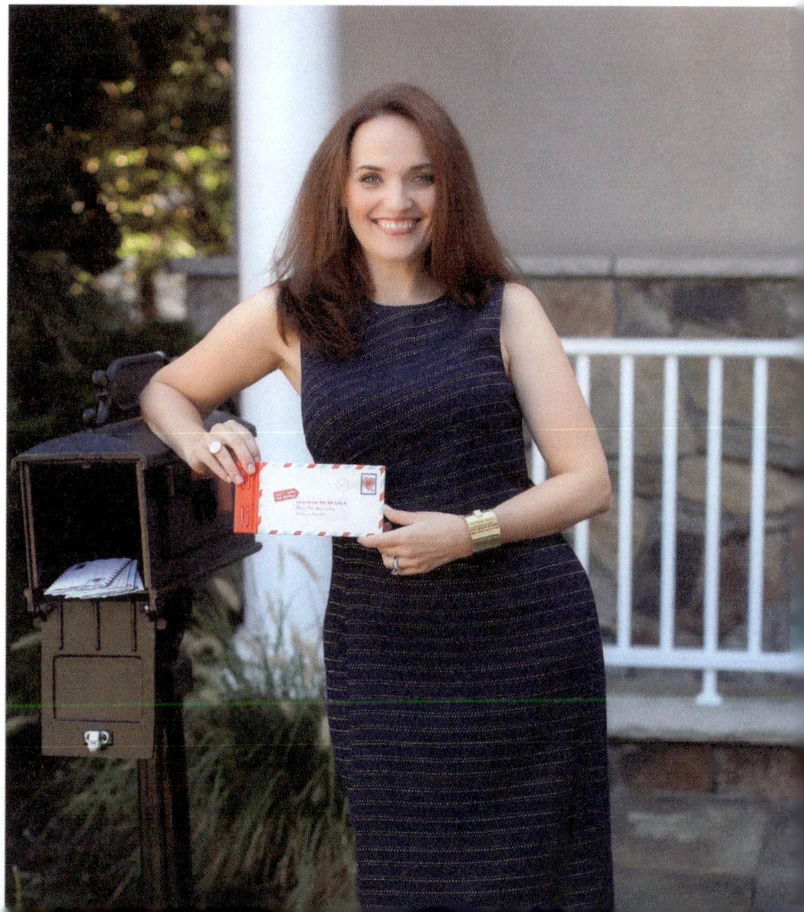

BRAND PHOTOGRAPHY LIBRARY

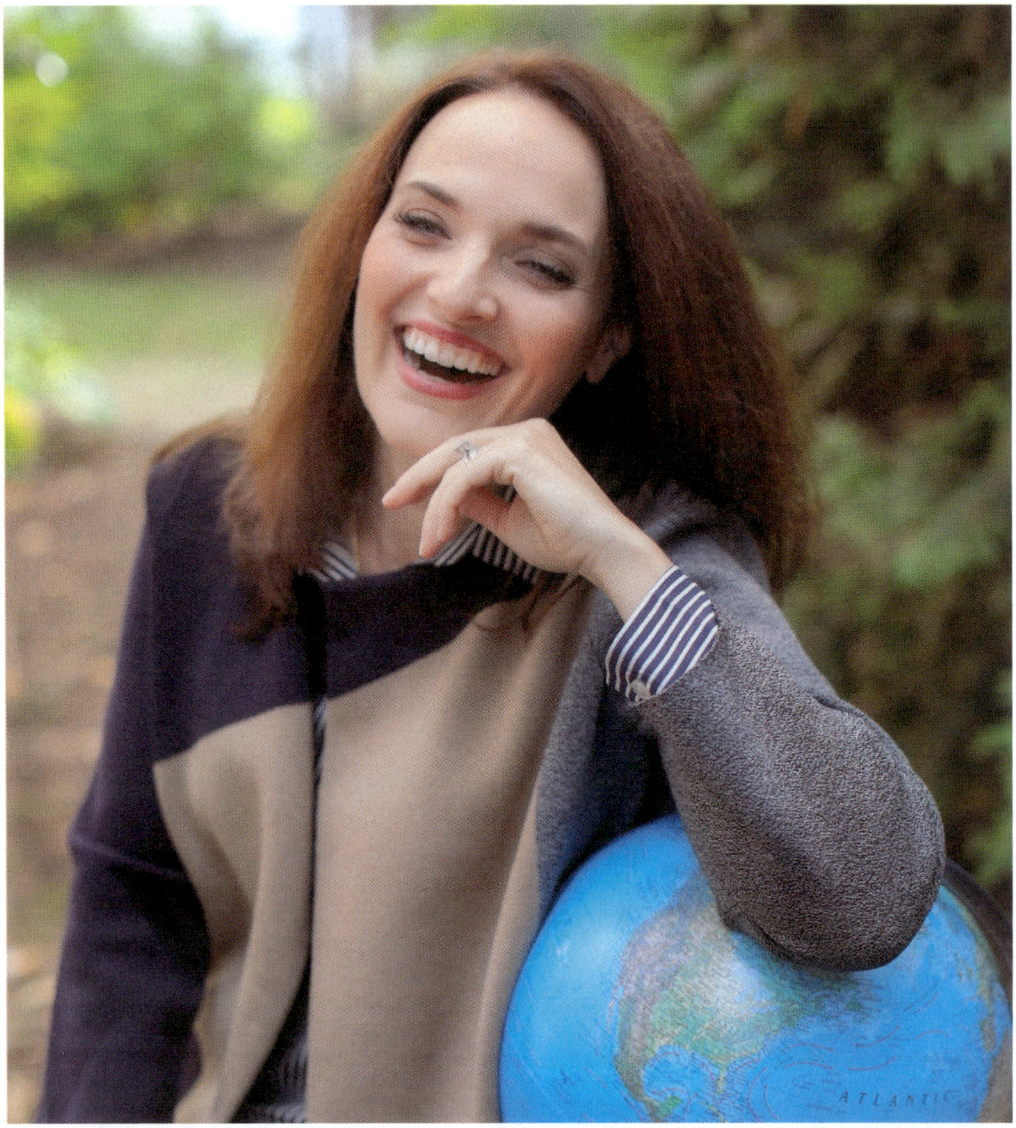

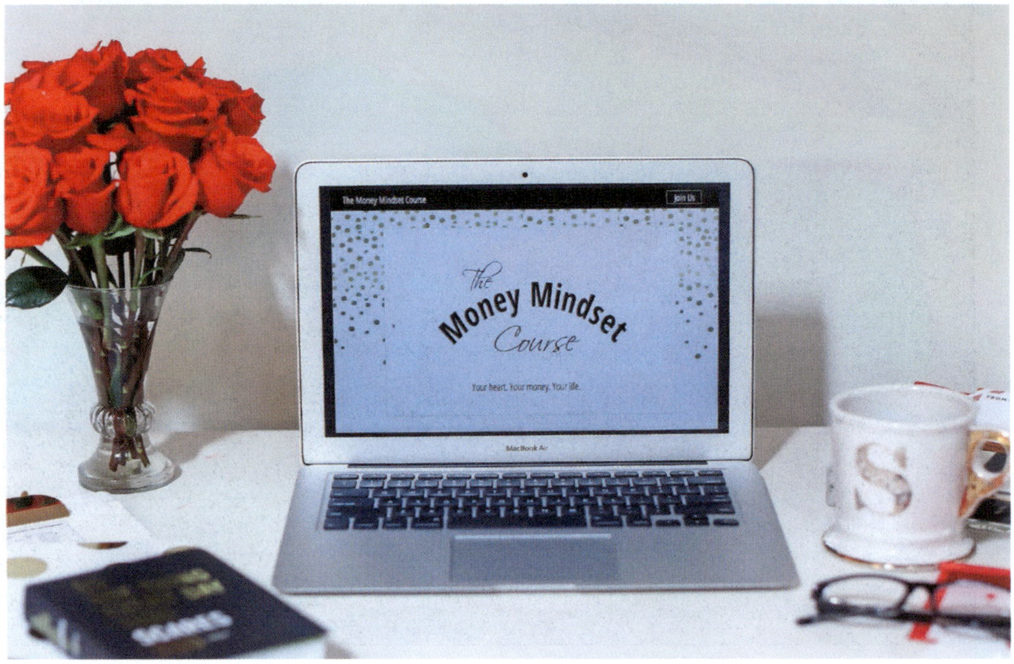

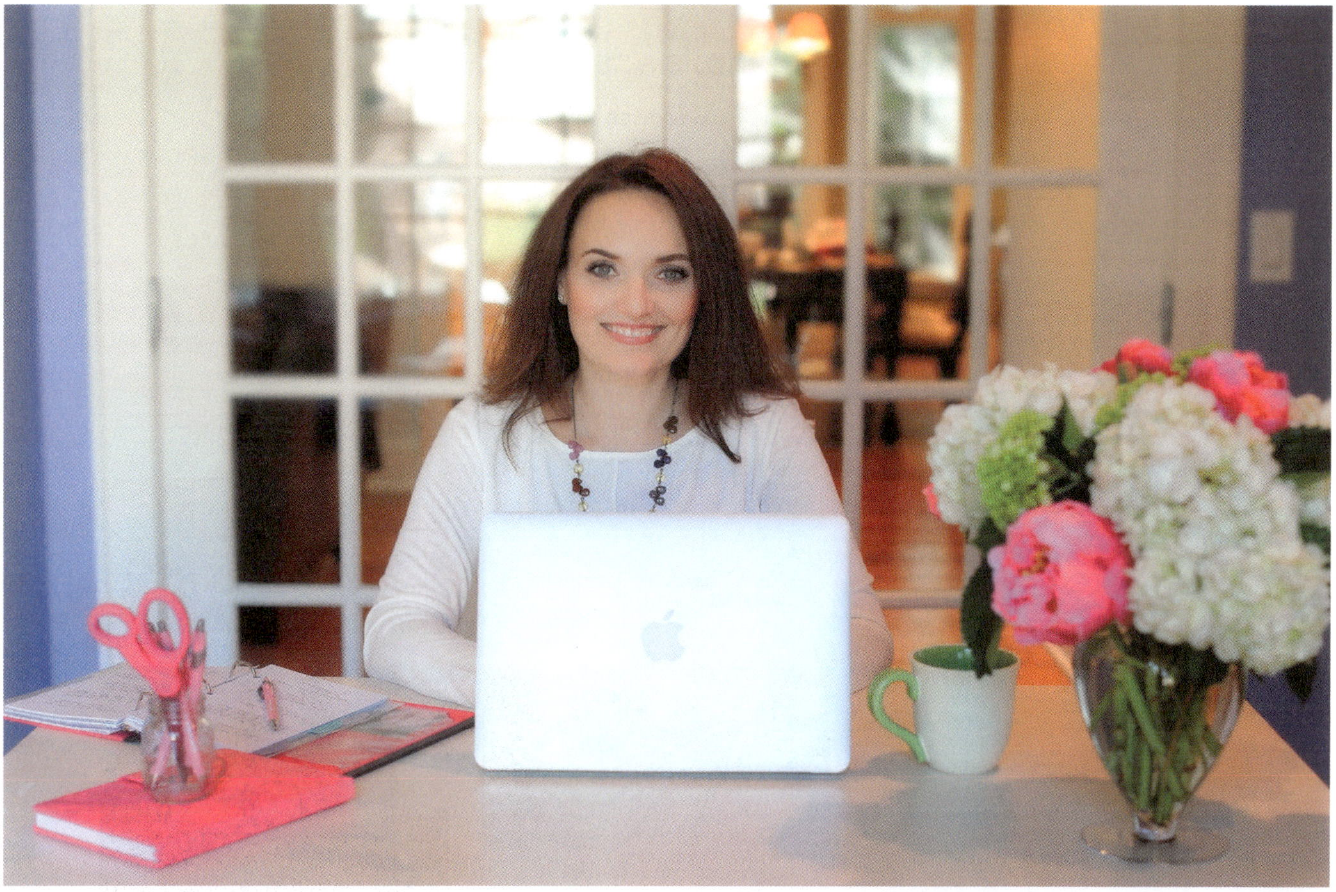

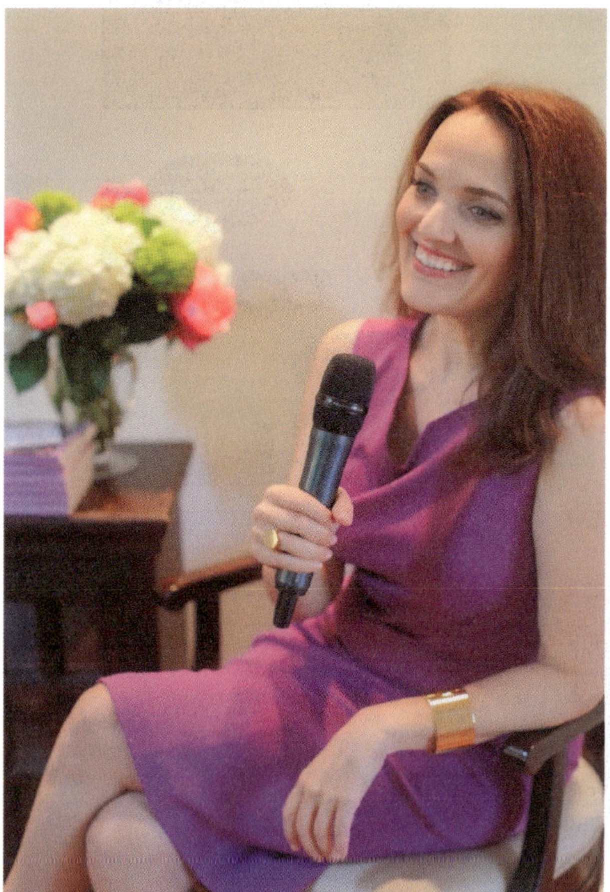

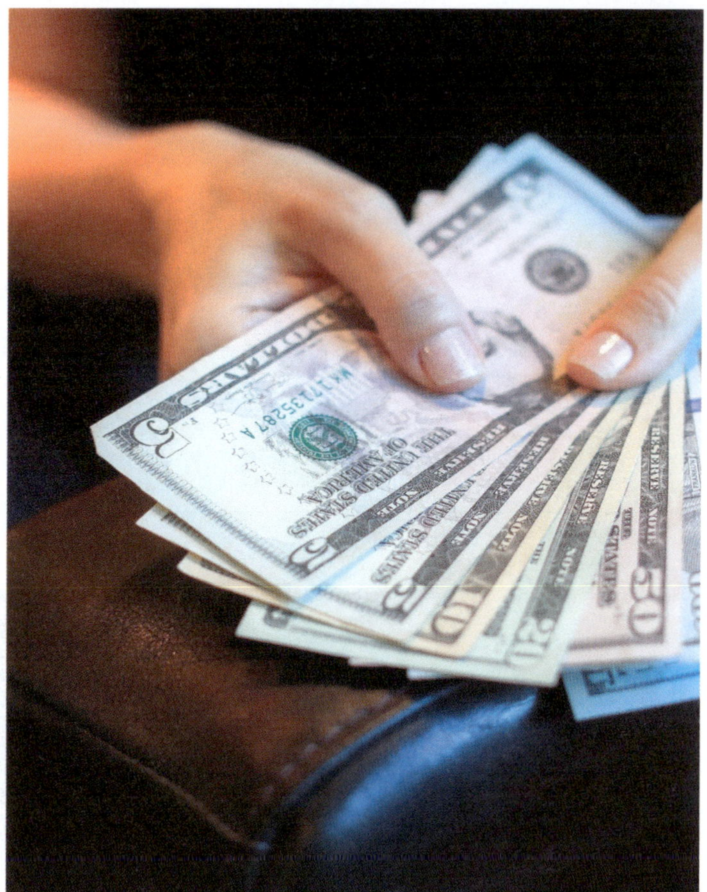

WEBSITE + SOCIAL MEDIA

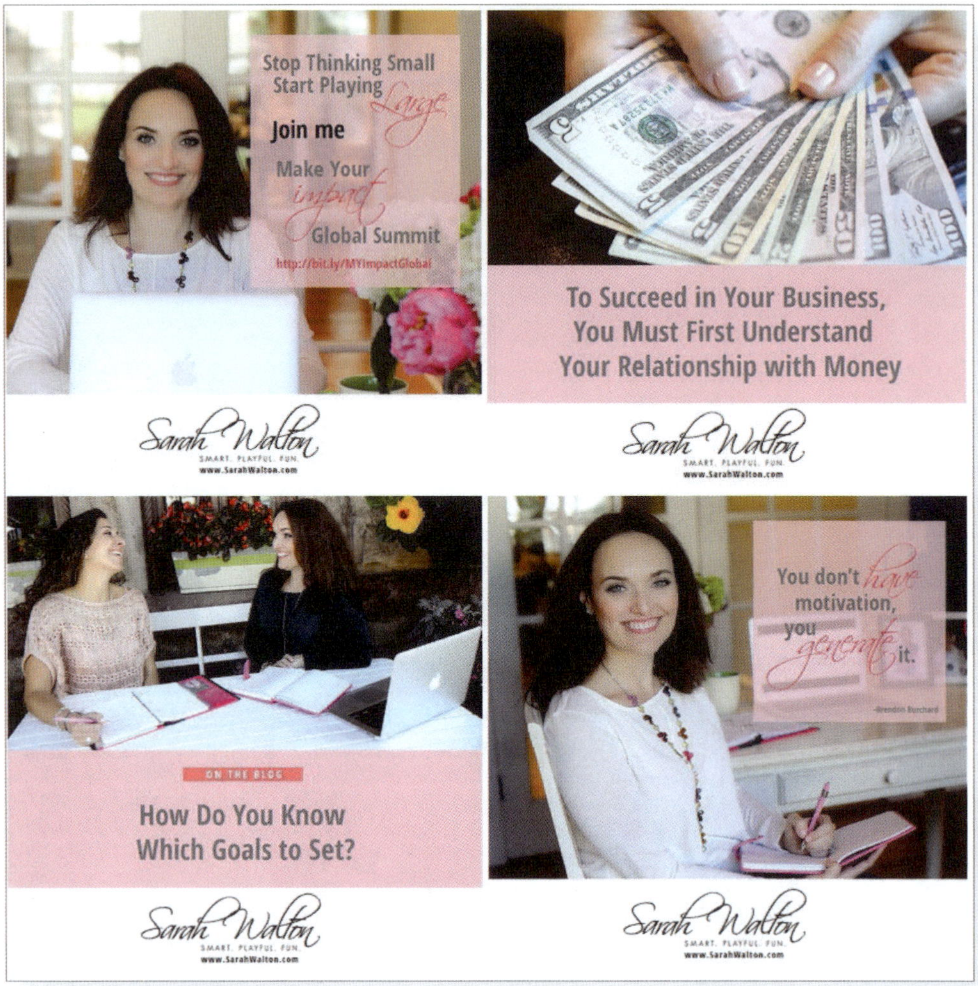

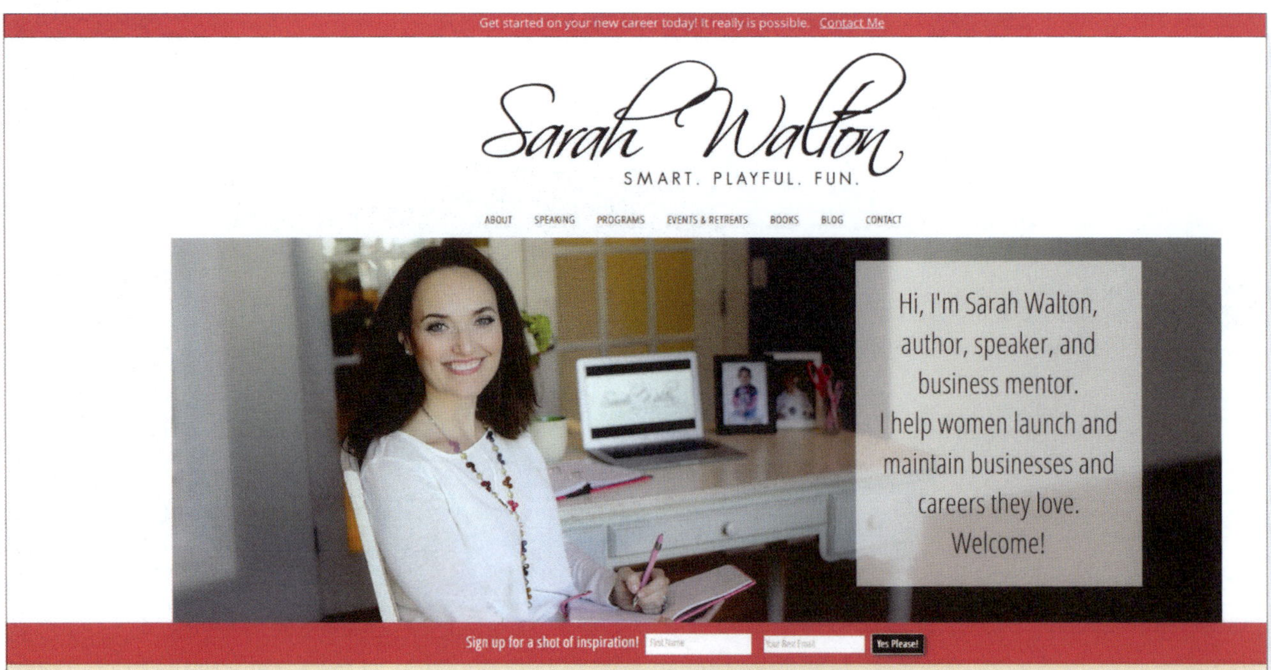

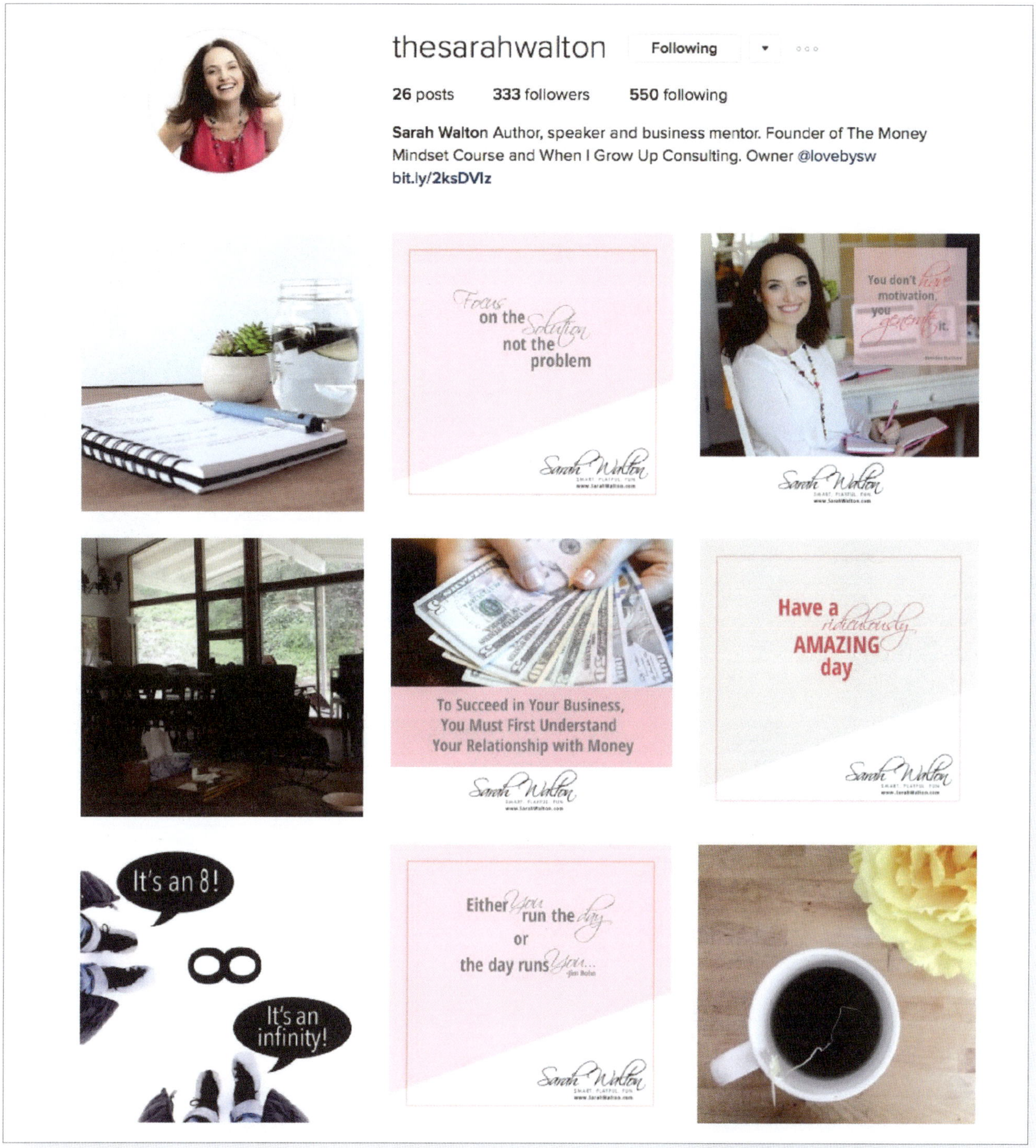
thesarahwalton
Following
26 posts
333 followers
550 following
Sarah Walton Author, speaker and business mentor. Founder of The Money Mindset Course and When I Grow Up Consulting. Owner @lovebysw
bit.ly/2ksDVlz
Focus on the Solution not the problem
Sarah Walton
You don't have motivation, you generate it.
Sarah Walton
To Succeed in Your Business, You Must First Understand Your Relationship with Money
Sarah Walton
Have a ridiculously AMAZING day
Sarah Walton
It's an 8!
It's an infinity!
Either you run the day or the day runs you...
Sarah Walton

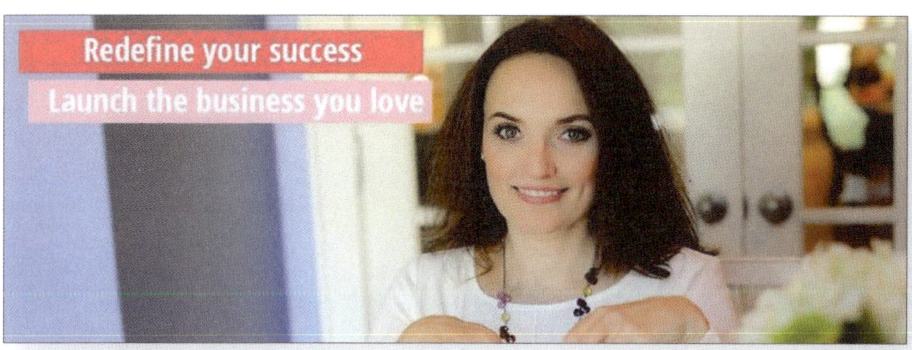
Redefine your success
Launch the business you love

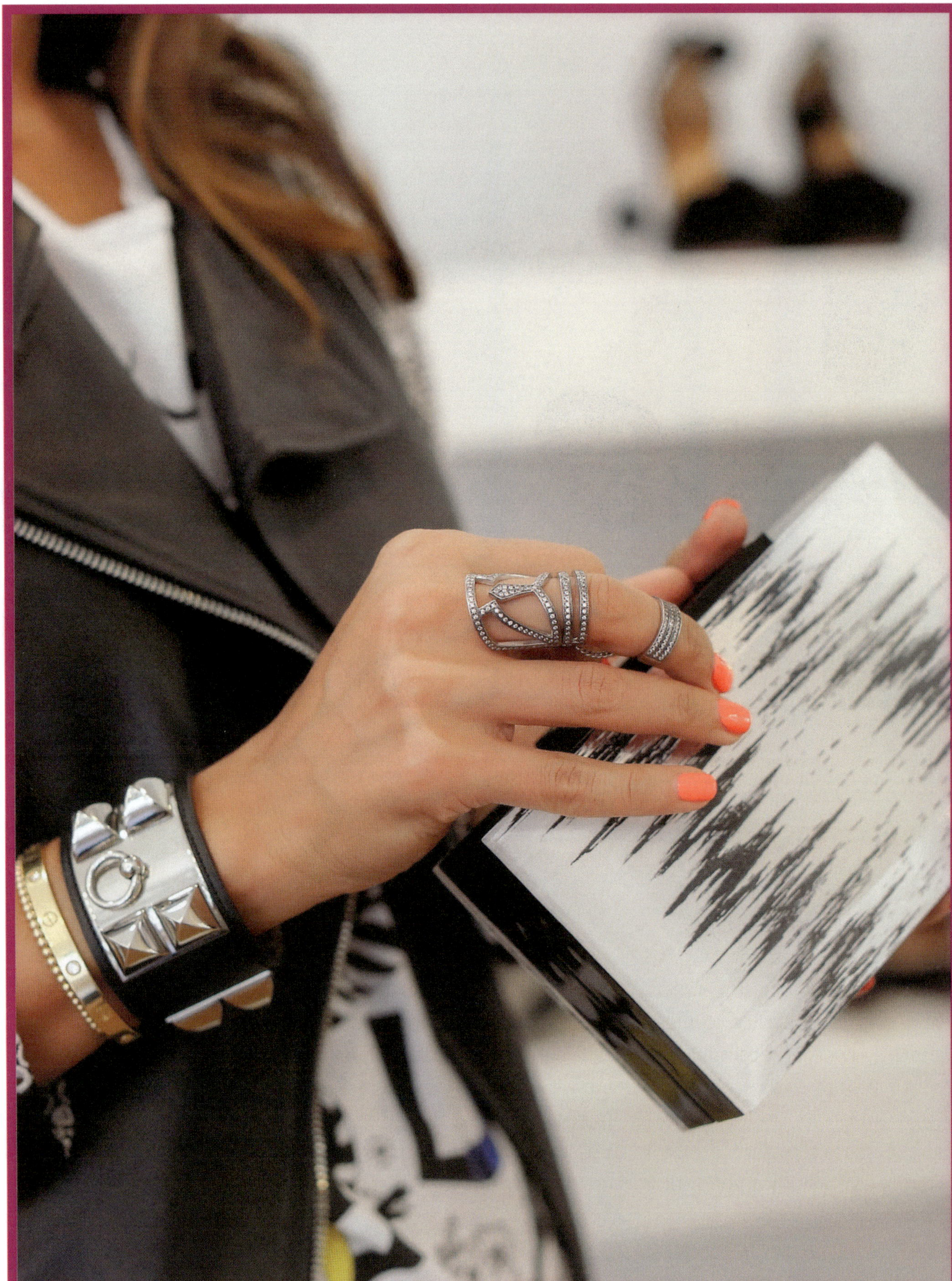

BRAND PHOTOGRAPHY

10

Lookbook

Want to see more brand photography examples of women in different industries? Here are three sample client brand photography libraries. Each was customized with the business owner's core message in mind. See how the visuals help the women stand out as leaders and take their audience on a deeper journey into their business.

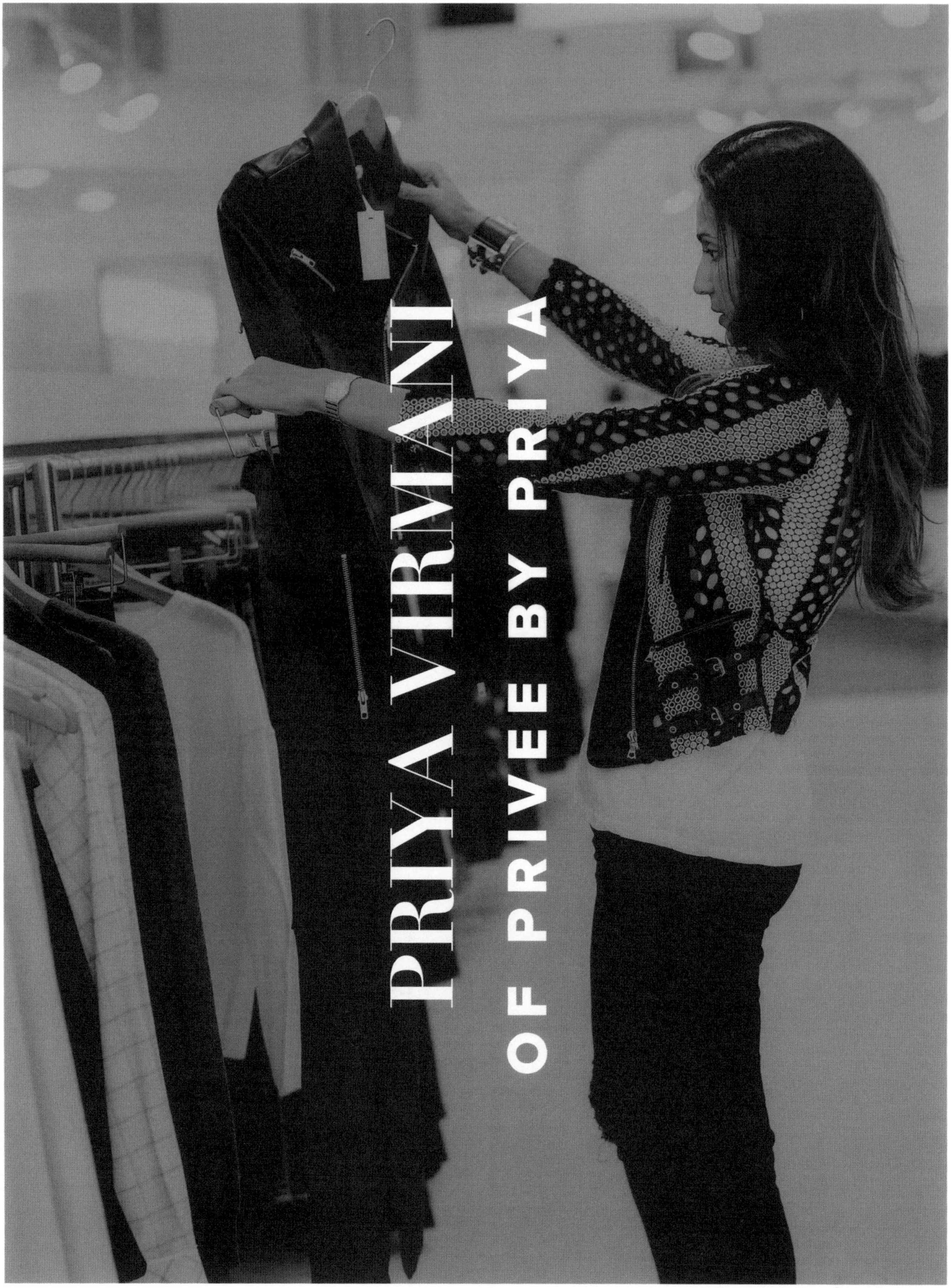

www.priveebypriya.com

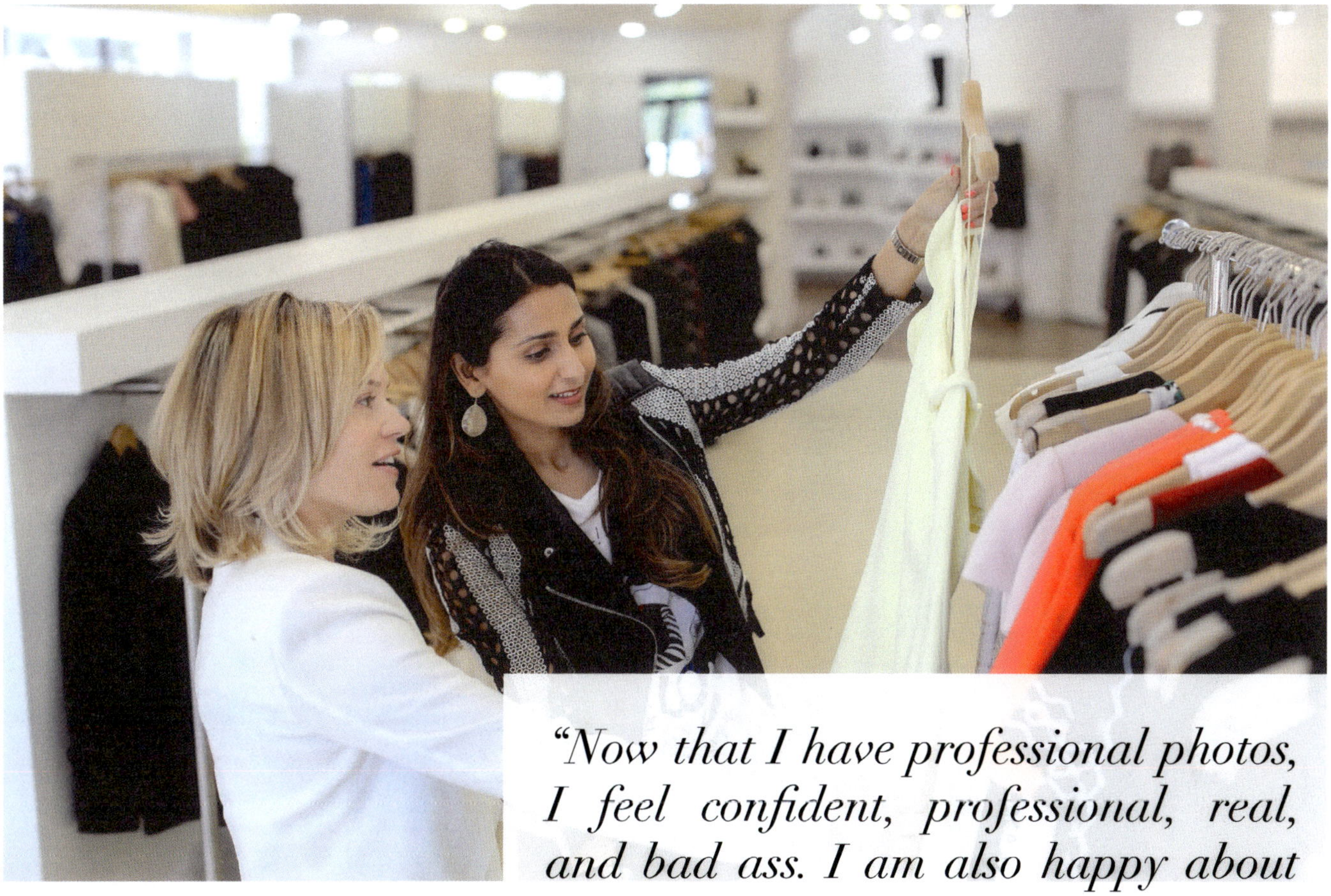

"Now that I have professional photos, I feel confident, professional, real, and bad ass. I am also happy about the additional views on Facebook and Instagram plus more website visits."

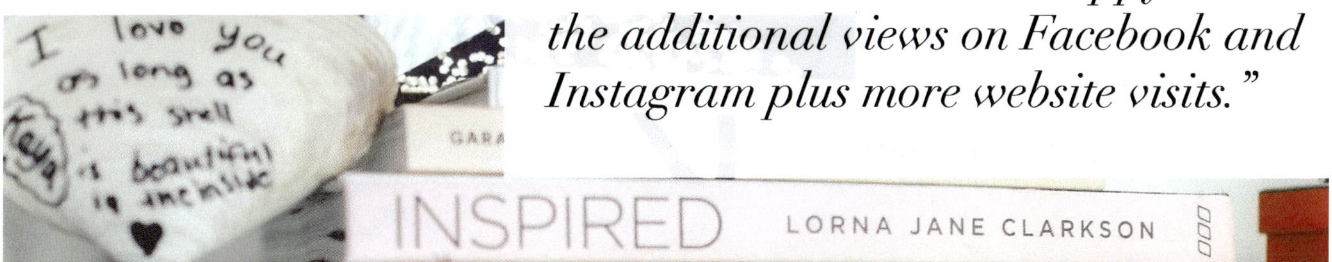

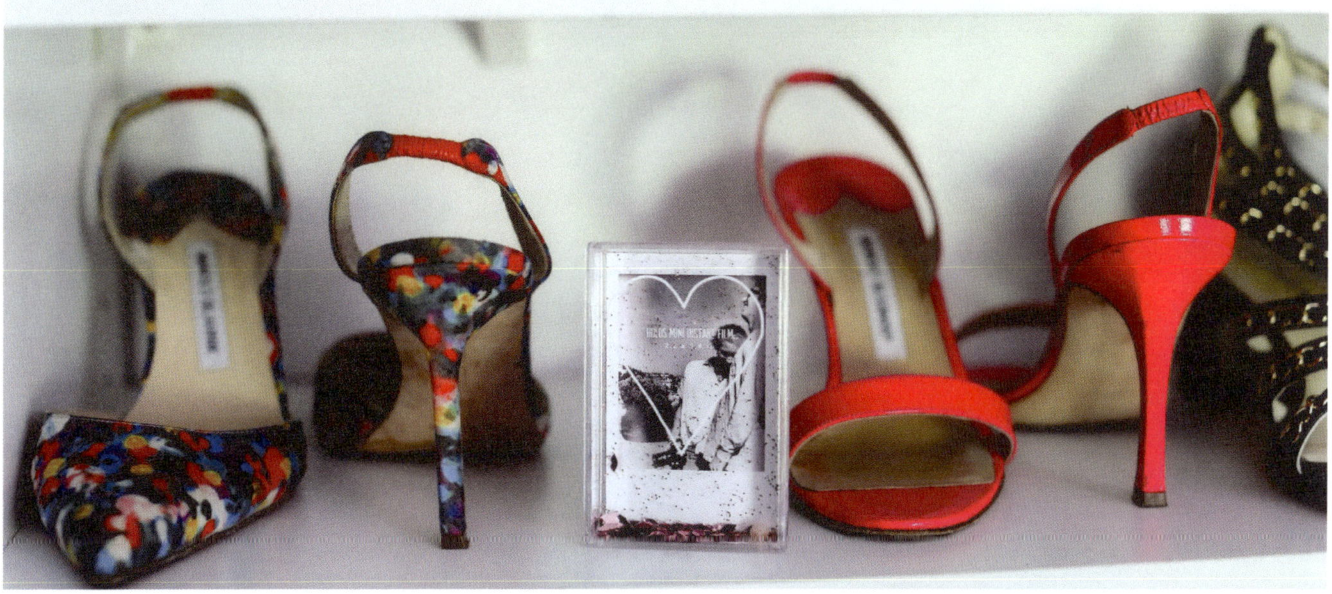

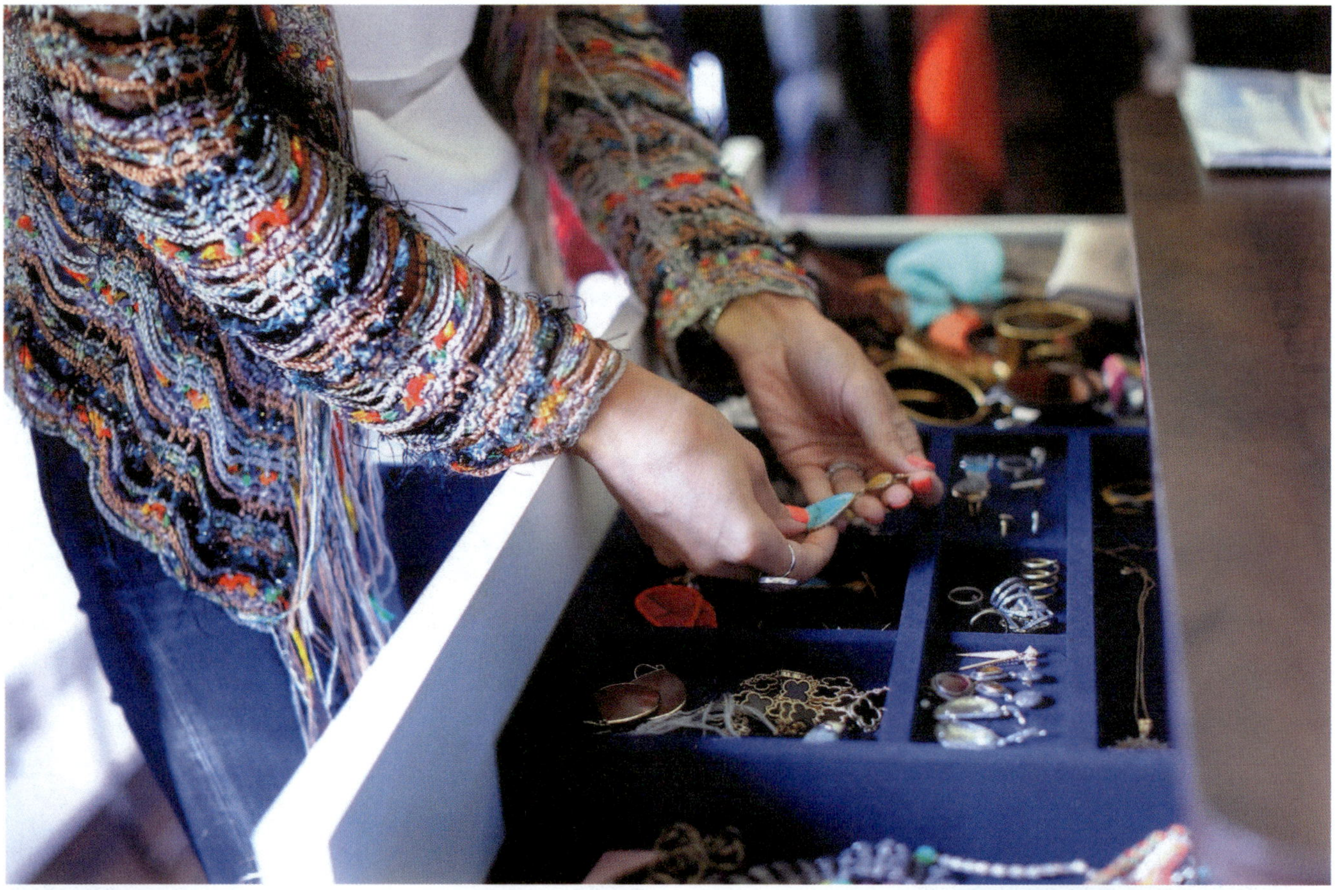

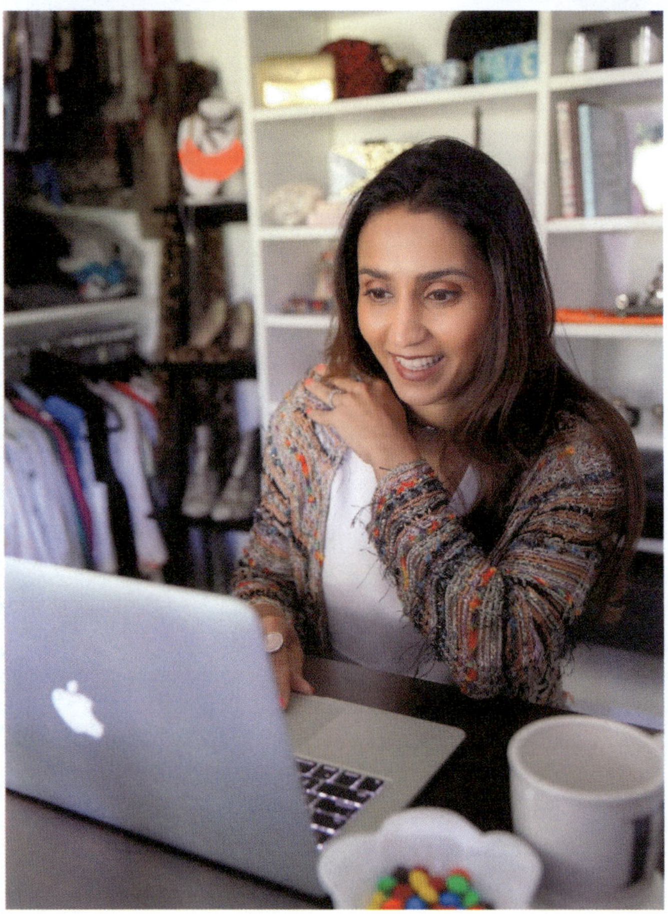

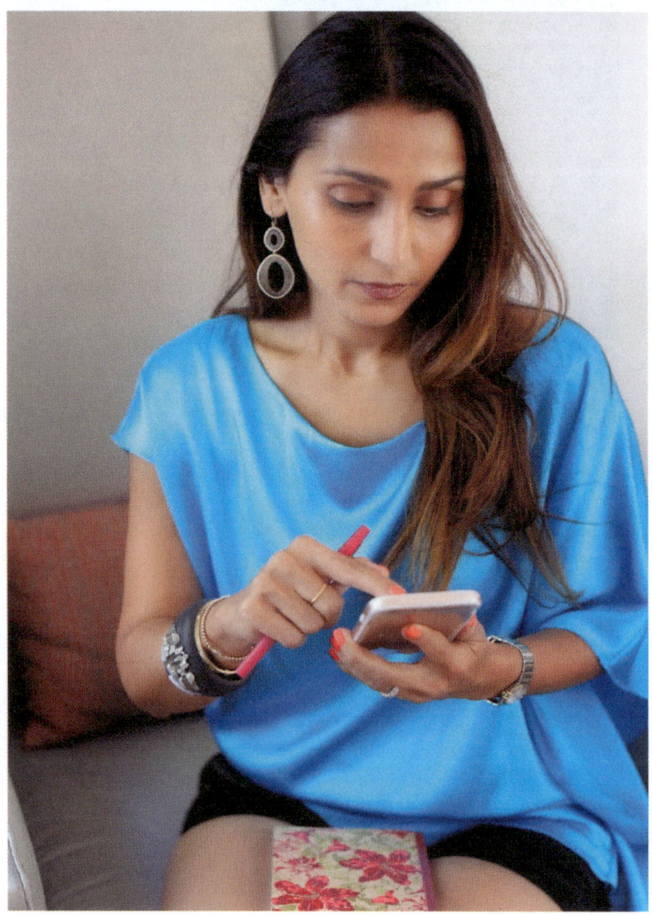

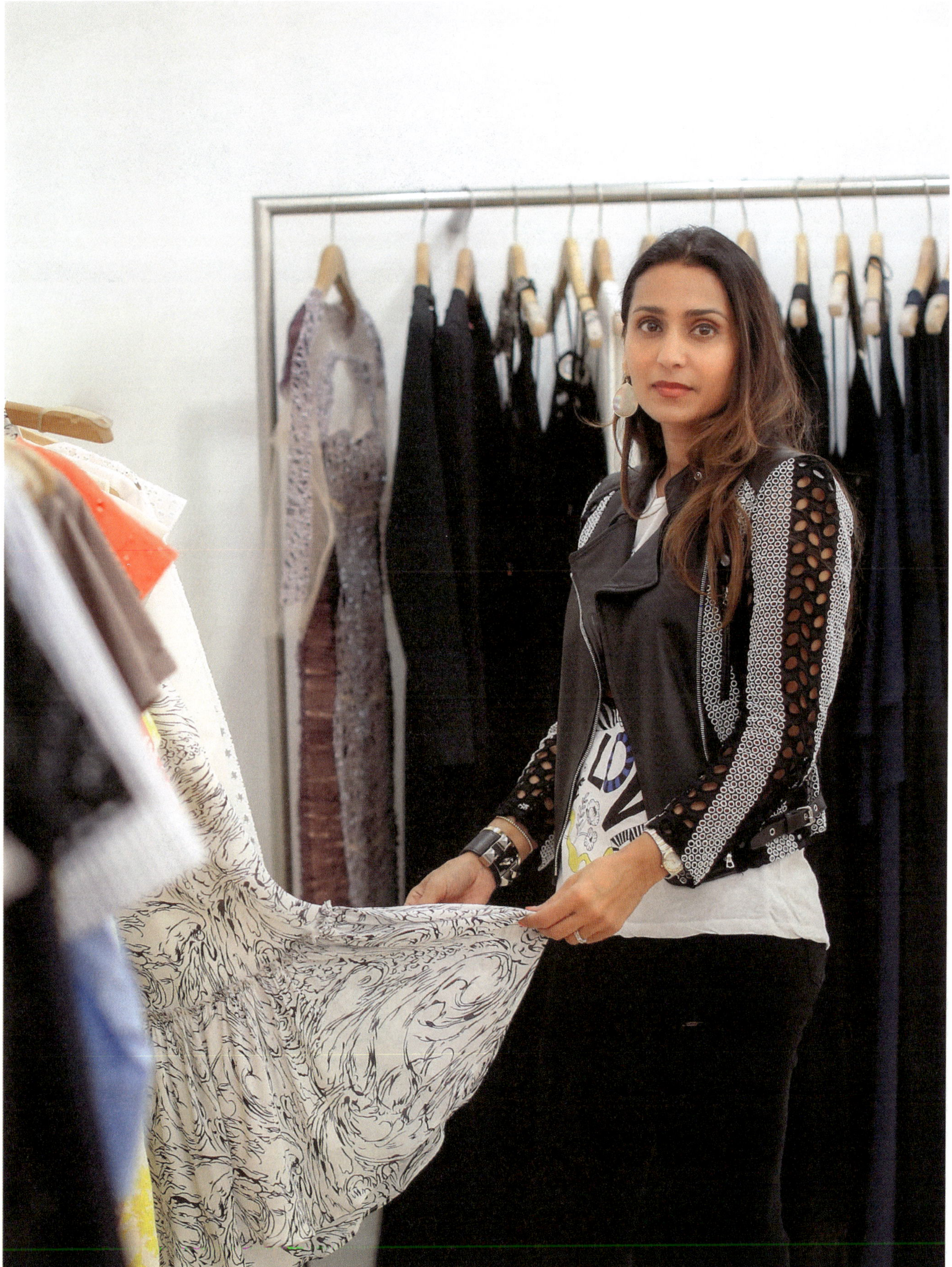

PROFESSIONAL ORGANIZER

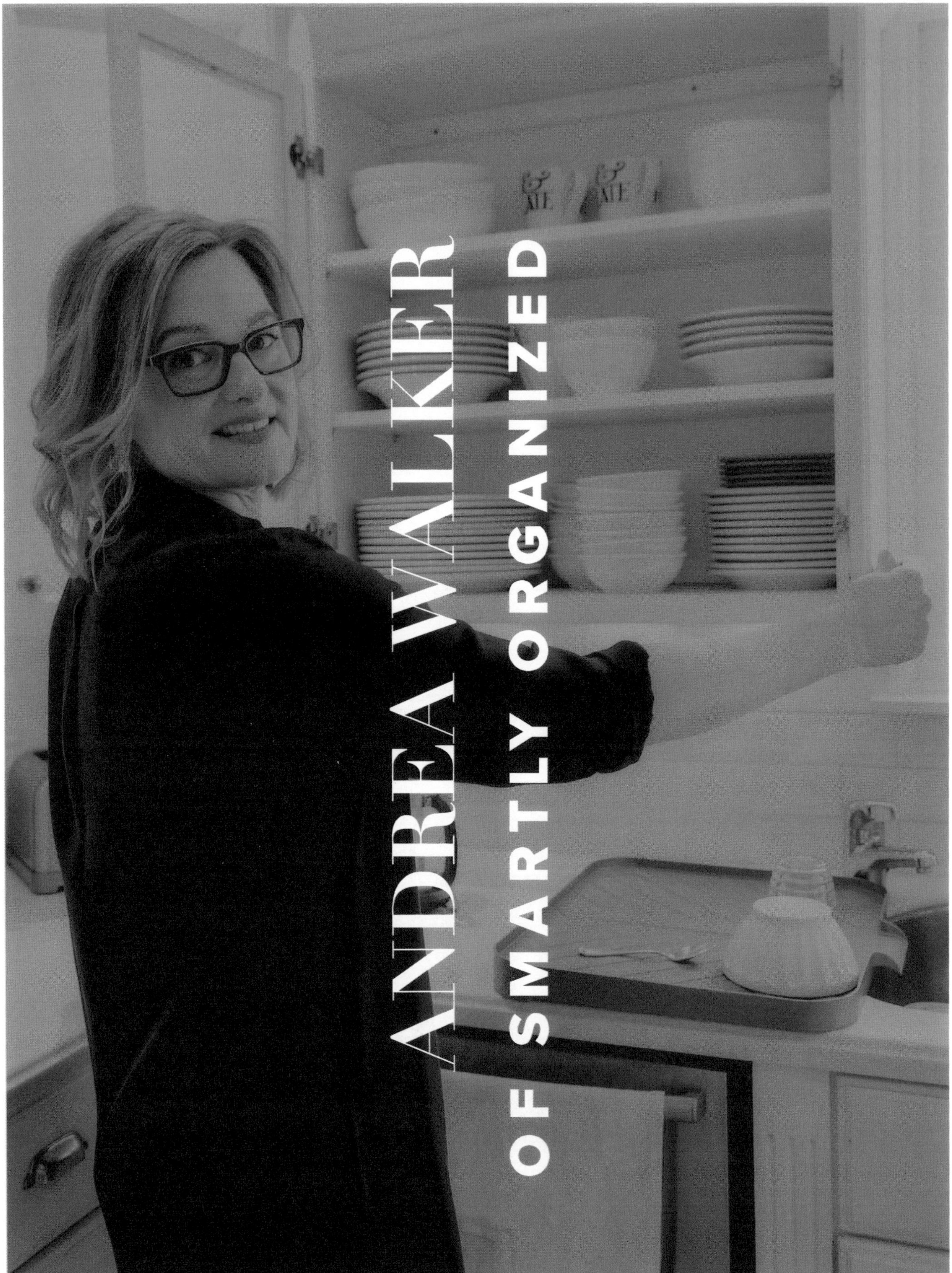

www.smartlyorganized.com

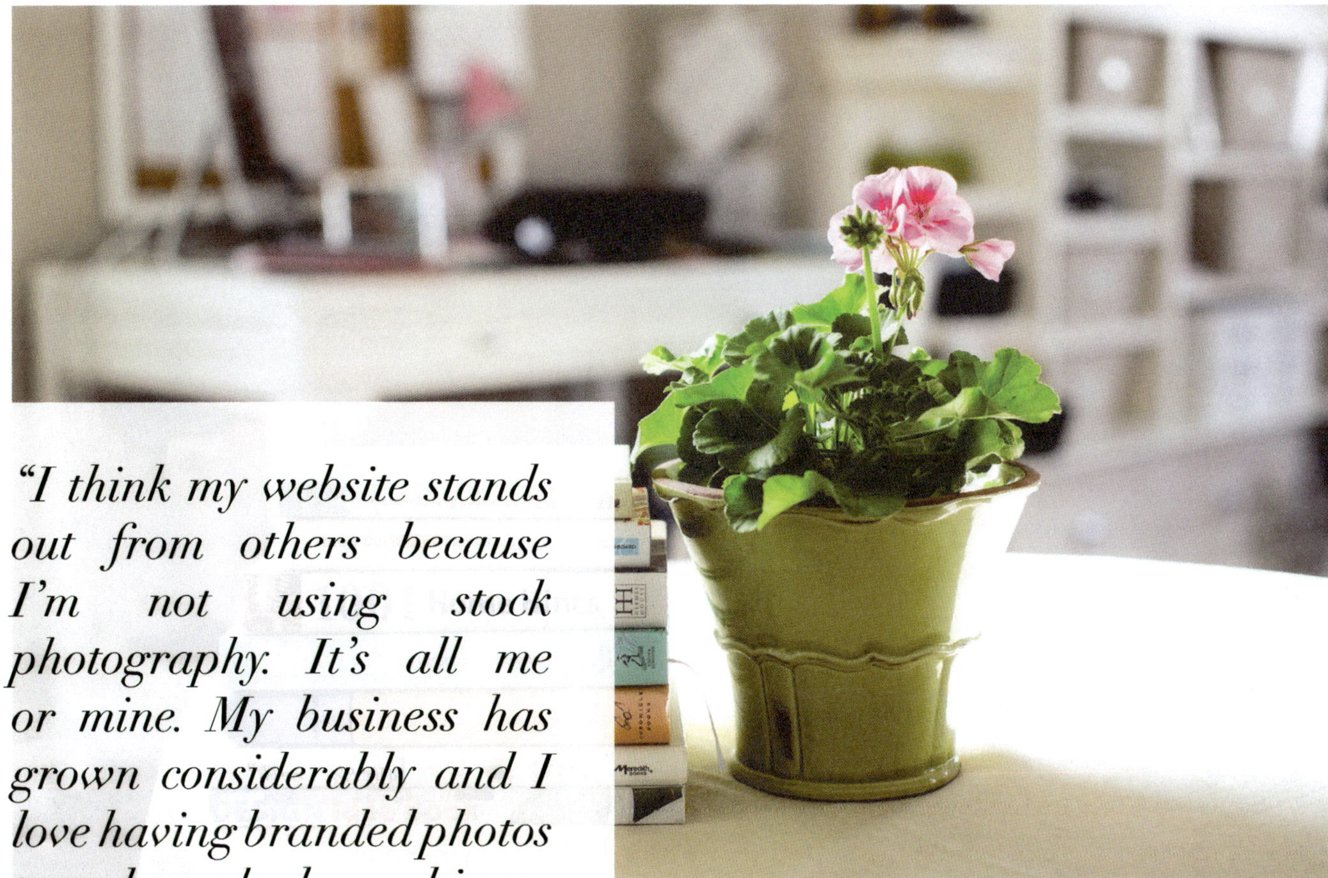

"I think my website stands out from others because I'm not using stock photography. It's all me or mine. My business has grown considerably and I love having branded photos to make me look even bigger than I am. I think it was the catalyst I needed to move me forward."

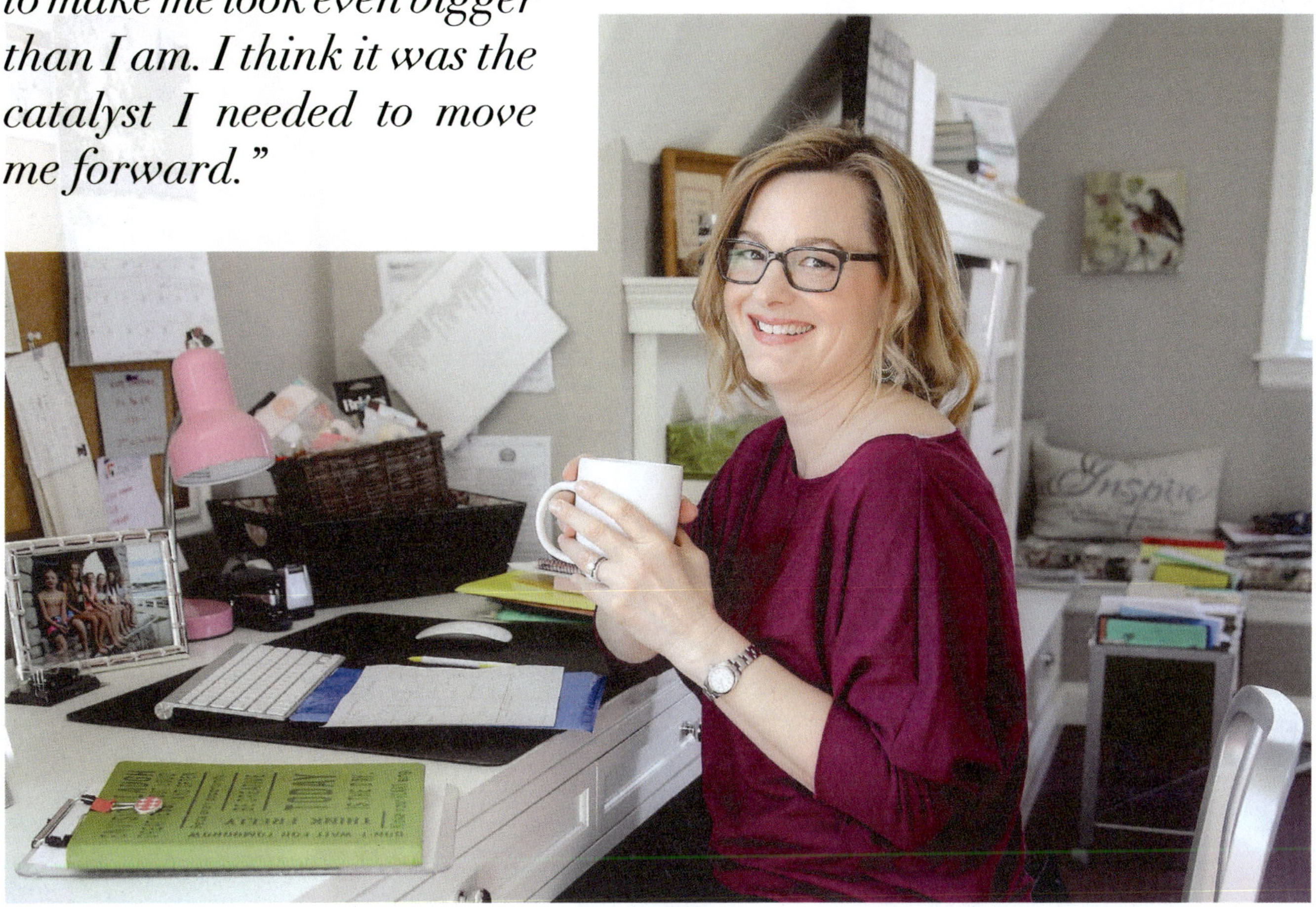

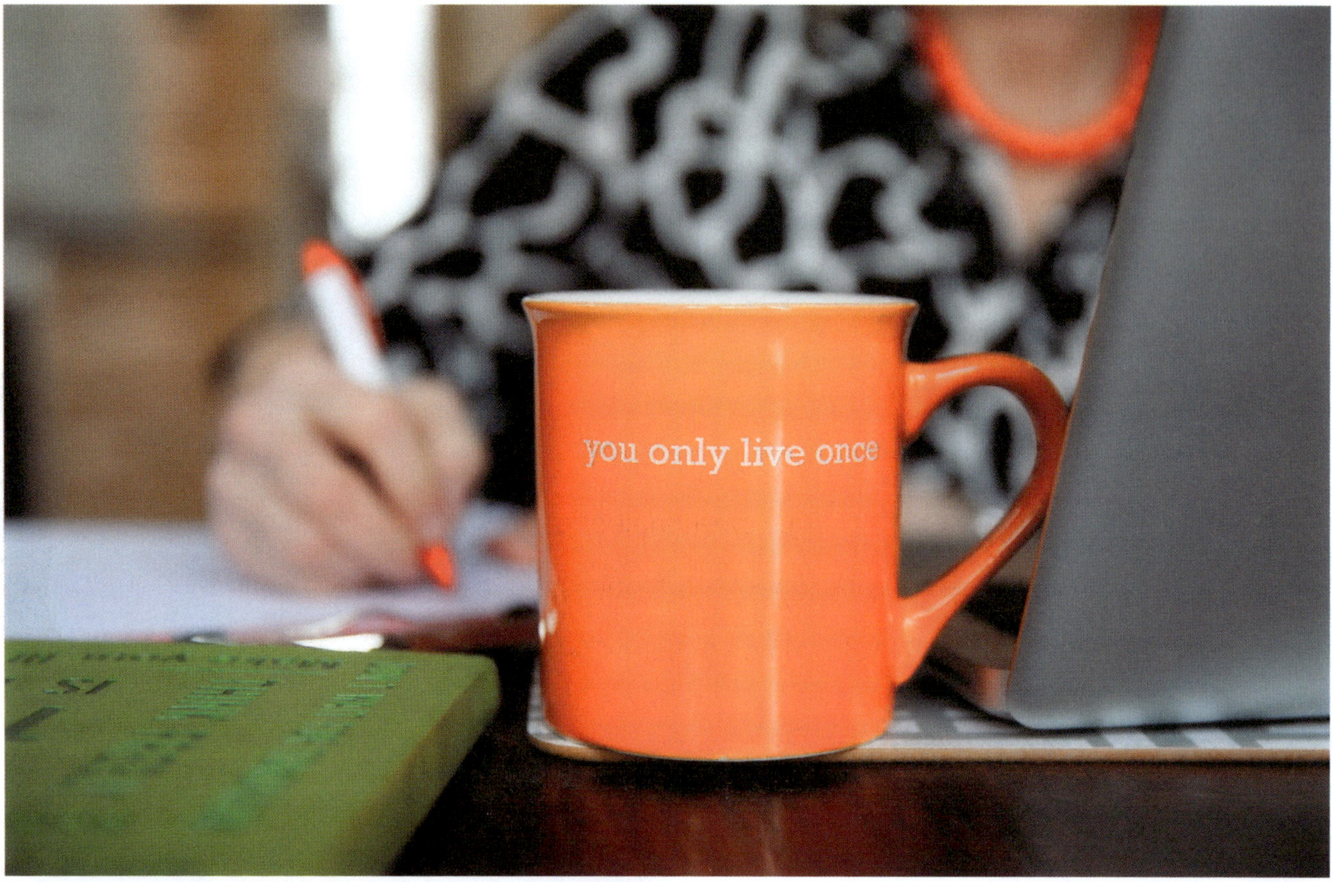
you only live once

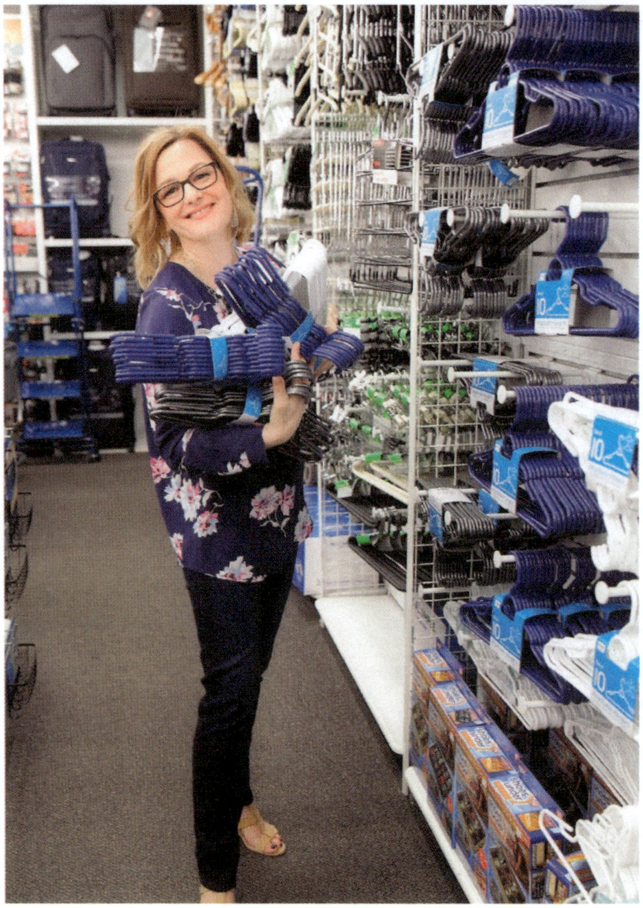

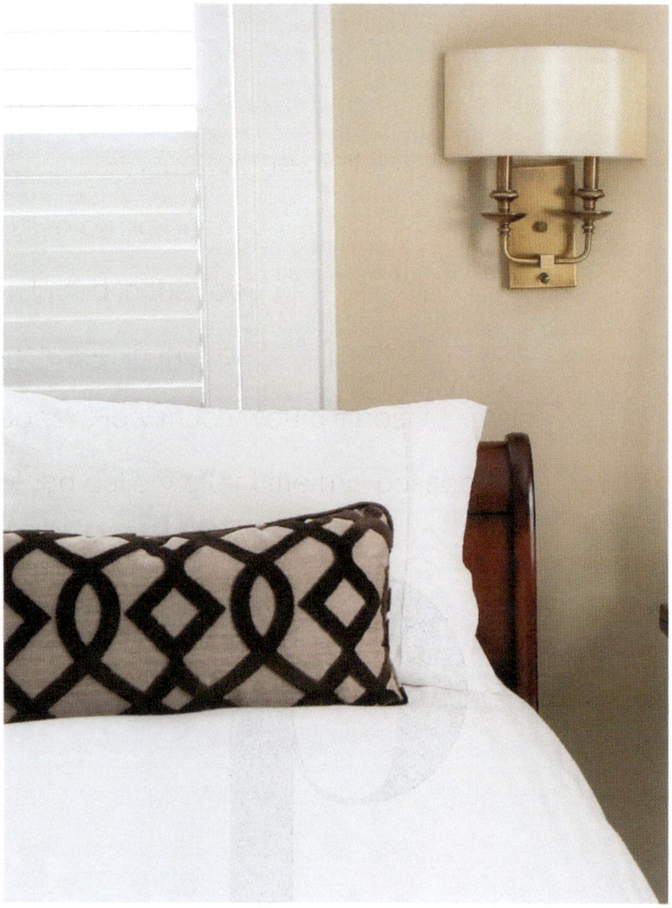

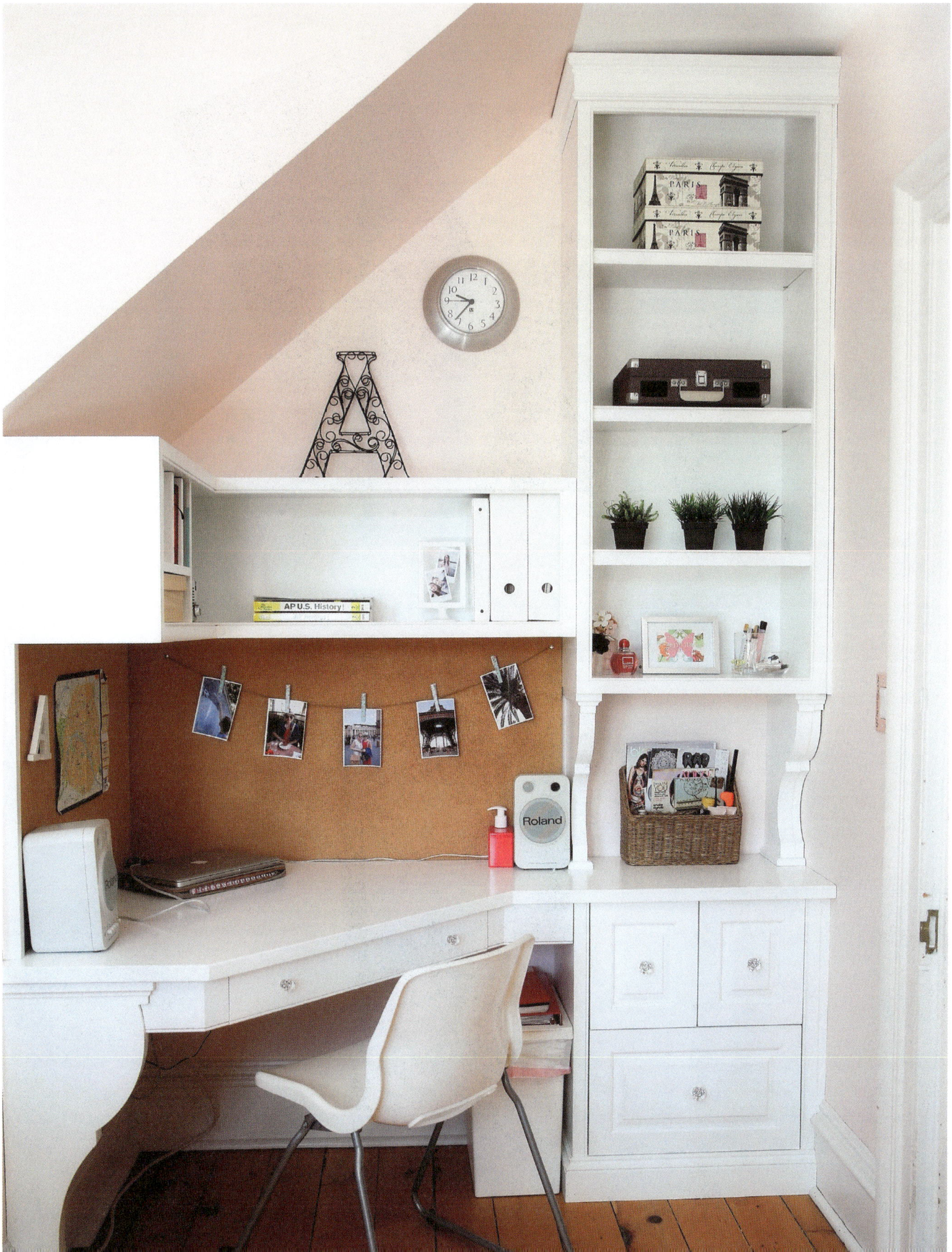
PARIS
PARIS
AP U.S. History
Roland

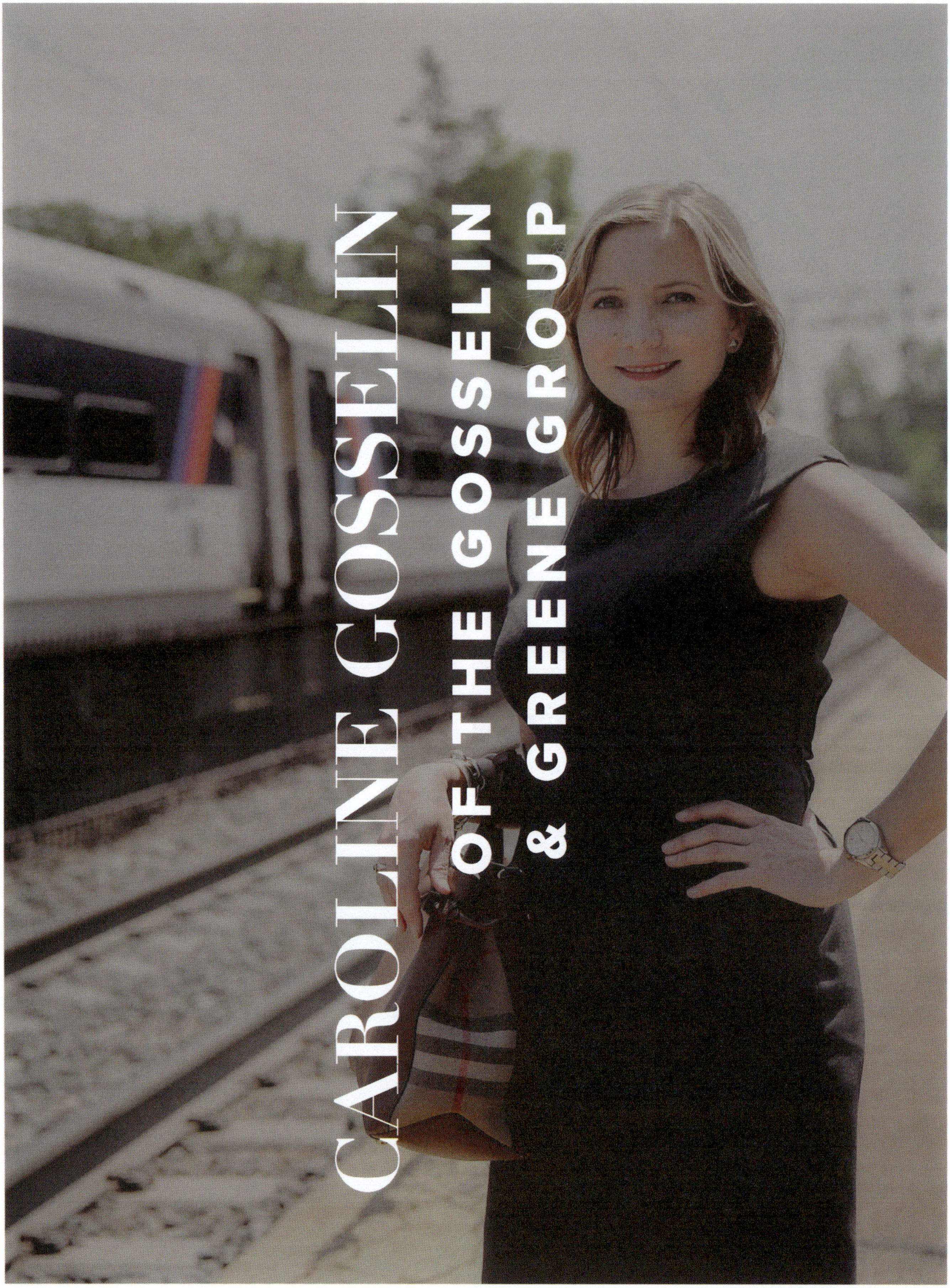

www.gosselingreene.com

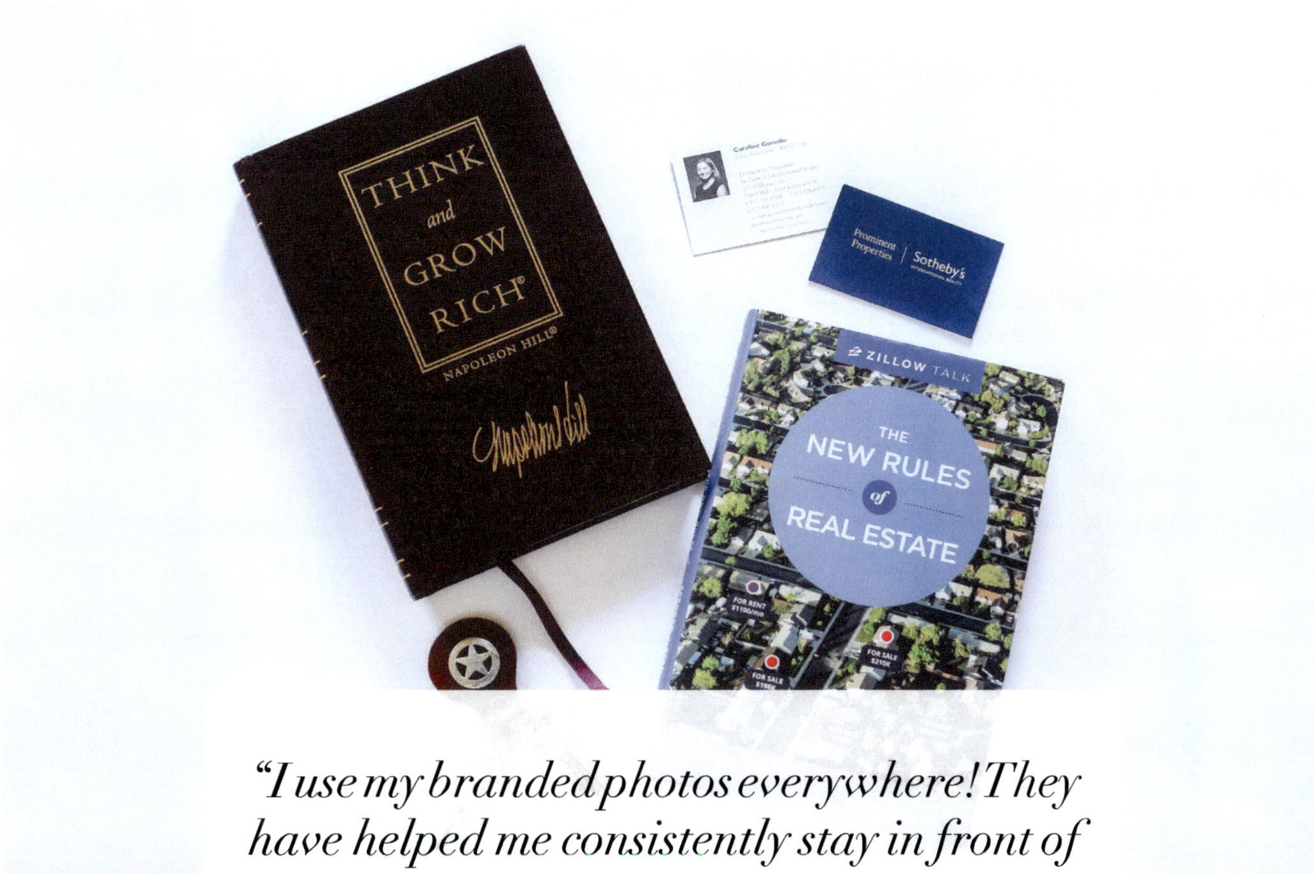

"I use my branded photos everywhere! They have helped me consistently stay in front of people in a fun, yet still professional way."

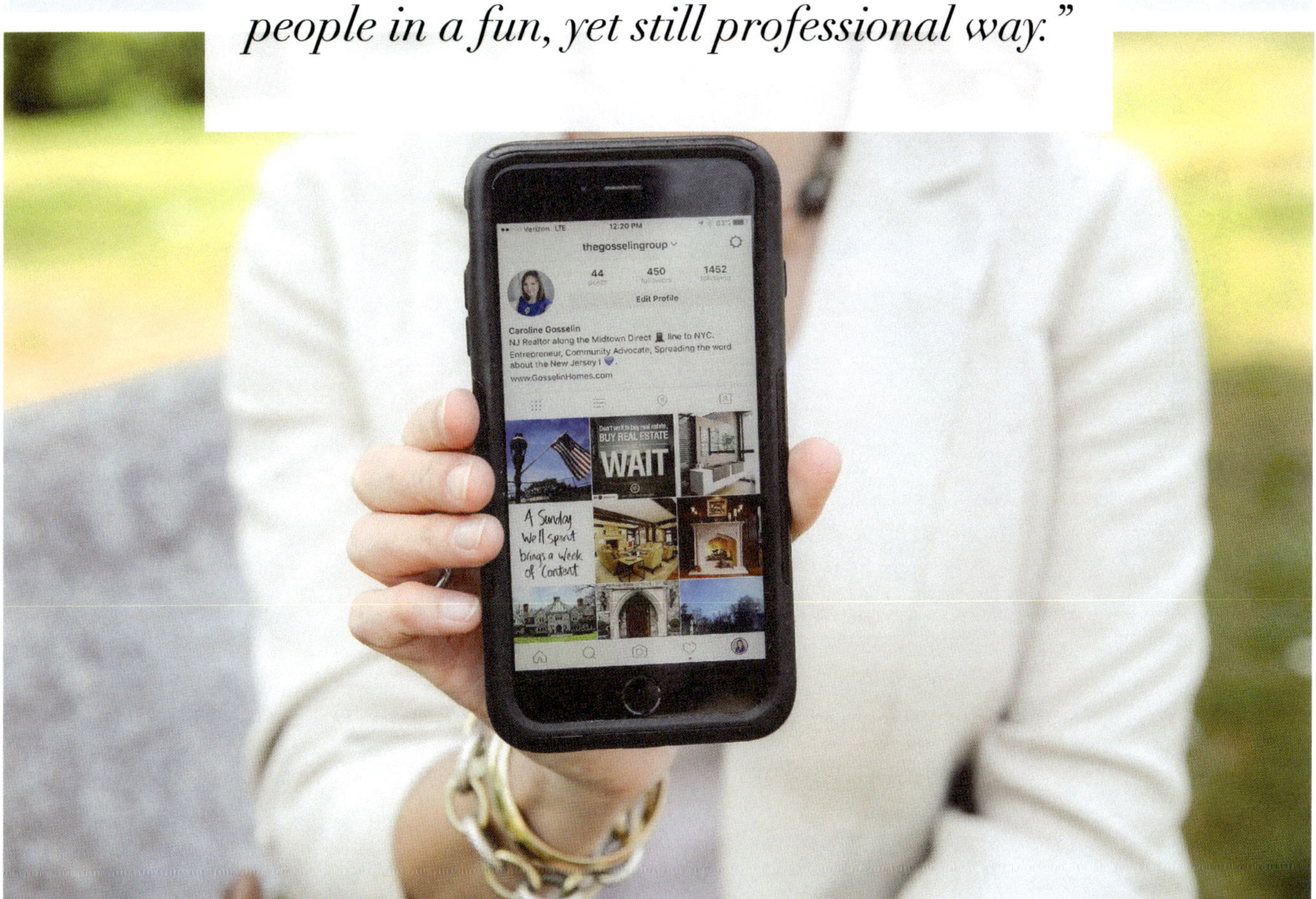

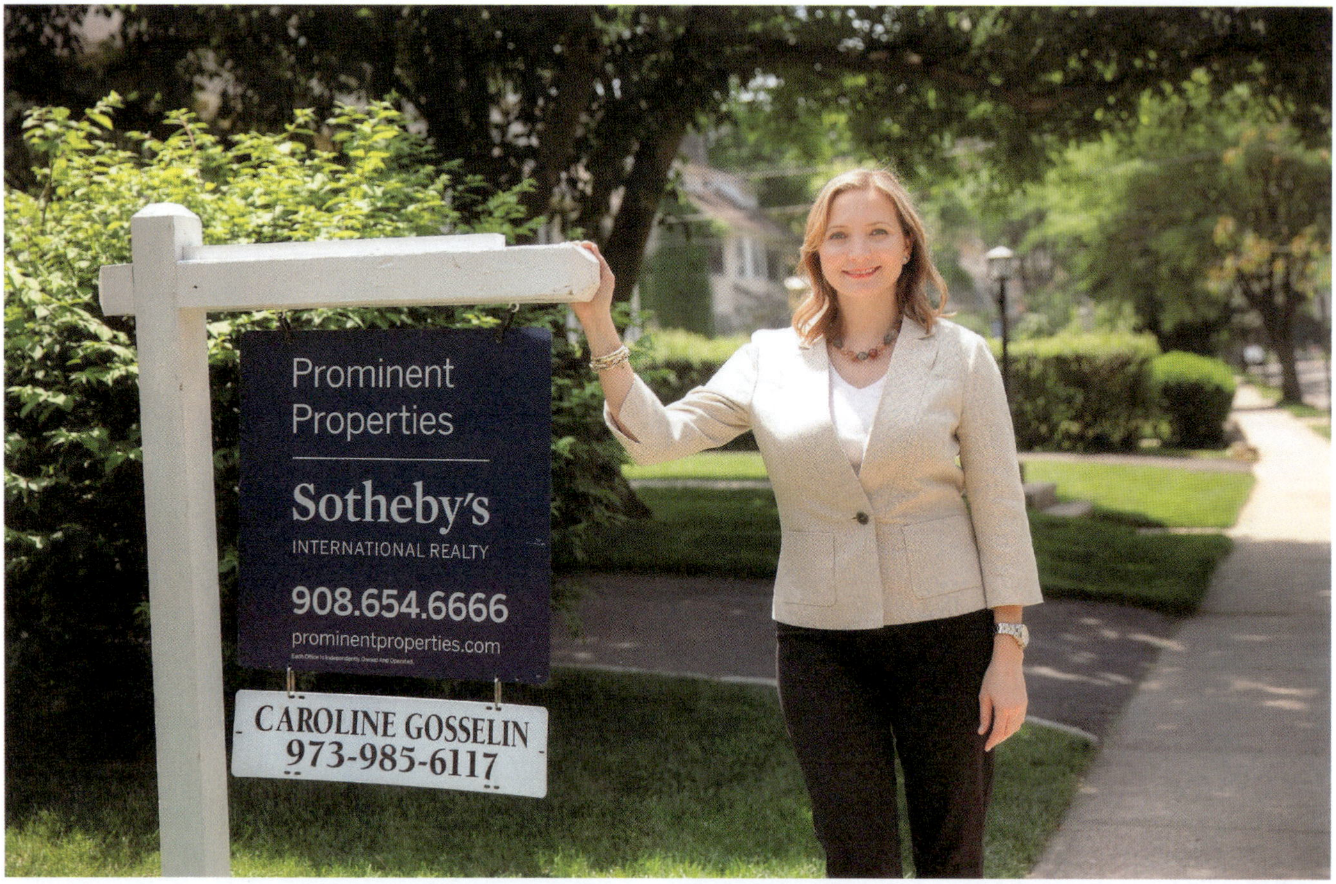
Prominent
Properties
Sotheby's
INTERNATIONAL REALTY
908.654.6666
prominentproperties.com
CAROLINE GOSSELIN
973-985-6117

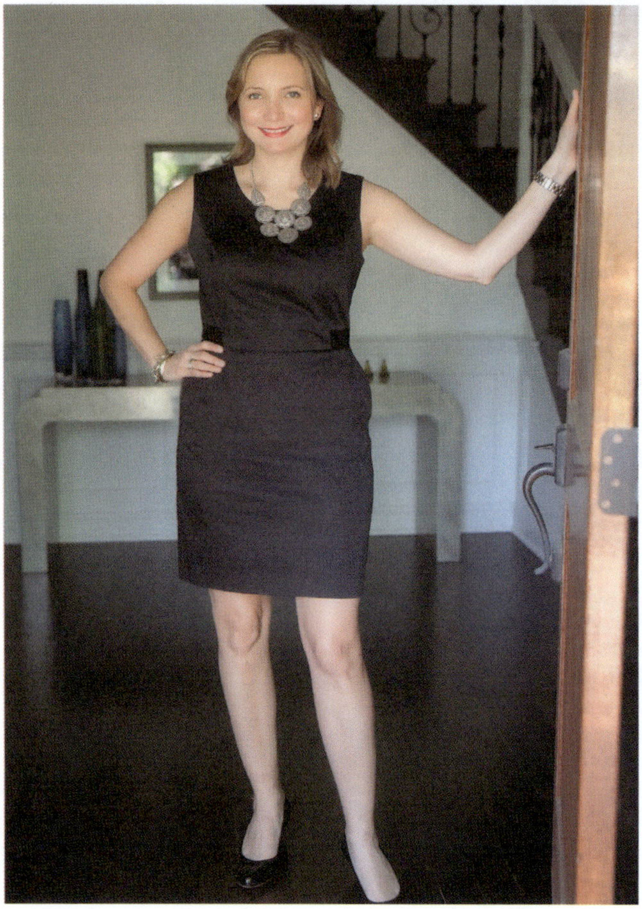

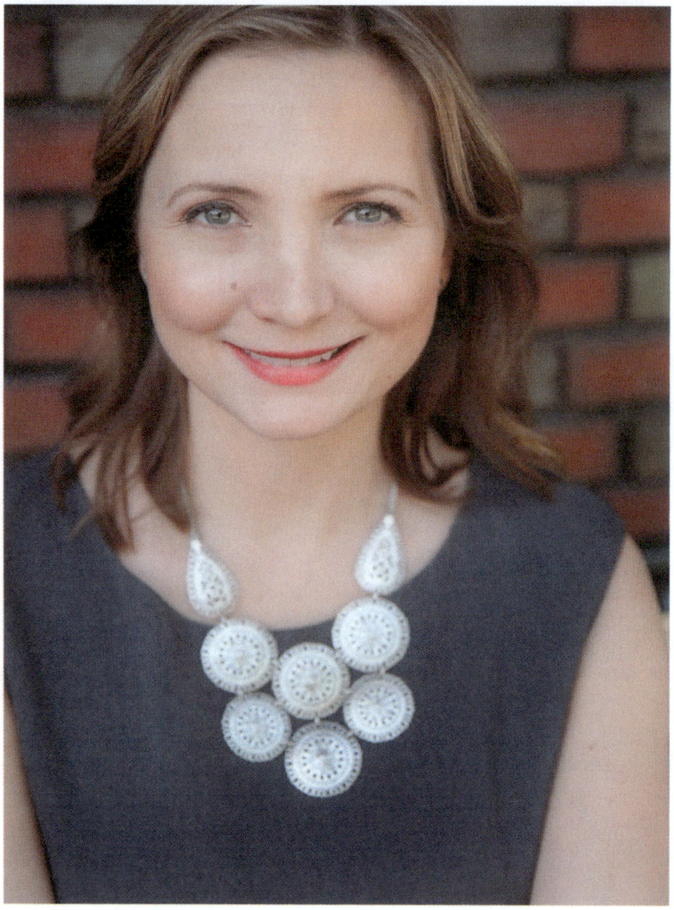

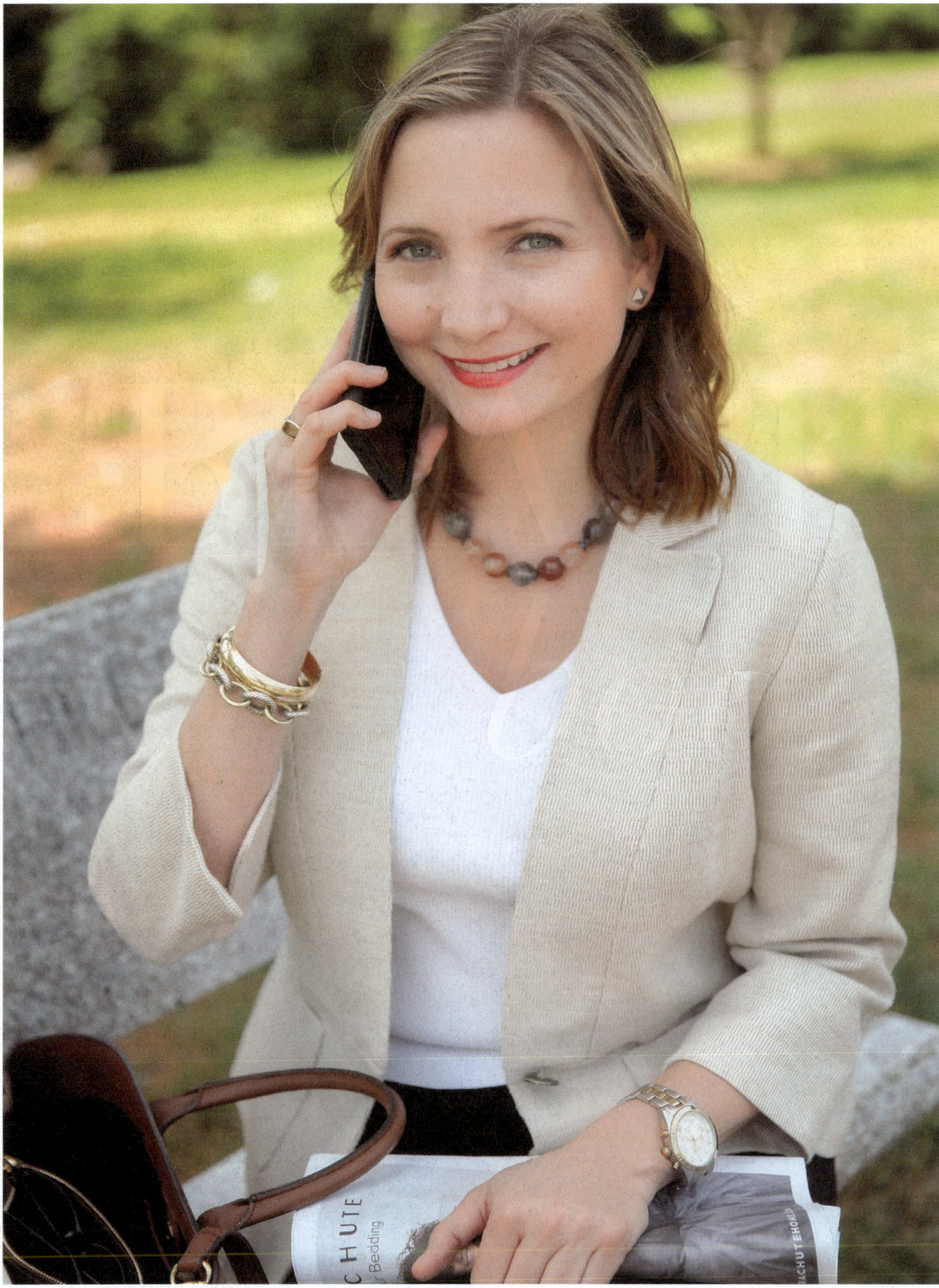

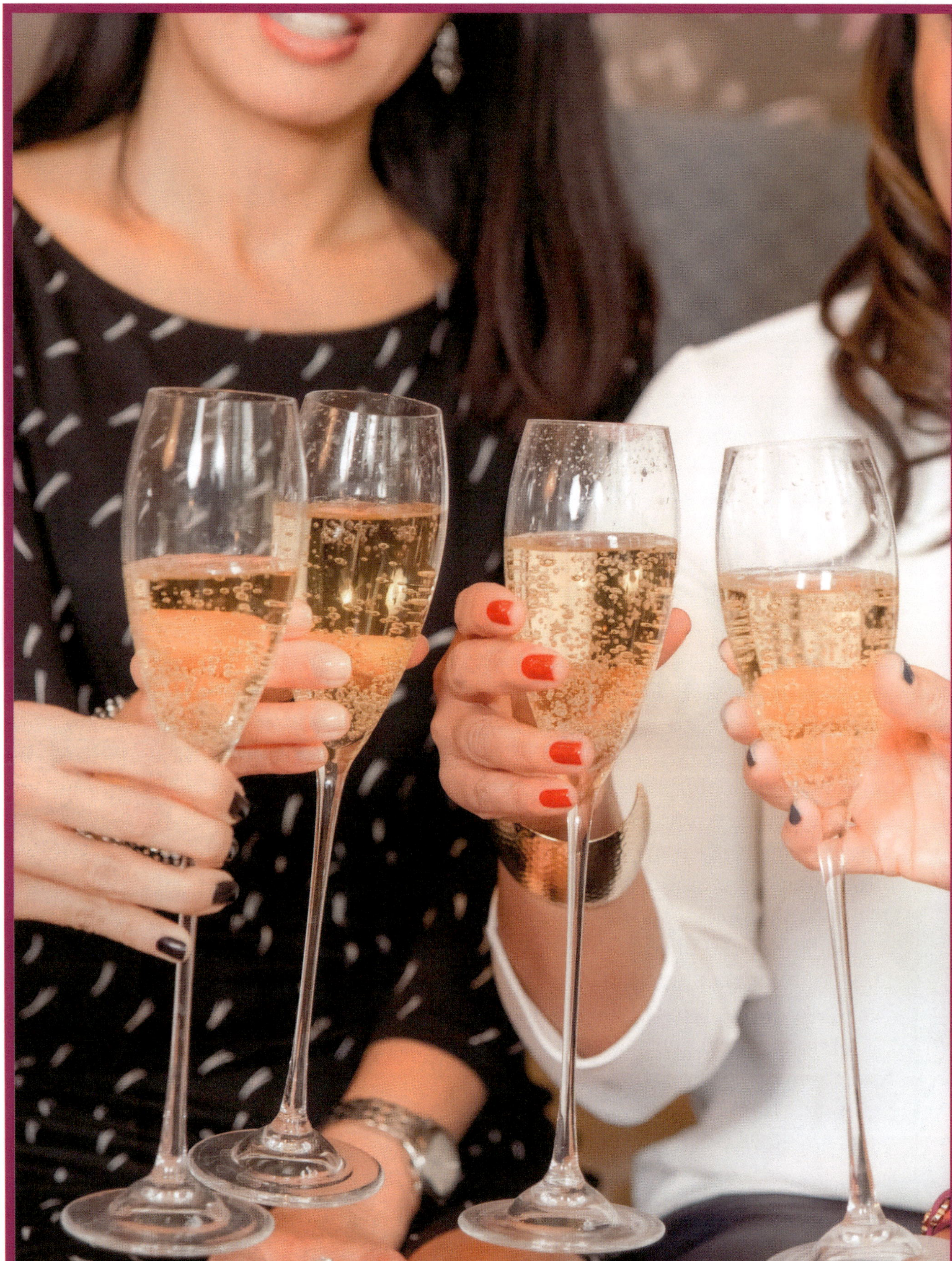

11

THE BLACK *book*

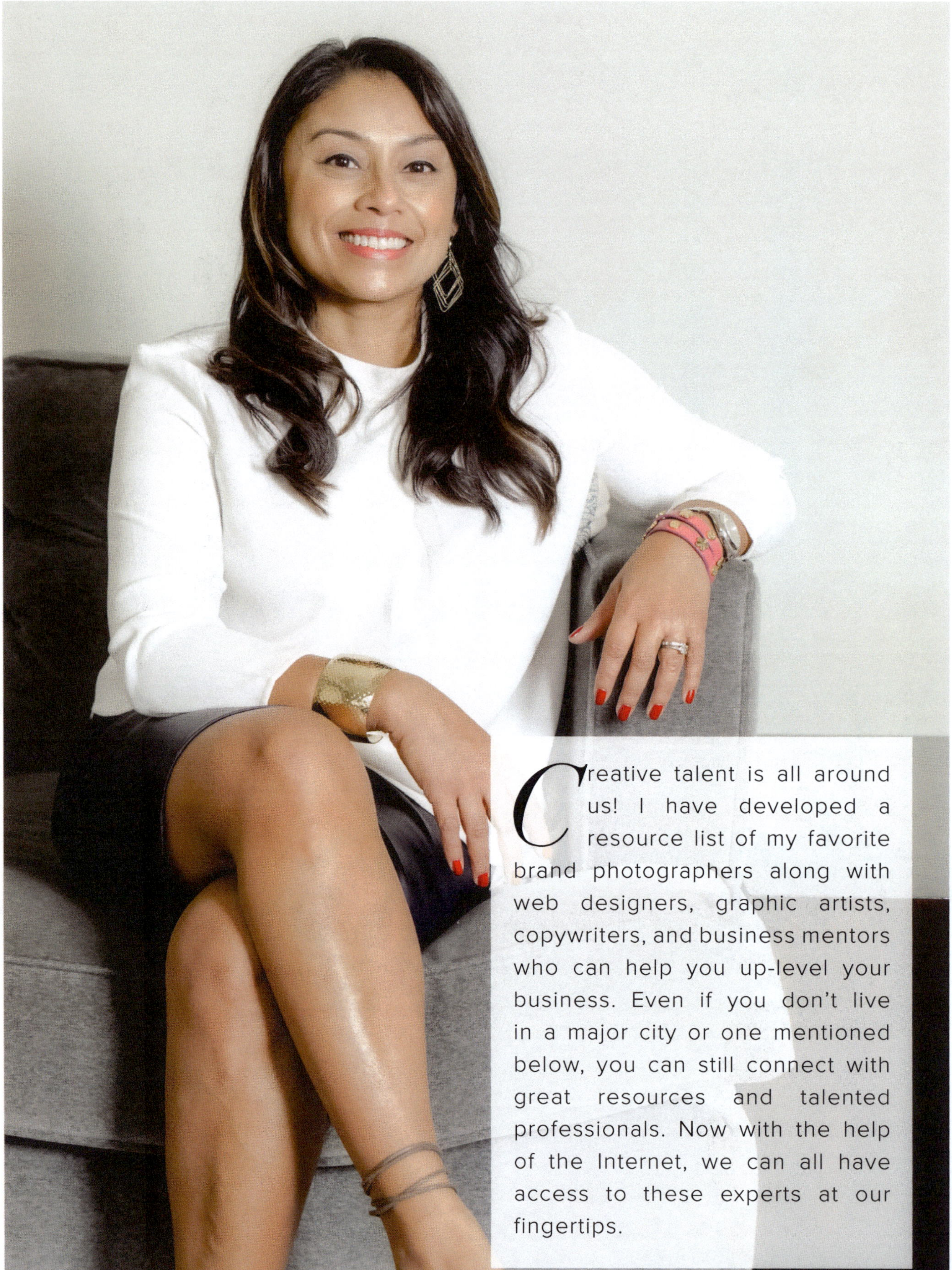

Creative talent is all around us! I have developed a resource list of my favorite brand photographers along with web designers, graphic artists, copywriters, and business mentors who can help you up-level your business. Even if you don't live in a major city or one mentioned below, you can still connect with great resources and talented professionals. Now with the help of the Internet, we can all have access to these experts at our fingertips.

BRAND
PHOTOGRAPHERS

Caroline White	*www.carolinewhitephotography.com*	*LA/NYC+*
Timothi	*www.timothi.com*	*LA/NYC*
Kelsey Lee	*www.thebrandgals.com*	*LA*
Wendy Yalom	*www.wendykyalom.com*	*San Francisco*
Britney Gardner	*www.britneygardner.com*	*Portland*
Heidi Hapanowicz	*www.heidihapanowicz.com*	*Miami/San Diego+*
Alyssa Peek	*www.peekphotography.nyc*	*NYC*
Laura Leff	*www.lauraleecreative.imlauralee.com*	*NJ*
Jessica Christian	*www.jessicasunshinephoto.com*	*Atlanta*
Naomi Epstein	*www.naomiepsteinheadshots.com*	*Chicago*
Chelsea Mazur	*www.chelseamazur.com*	*Chicago*
Anna Argiropoulos	*www.annawithlovephotography.com*	*Toronto*
Jessica Charuk	*www.charukstudios.com*	*Toronto*
Jess Kornacki	*www.artofher.com*	*Denver*
Amalie Orrange	*www.thebrandedbosslady.com*	*Orlando*
Stacy Pierce	*www.stacypierce.com*	*Orlando*
Megan Weaver	*www.megan-weaver.com*	*Dallas*
Danielle Finney	*www.dfinneyphoto.co*	*Washington, DC*
Aliyah	*www.alimondphotography.com*	*Northern VA*
Carla Coulson	*www.carlacoulson.com*	*Europe*
Zahrina	*www.zahrinaphotography.com*	*Australia*
Lauren	*www.studiosolandco.com*	*Australia*
Rebecca Taylor	*www.rebeccataylor.com.au*	*Australia*

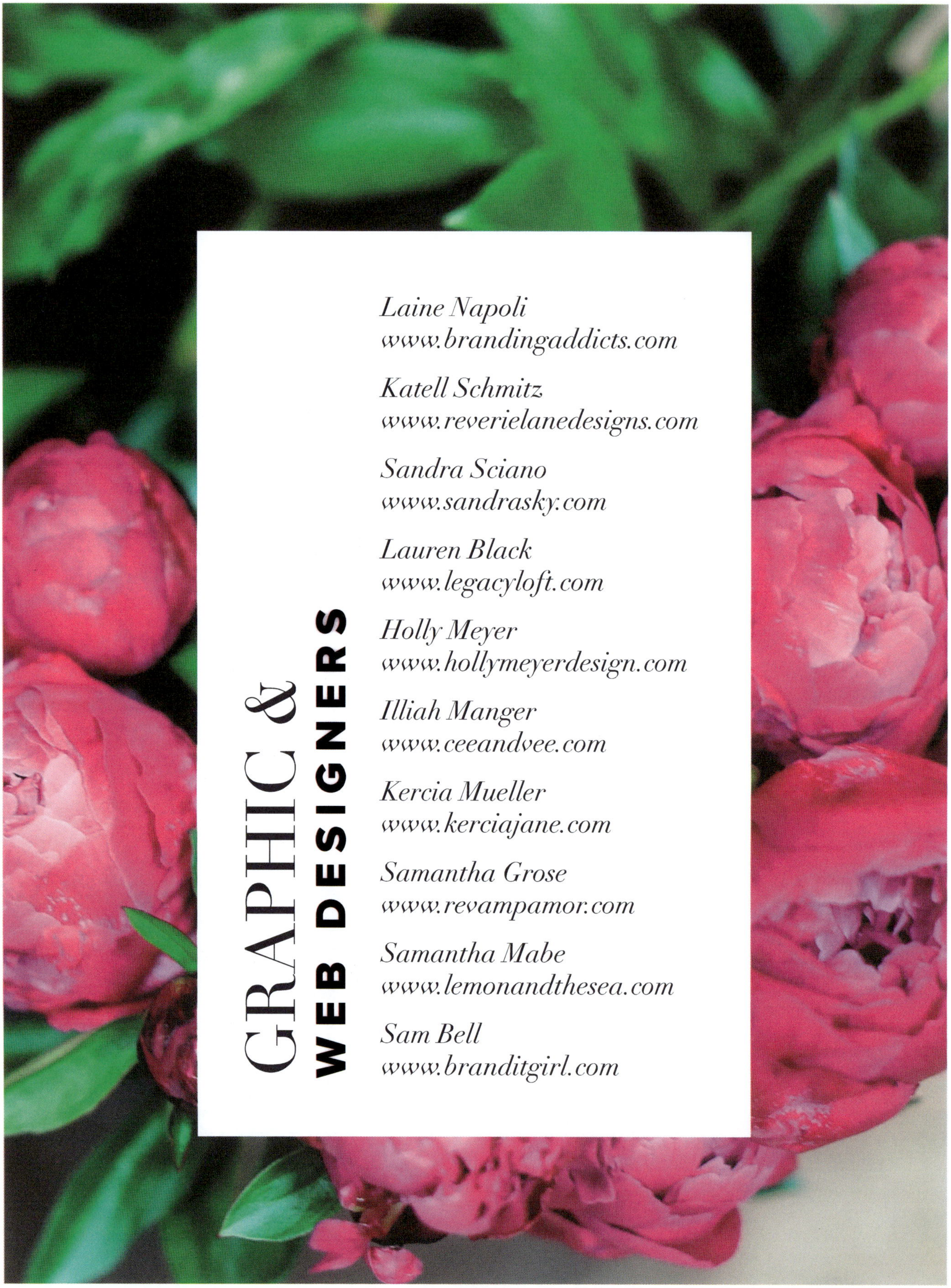

GRAPHIC & WEB DESIGNERS

Laine Napoli
www.brandingaddicts.com

Katell Schmitz
www.reverielanedesigns.com

Sandra Sciano
www.sandrasky.com

Lauren Black
www.legacyloft.com

Holly Meyer
www.hollymeyerdesign.com

Illiah Manger
www.ceeandvee.com

Kercia Mueller
www.kerciajane.com

Samantha Grose
www.revampamor.com

Samantha Mabe
www.lemonandthesea.com

Sam Bell
www.branditgirl.com

PERSONAL
STYLIST

Neepa Sidkar
www.accessiblestyle.net

Priya Virmani
www.priveebypriya.com

Elaine Yu
www.simplychicstyling.com

Phylicia Bernard
www.styleingenewity.com

VIDEO
EXPERT

Holly G Studios
www.hollygstudios.com

Trena Little
www.trenalittle.com

SOCIAL MEDIA
STRATEGIST

Kaitlyn Pierce
www.piercesocial.com

Erin Montgomery
www.pipersocialmedia.com

Christina Ochoa
www.thesocialbutterflygal.net

BOOK EDITOR &
WRITING COACH

Jodi Brandon
www.jodibrandoneditorial.com

Alexa Haddock Bigwarfe
www.writepublishsell.com

COPYWRITER

Ashley Beaudin
www.ashleybeaudin.com

Janine Duff
www.janineduff.com

Tara Bosler
www.tboslerwriting.com

CONTENT
STRATEGIST

Abby Herman
www.abbymherman.com

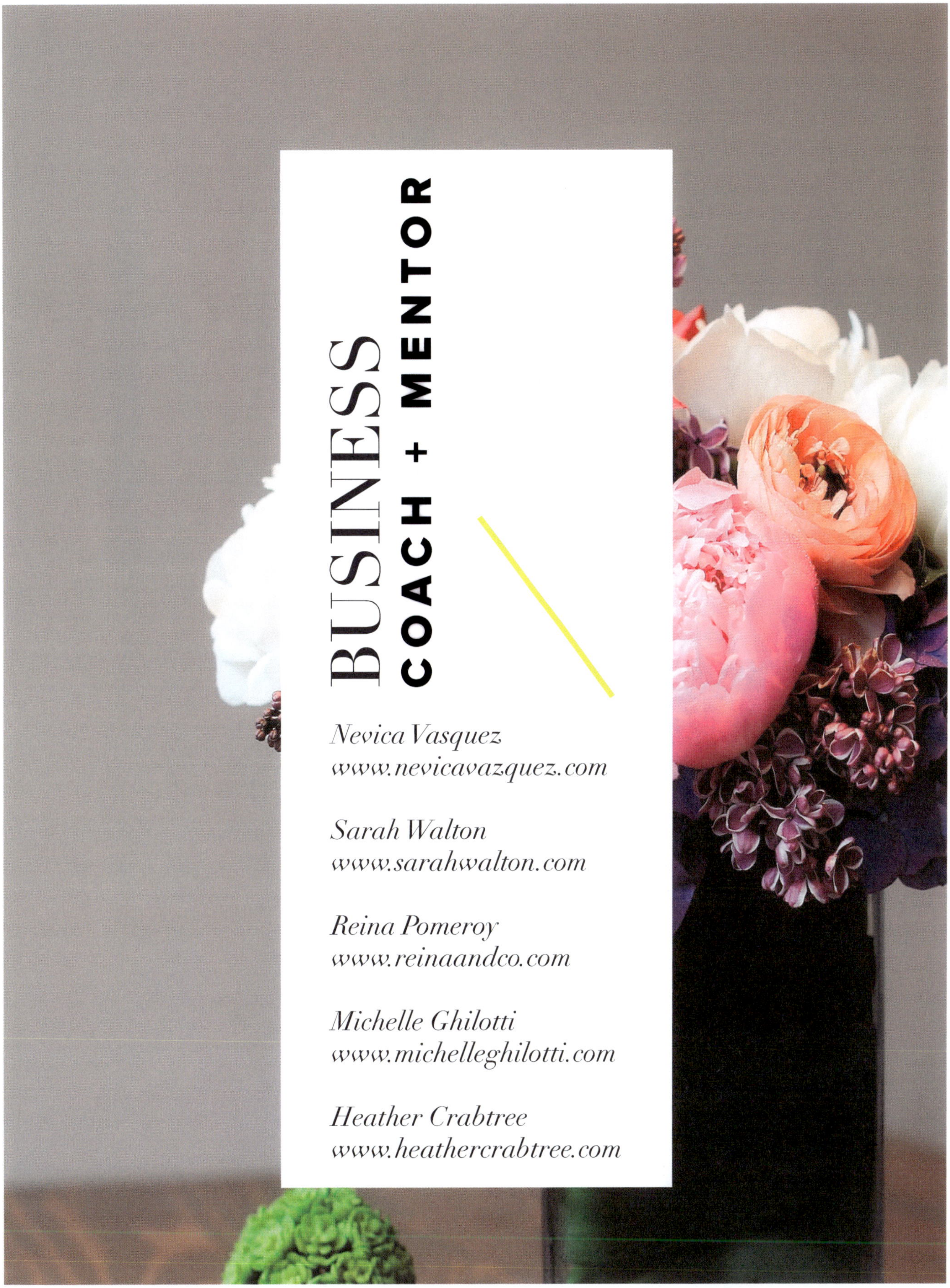

BUSINESS COACH + MENTOR

Nevica Vasquez
www.nevicavazquez.com

Sarah Walton
www.sarahwalton.com

Reina Pomeroy
www.reinaandco.com

Michelle Ghilotti
www.michelleghilotti.com

Heather Crabtree
www.heathercrabtree.com

PUBLIC RELATIONS
EXPERT

Amanda Berlin
www.amandaberlin.com

Moni Jefferson
www.monijeffersonpr.com

PUBLIC SPEAKING
STRATEGIST

Jessica Rasdall
www.jessicarasdall.com

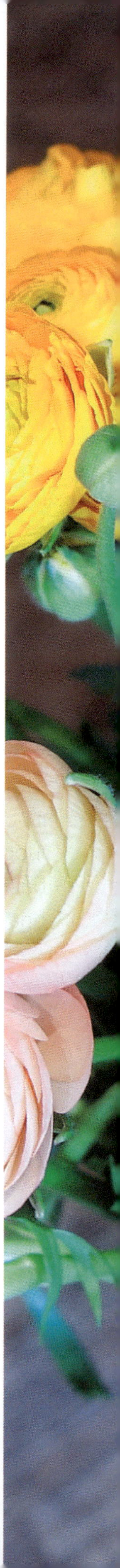

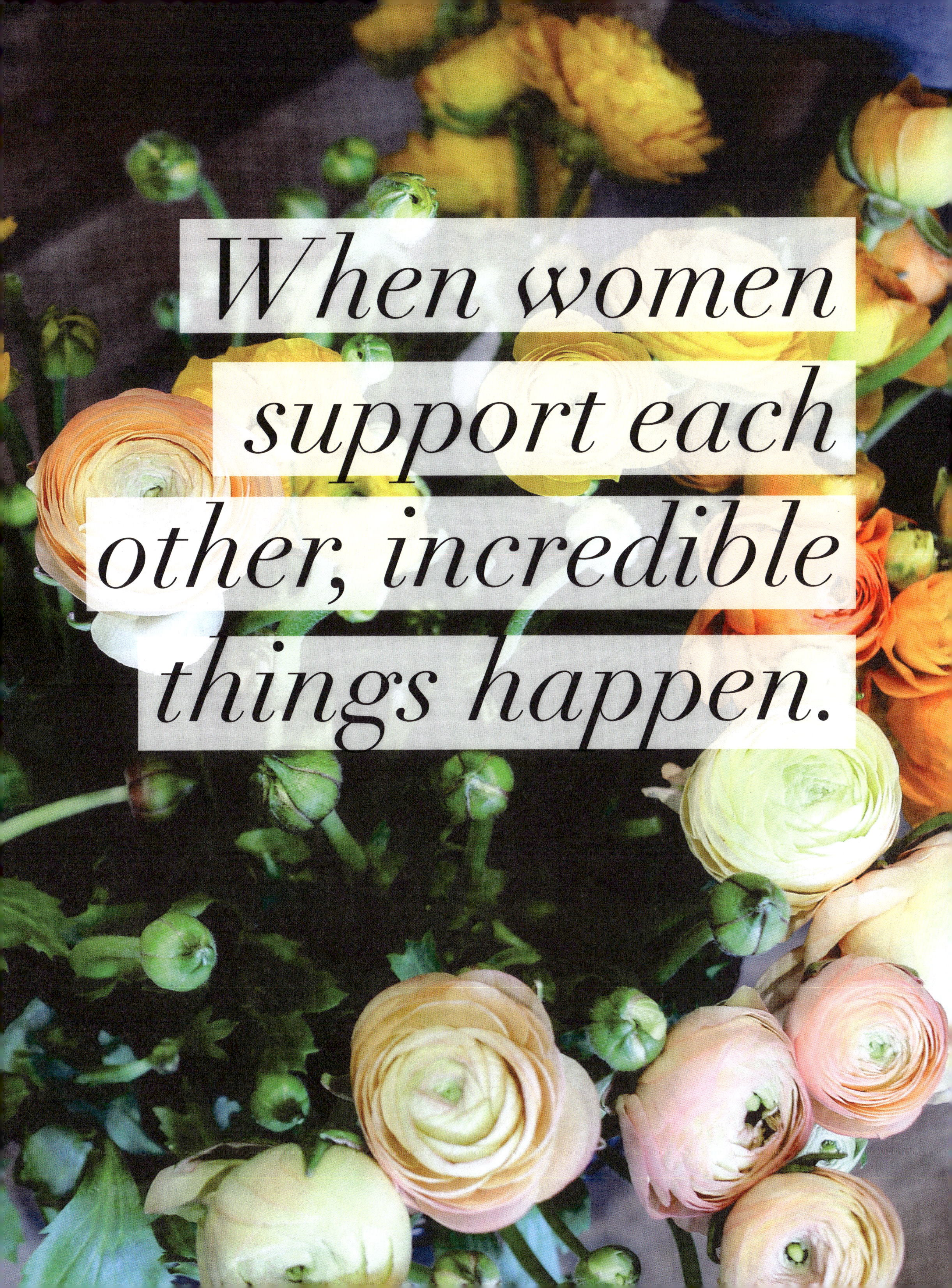
When women
support each
other, incredible
things happen.

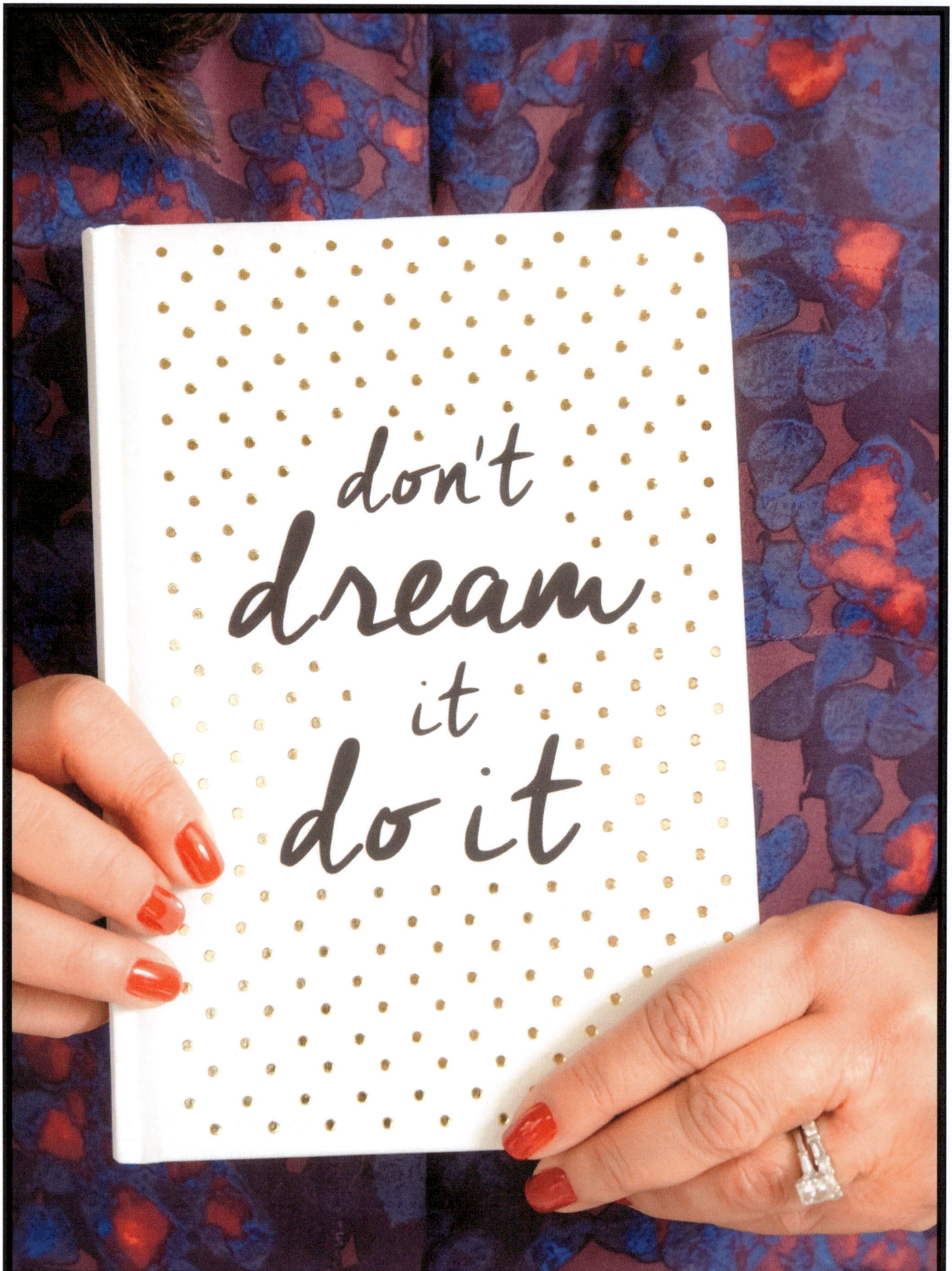
don't
dream
it
do it

GLOSSARY

BRAND - The relationship and perception your audience has with your products and services. Any name, design, style, words, symbols, or icons used to represent and differentiate your product or service from another.

BRAND PHOTOGRAPHY - A collection of customized, storytelling images that communicate the essence of your brand message.

BRAND STRATEGY - A plan used by a businesses to create a particular image for their brand and to meet certain goals.

COMMERCIAL PHOTOGRAPHY - A style of photography that focuses on selling products and services.

CROPPING - The removal of the outer parts of an image to improve framing, accentuate subject matter, or change the dimensions of the image.

DROPBOX - A file-hosting service that allows for easy and electronic transfer of files, photos, documents, and videos.

EDITING - The process of altering images through software like Photoshop or Lightroom or through smartphone apps.

EDITORIAL PHOTOGRAPHY - A style of photography found in magazines that sells a story.

HEADSHOT - A specific type of portrait focusing on the face and usually shot from the shoulders up.

HIGH-RESOLUTION PHOTOS - The type of photos needed to produce the best quality and sharpest prints. 300 dpi is recommended.

LIFESTYLE PHOTOGRAPHY - A style of photography that focuses on capturing portraits and people in real-life, everyday events in a creative manner.

LOCATION SCOUTING - The process of looking for locations before a shoot.

MOOD BOARD - A collection of images, materials, pieces of text, etc., intended to inspire the creative process.

PERSONAL BRANDING - The act of marketing people as brands.

PHOTOSHOP - An editing software program used to enhance photos.

PROOFS - Digital photo images that are not fully edited and finished; often used in the gallery viewing process.

PROPS - Things or objects that support the overall story theme of your photo shoot.

RETOUCHING - The process of manipulating photographs in order to slightly change the looks of the subject, like erasing pimples or making evening out skin tone.

STOCK PHOTOS - Professional photographs of common places, nature, or people that are styled with a broad appeal to be used by several businesses or for commercial purposes.

STYLIST - A person whose job is to select and put together clothes and accessories in a stylish way.

WEB-SIZED PHOTOS - A lower-resolution photo used strictly for online and not suitable for printing. 72 dpi is recommended for quick uploading.

FEATURED BUSINESSES

www.accessiblestyle.net
www.acolorstory.com
www.airbnb.com
www.amynicolewellness.com
www.beautycounter.com/maggiezakhary
www.belong-mag.com
www.bloguettes.com
www.blowin-blowout.com
www. breather.com
www.bungalow63.com
www.canva.com
www.ckomaplewood.com
www.claudiapetrilli.com
www. deathtothestockphoto.com
www.dressedbylori.com
www.elizabethjonespersonalstyling.com
www.elladesigngroup.com
www.facebook.com/adornmarket
www.facebook.com/Blingitupjewels
www.GosselinGreene.com
www.hautechocolate.ca
www.instagram.com
www.iomwellness.com
www.jellybus.com/moldiv
www.jennifermchenry.cabionline.com
www.lauraleecreative.imlauralee.com
www.linkedin.com/in/kimberleyhaley
www.lucychambersmakeup.com
www.madewithover.com
www.millburnflorist.com
www.myfriendbettysays.com
www.natalyapricegroup.com
www.newjerseyluxuryrealestate.com
www.norahlovesmakeup.com
www.nourishandflourishhealth.com
www.oharaproject.com
www.pictapgo.com
www.priveebypriya.com
www.reelstylebeauty.com
www.ruvololaw.com
www.sarahwalton.com
www.simplychicstyling.com
www.smartlyorganized.com
www.stelladot.com/swapnapatel
www.tashablasi.com
www.thebaristudio.com
www.thedanishbakinggirl.com
www.thesusanparker.com
www.thredup.com
www.turquoiseandpalm.com
www.unsplash.com
www.upglo.org
www.vsco.co

WITH GRATITUDE

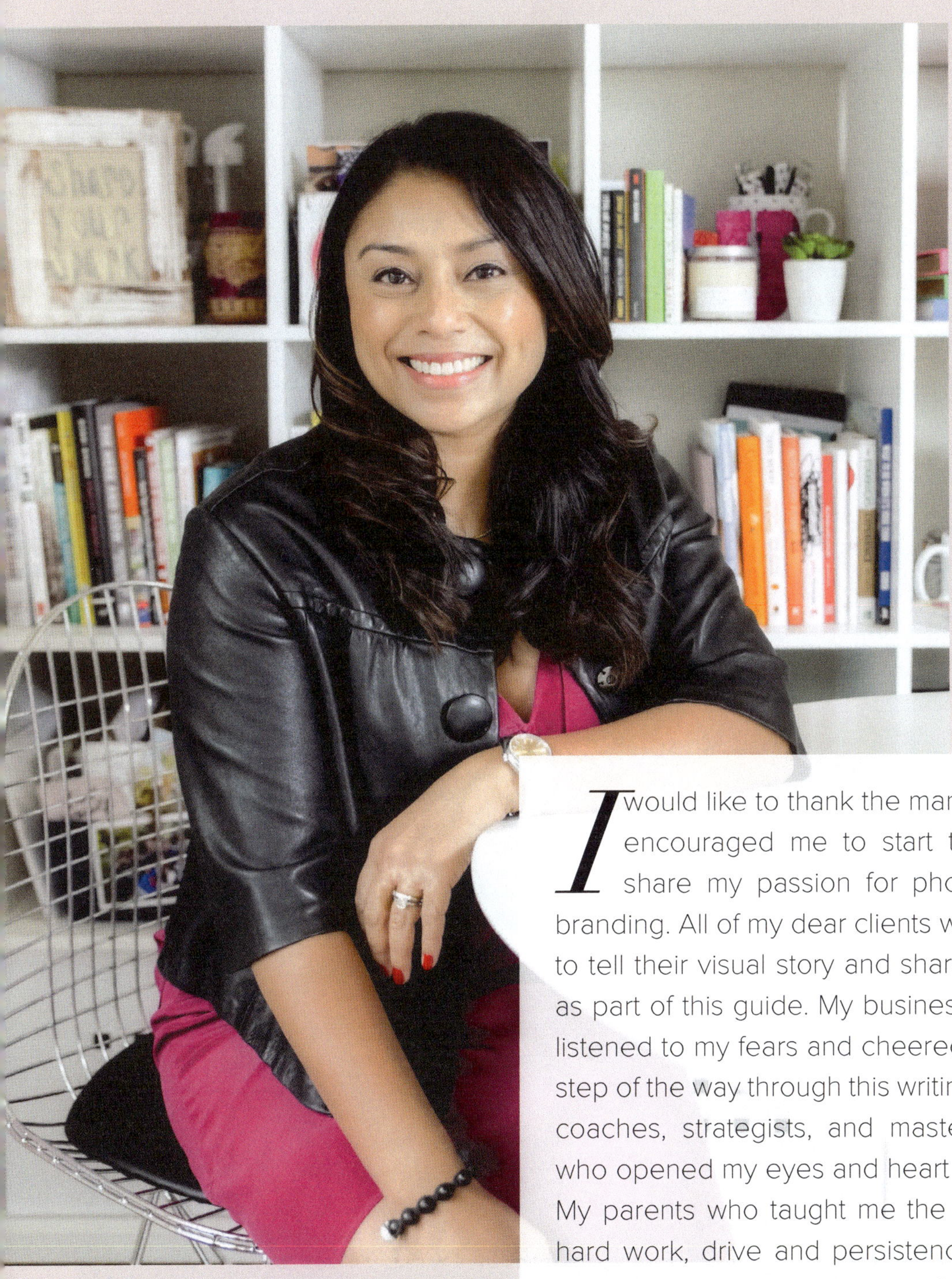

I would like to thank the many people who encouraged me to start this book and share my passion for photography and branding. All of my dear clients who trusted me to tell their visual story and share their images as part of this guide. My business besties who listened to my fears and cheered me on every step of the way through this writing process. My coaches, strategists, and mastermind friends who opened my eyes and heart to this project. My parents who taught me the importance of hard work, drive and persistence. Above all, I am grateful to my husband, Sunil, and three sons, Niko, Kishan, and Shay — my beloved fam-jam. In spite of my many days in front of the computer and our dinners ordered in, thank you for always supporting my crazy ideas and big dreams.

ABOUT MALLIKA

My name is Mallika Malhotra and I am a brand photographer and branding mentor in New Jersey. I help women in business who feel frustrated, lost, and invisible to get noticed as a leader in their industry by crafting a highly personalized visual brand.

For nine years, I have been telling visual stories with my camera. I leverage my experience as an advertising executive on big beauty brands like L'Oreal and Oil of Olay, along with my creative eye for photography and business strategy skills, to create storytelling images that build stand-out brands.

I am passionate about empowering women to share their message with confidence. When women tap into their unique story, their brand stands out and deeply connects with their audience, resulting in a passionate, purpose-driven, and profitable business.

I understand that the brand photography process can seem complicated, stressful, and overwhelming. After working with hundreds of women, I see this with my own clients and have even felt it at my own brand photo shoot. I created this playbook to help you feel more confident and organized as you prepare for your big photography shoot. It is a big investment, and I hope this tool helps answers many of your questions about both the strategic and logistical parts of your shoot. I hope you feel more prepared and at ease, so you can enjoy the day of the photo session.

Remember: Your best photos and your clearest message will all be a result of a well-planned shoot!

I encourage you to share information from this guide with your photographer, specifically the brand story and the photo stories guide. It will be a great way to work together, get on the same page, and start brainstorming creative ideas as partners.

If you are local to NJ or NYC and would like to learn more about my brand photography shoots, please reach out to me at mallika@mikifoto.com. You can also learn more at www.mikifoto.com or on Instagram @mikifotoco. If you are not local and would like to work together, I also offer one-on-one consultations calls in which I can help you with your brand photography strategy and creative direction for your photo shoot. I am currently creating an online course to help you define your brand story and develop your visual strategy. (Coming soon!)

I would love to learn more about you, your business, and your story.

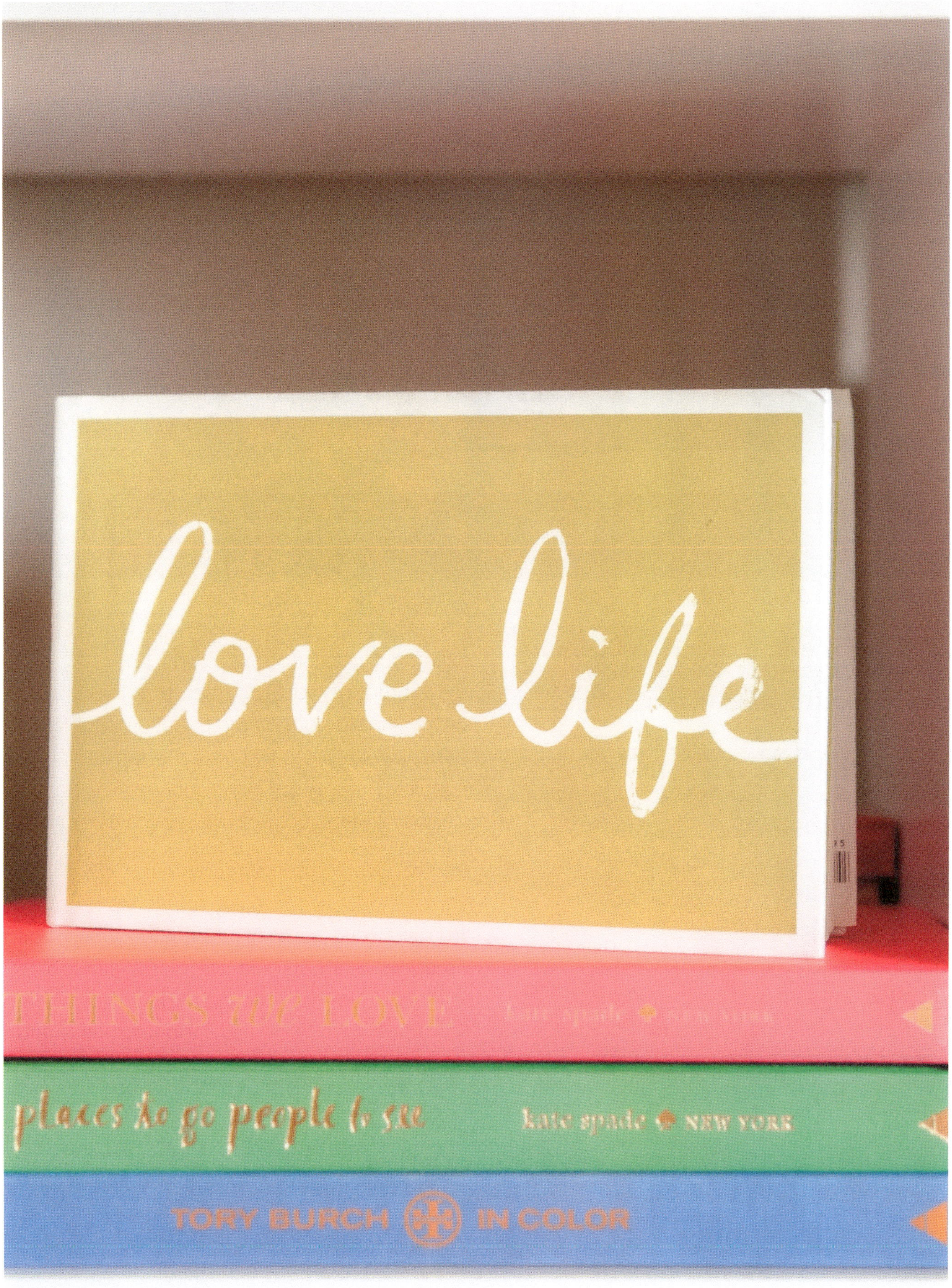
love life
THINGS we LOVE
places to go people to see
kate spade NEW YORK
TORY BURCH IN COLOR

THE MOST ALLURING THING A WOMAN CAN HAVE IS CONFIDENCE.

– Beyoncé

Printed in Great Britain
by Amazon

61221639R00087